AS

Dan Clayton
Beth Kemp
Series editor
Adam Leyburn

Nelson Thornes

Published in 2008 by:
Nelson Thornes Ltd
Delta Place
27 Bath Road
CHELTENHAM
GL53 7TH
United Kingdom

08 09 10 11 12 / 10 9 8 7 6 5 4 3 2

A catalogue record for this book is available from the British Library

ISBN 978 0 7487 9848 3

Cover photograph by Corbis
Illustrations include artwork drawn Harry Venning and Pantek Arts Ltd
Page make-up by Pantek Arts Ltd, Maidstone, Kent
Printed in Great Britain by Scotprint

Acknowledgements
The authors and publishers wish to thank the following for permission to use copyright material:

p4: © Digital vision/Alamy; p8: The Vegan Society for its advert 'Vegetarian? Cut the crap'; p9: Rubicon Drinks Ltd for its advertisement, 'New Rubicon Papaya'; pp12–13, p32: The Assessment and Qualifications Alliance for extracts from AQA English Language A Specification, 'Transcription key ENA3 June 2006' and 'Transcription key ENA3 June 2005'; p17: Innocent Drinks Ltd for its label 'innocent breakfast thickie'; p22: Gaggle.net Inc for an extract from its website; p25: Profile Books Ltd for an extract from the inside front jacket flap in Richard Ingrams, *Bling, Blogs and Bluetooth* (2006); p29: Scholastic Ltd for an extract from Nick Arnold and Tony De Saulles, *Horrible Science: Disgusting Digestion*, Scholastic Children's Books (2002), p12. Text copyright © Nick Arnold 2002. Illustrations copyright © Tony De Saulles 2002; p32: Pearson Education for an extract from A. D. Edwards and V. J. Furlong, *The Language of Teaching*, Heinemann (1978); p34: Mallinson Rendel Publishers Ltd for an extract from Lynley Dodd, *Hairy Maclary and Zachary Quack*, Puffin (2004), p1; p38: www.recipes4us.co.uk for a recipe from its website, Friends of the Earth and Everyclick Ltd for an advertisement on the Everyclick website; p40: Cambridge University Press for an extract from John Gumperz, 'Discourse Strategies' in *Talk at Work*, eds P. Drew and J. Heritage (1982); p43: Kate Raworth at Oxfam GB for an extract from her article, 'Wear your ethics with pride', *The Guardian*, 23.2.04; p41: © Chris Bland; Eye Ubiquitous/CORBIS; p60: Jane Hale; p77: Jean Berko, for the Wug illustration from her article, 'The child's learning of English morphology', *Word* 14 (1958), pp150–177. Copyright © Jean Berko Gleason 2006; p134: Trinity Mirror plc for 'Destiny's Hour', *Daily Mirror*, 7th June 1944. Copyright © Daily Mirror/Mirrorpix; p137: News International Syndication Ltd for extracts from John Gaunt, 'How about a Dangerous People Act', *The Sun*, 9.1.07. Copyright © The Sun; p143: Douglas Harper for the definition of 'bitch' on the website www.etymonline.com; p143: © tbkmedia.de; p144: Guardian News & Media Ltd for an extract from Eve Kay, 'Call me Ms', *The Guardian*, 29.6.07. Copyright © Guardian News & Media Ltd 2007; p148: © *The Sun*/nisyndication; p152: © Heide Benser/Corbis; p154: Melissa Lorraine, 'Drug Addled Serial Swordsman', *The News of the World*, 19.8.07. Copyright © The News of the World; p154: © Rex Features; p155: © Geoffrey Swaine/Rex Features; p156: © Leonard de Selva/CORBIS; p157: Metropolitan Police Service for an extract from the Dimbleby Lecture, November 2005, given by Commissioner Sir Ian Blair. Copyright © Metropolitan Police Service; p158: Henry Holt and Company, LLC for an extract and cover from David Simon, *HOMICIDE: A Year on the Killing Streets* (2006), pp14–15. Copyright © 1991 by David Simon. Cover copyright © 2006 by Henry Holt & Company; p159: *The Belfast Telegraph* for an extract from 'Basra: The soldiers' tales', The Belfast Telegraph, 5.9.07; p160: © Nigel Sawtell/Alamy; p162: Trevor Kavanagh, 'Article on Crime Figures', The Sun, 19.7.03. Copyright © The Sun; p184: PinkUnlimited for extracts from Tony Grew, 'Not all representation is positive' and its editorial policy on www.pinknews.co.uk; p186: © John Stillwell/Rex Features; p189: The Watts Publishing Group Ltd for an extract from Pete Sanders and Steve Myers, What do you know about: *People with Disabilities*, Franklin Watts (2000), pp4–5; pp193–4: Little, Brown Book Group Limited for an extract from Angela Carter, *The Passion of New Eve*, Virago (1982), pp176–7.

Every effort has been made to contact the copyright holders and we apologise if any have been overlooked. Should copyright have been unwittingly infringed in this book, the owners should contact the publishers, who will make the corrections at reprint.

Contents

AQA introduction

Nelson Thornes and AQA

Nelson Thornes has worked in collaboration with AQA to ensure that this book offers you the best support for your AS or A Level course and helps you to prepare for your exams. The partnership means you can be confident that the range of learning, teaching and assessment practice materials has been checked by the senior examining team at AQA before formal approval, and is closely matched to the requirements of your specification.

Blended learning

Printed and electronic resources are blended: this means that links between topics and activities between the book and the electronic resources help you to work in the way that suits you best and enable extra support to be provided online. For example, you can test yourself online, and feedback from the test will direct you back to the relevant parts of the book.

Electronic resources are available in a simple-to-use online platform called Nelson Thornes learning space. If your school or college has a licence to use the service, you will be given a password through which you can access the materials through any internet connection.

Icons in this book indicate where there is material online related to that topic. The following icons are used:

🔆 Learning activity

These resources include a variety of interactive and non-interactive activities to support your learning.

☑ Progress tracking

These resources include a variety of tests that you can use to check your knowledge on particular topics (Test yourself) and a range of resources that enable you to analyse and understand examination questions (On your marks…).

🔁 Research support

These resources include WebQuests, in which you are assigned a task and provided with a range of weblinks to use as source material for research.

🔳 Study skills

These resources support you and help develop a skill that is key for your course, for example planning essays.

🔍 Analysis tool

These resources feature text extracts that can be highlighted and annotated by the user according to specific objectives.

When you see an icon, go to Nelson Thornes learning space at **www.nelsonthornes.com/aqagce**, enter your access details and select your course. The materials are arranged in the same order as the topics in the book, so you can easily find the resources you need.

How to use this book

This book covers the specification for your course and is arranged in a sequence approved by AQA.

Its structure mirrors the specification exactly: it is split into two units (Unit 1 Seeing through language and Unit 2 Representation and language), which are then broken down further into Sections A and B. Each section begins with an introduction to the topics that will be covered and concludes with exam (Unit 1) or coursework (Unit 2) preparation and suggestions for further reading. This is followed by feedback on the Language around you and Classroom activities, as well as the Data response exercises. At the back of the book, you will find answers to the Topic revision exercises, alongside The linguistic frameworks toolkit (a reference guide containing the frameworks that will be useful to you in your language analysis work) and a glossary of key terms.

Learning objectives

At the beginning of each section you will find a list of learning objectives that contain targets linked to the requirements of the specification.

The features in this book include:

Key terms

Terms that you will need to be able to define and understand.

Theories

Key language theories – the main points summarised.

Research points

Linguistic research that has been carried out in the area you are studying.

Thinking points

Questions that check your understanding of the research point.

Activities

Language around you, Classroom and Extension activities all appear throughout. Coursework activities appear throughout Unit 2.

Links

Links to other areas in the textbook which are relevant to what you are reading.

Data response exercises

Questions based on given data.

Topic revision exercises/Topic summaries

Brief revision exercises to test your knowledge of each topic in Unit 1. Key points which summarise topics in Unit 2.

AQA Examiner's tip

Hints from AQA examiners to help you with your study and to prepare for your exam.

AQA Examination-style questions

Questions in the style that you can expect in your exam. AQA examination questions are reproduced by permission of the Assessment and Qualifications Alliance.

Nelson Thornes is responsible for the solution(s) given and they may not constitute the only possible solution(s).

Weblinks in the book

Because Nelson Thornes is not responsible for third-party content online, there may be some changes to this material that are beyond our control. In order for us to ensure that the links referred to in the book are as up-to-date and stable as possible, the websites provided are usually homepages with supporting instructions on how to reach the relevant pages if necessary.

Although most key terms can be found in The linguistic frameworks toolkit towards the back of this book, a full glossary of terms is available at: **nelsonthornes.com/aqagce/english_lang_a.htm**

Please let us know at **webadmin@nelsonthornes.com** if you find a link that doesn't work and we will do our best to correct this at reprint, or to list an alternative site.

Introduction to this book

Why study English Language?

As a user of English, you will already have an idea of its size and influence. English is a big language: the *Oxford English Dictionary* contains over 600,000 words, and around 25,000 words are added to the language each year, some of which last for years, while others appear and disappear almost overnight. New words are always joining and old words disappearing (we now listen to 'podcasts', but not the 'wireless'). English is an exciting and modern language, a mixture of cultures and traditions: it contains words originating from hundreds of other languages, and this gives it its variety, colour and downright quirkiness. (Did you know that 'ukulele' means 'jumping flea' in Hawaiian?) English is a world language that one out of every five people on earth can use and that is spoken as a main language by over a billion people. So, as a user of English, you are certainly not alone.

In beginning your A Level in English Language, though, you are moving up a level – from being simply a user of English to becoming a student of English.

The good news is that English is a language you have been thinking about (even if you didn't realise it) for many years. Every time you have a conversation, read an advert or go shopping, you are thinking about English. In fact, if you did a GCSE in the subject, you have already started studying English. You probably looked at different types of writing, to persuade, to inform or describe. You perhaps began to look at some technical terms we use to describe how words work and have learned to label words with terms like 'noun' and 'verb'. At A Level, this will continue, but you will move towards a deeper understanding of how the language succeeds in doing so many things for so many people.

Some more good news about studying English Language is that many of the skills you'll learn will build on things that you already know, though on this course you will begin to look at them in a different way. This makes it different from many A Levels where you are thrown into something completely new. Also, the course revolves around understanding some key ideas that tie in and link to all its modules. This makes the learning feel like a process in which you revisit ideas, building your understanding piece by piece as the weeks go by, rather than through a series of separate and unrelated topics. After all, despite the range and breadth of the English language, what it all comes down to in the end is words.

English has its own technical terms like many other areas of life, and one job you will have is to learn some of these terms. But this is not something new. You probably use highly technical terms already, but in other areas, and again without realising it. For instance, if you wanted to talk about music technology to someone else who knew about it, you would use particular specialist words to make yourself clearer: 'downloading' and 'file-sharing' , 'MP3s' and 'USBs'. By using these terms you can say what you want to more quickly and more precisely. With English Language this is no different. You will learn a whole set of words that will help you to discuss the subject in a similarly detailed way. Although the number and complexity of these terms can at first be off-putting, by the end of your course you will be able to use them in the same way that you use other groups of terms to discuss hobbies or interests.

One key difference between GCSE and A Level is that, whereas before you have focused mainly on written English, you will now study how English works as speech, and how new types of communication, such as internet chatrooms or text messaging, are altering the ways we discuss ideas about speech and writing. English is in a constant state of change, and although your course will look back to the past, it will also look at what is happening to language now, and how you and your generation are changing the language. Because of this, you may well have a more up-to-date and accurate view of the way English is *actually* used than your teachers do!

Like many other A Levels, English Language focuses on a number of topics. You will study questions like 'why do children learn language at such a pace?' and 'how is language used to label different social groups?' and will be encouraged to look at the ideas of other language experts. In many of these areas, though, there are no right answers, and whereas at GCSE things were often seen as correct or incorrect, at A level you will be encouraged to consider and weigh up different opinions to come to your own conclusions.

As well as studying other people's use of English, you will also have the opportunity to produce your own writing and reflect more deeply about your own language use. This will lead you to improve your own English – something that will help you with all of your courses.

How is English Language A assessed?

At GCSE, you probably got used to two main kinds of assessment – exams and coursework. This continues at A Level, where both the AS and A2 years contain one exam and one coursework module. Coursework assessment represents 40 per cent of the course with 60 per cent assessed by an exam that you will take at the end of the course. This gives a variety to the tasks you will undertake and will allow you to work in different ways.

There are four assessment objectives (AOs) on which your actual marks will be based, and these vary in importance from task to task. These AOs refer to the different skills that are needed in each module. Broadly, they cover four main areas: writing about language itself; writing about the effects of language; understanding other people's ideas about language; and using language yourself.

It is not vital that you know in detail which AOs apply to which tasks, but understanding what examiners are looking for in each area of the course will help you, and it would be a good idea to spend some time getting to know them. You will find explanations of the AOs later in this book and we have also tried to show you how they relate specifically to different parts of the course.

What does each unit cover?

We have structured this book to reflect how we think the units of the course work best. This should make it easier for you to get to grips with each part. We have also tried to split up the units into smaller parts, and to put them in an order that we think will help you build up your knowledge in a logical way. On page 206, you will find something called The linguistic frameworks toolkit. Don't let the name or the size of it put you off. The toolkit, as the name suggests, contains terms that will act as tools, helping you to describe language more precisely. Don't try to understand them all at once. The toolkit is something you will be encouraged to refer to throughout the book, and it will help you to build up your understanding gradually and in a manageable way. It is by no means necessary that, even at the end of your course, you will need to have learned and memorised it all.

You will begin to look at some of the most basic terms in the toolkit in Unit 1, Seeing through language. In Section A of this unit, Language and mode, you will start to look at how we can talk and write about language in a more technical way. You will begin to use a system for looking at language where you will think about a number of things: how the sounds of words or how they look on a page can alter our reaction

to them; how words themselves are made up of even smaller bits of language; and how groups of words fit together to create meanings. You will also look at how language can be encountered in different forms – as writing, speech or a mixture of both – and how these forms change the way language affects us. In Section B, Language development, you will study ideas behind how and why children learn language at such a quick rate. You will examine many examples of child language data – what children actually say and write – and different theories about this. In addition, you will look at how children's language develops over the first years of their lives.

Unit 2 is the coursework unit, Representation and language; it is not as complicated as it sounds. In it you will think about how we talk or write about people and things in certain ways, and how, if we change the words we use, we can often change the way we think about or view them. It is concerned with how the image of, say, a sportsperson or TV celebrity can change from week to week, not because of *what* people say about them but because of *how* they say it. For instance, do we think of Madonna in a different way if some parts of the media refer to her as Madge? In the coursework, you will be able to choose your own topics, so you can focus on areas that interest you.

Where could it take you?

We very much hope that through your AS course you will develop a passion for the study of the English language and that this will lead you on to continue with the course at A2. Many of the things you will learn on this course lead directly into the A2 units and these will develop your understanding further. Afterwards, your A Level will give you a good grounding to move on to higher education in a whole range of areas: you may look to continue with English, focusing on one of a wide range of related courses offered by universities: sociolinguistics, for example, which looks at language and society, or applied linguistics, one part of which looks at how different languages work in different ways. Alternatively, the course will help you in other areas, such as psychology, law, medicine, journalism, advertising and teaching.

Even if you decide to move totally beyond the subject, your course will have helped you to become a better language user, to express your thoughts more precisely and persuasively – skills valued in all areas of life.

The English Language A series

This book has been written specifically for the new 2008 A Level courses. AQA and Nelson Thornes have worked together to produce a textbook that will guide you through the essential content and assessment of your course. The online e-resources that accompany the book build on its content and will give you the opportunity to stretch yourself and to approach your study using different types of learning.

The writers of this book are experienced teachers and AQA examiners. Their teaching experience means that they have an understanding of the best ways to explain the ideas you will encounter, and this knowledge has affected and influenced the design of the book. As examiners, they have seen thousands of student answers, and this experience is reflected in the Examiner's tips that give you advice on how to approach the exam and coursework tasks.

Of course, we could not put everything into the book, and you will need to look beyond it to your teachers, fellow students and other sources. We have tried helping you in this by referring you to places where you can extend your study further. In wishing you the best for your course, we will offer one last piece of advice: in studying English Language, some of the best resources are all around you. When you pick up a magazine, watch a film, send a text message or use the internet, you are engaging with language on one of its many levels. Although previously you may have done these things without considering language issues, as a student of language you will understand how language underpins daily life.

Seeing through language

Assessment objectives:

- **AO1** Select and apply a range of linguistic methods to communicate relevant knowledge using appropriate terminology and coherent, accurate written expression.

- **AO2** Demonstrate critical understanding of a range of concepts and issues related to the construction and analysis of meanings in spoken and written language, using knowledge of linguistic approaches.

- **AO3** Analyse and evaluate the influence of contextual factors on the production and reception of spoken and written language, showing knowledge of the key constituents of language.

The study of English Language at AS Level requires you to 'step back' from language and examine it in a new way. You already use the English language fluently or you wouldn't be beginning this study, but now you will need to acquire new ways of looking at and talking about language.

The first part of this book relates to Unit 1 of the AQA English Language A specification. It is called Seeing through language because that is what you are being asked to do. The material here is designed to prepare you for the Unit 1 examination, which is split into two sections: Section A Language and mode; and Section B Language development.

Section A Language and mode

This section explores how language varies when used for writing, speaking and in electronic contexts. In this section, through reference to The linguistic frameworks toolkit on page 206, you will learn a range of terminology and approaches for looking at different kinds of text. The exam on Language and mode requires you to analyse two texts from different modes, so you will work through different frameworks for looking at language, considering written, spoken and electronic texts in each topic. The frameworks used here form a foundation for all the work undertaken at AS and A2 in English Language.

Section B Language development

This section is the first language topic or issue you study on this course, and it refers to how children develop their ability to use language. In this section, you will use the frameworks to examine how children learn to speak and understand their native tongue, and how they learn to read and write. You will encounter and think about a range of theories about how language is learned. This section of the book also offers examples of children's uses of language – spoken and written, and from different ages. The exam on Language development asks you to comment on some language produced by a child or children, and to write an essay. These tasks require you to use linguistic frameworks and examples of children's language, and to discuss the different concepts and theories.

A Language and mode

Introduction

This section will get you used to looking at **texts** in a certain way and to the required depth. The focus is on language and **mode**, but you will also be introduced to **linguistic frameworks** and practise applying them to different kinds of text.

The section is divided into different topics (as are all the sections of this book). Each topic looks at a different aspect of mode and textual analysis. As you can see on this page, key terms are highlighted in the text with a brief explanation in the margin. For more detail and examples of the terms, look in The linguistic frameworks toolkit on page 206. This is grouped by category or framework, so you can check what belongs where.

Different levels of analysis

We are concerned with texts here, but will broaden the definition of a text that you've probably used in studying English up to now. You also need to be clearer and more precise about how texts achieve what they do. This means learning a lot of new terminology and developing the knowledge you already have. Some concepts will be familiar to you – like audience and purpose – and these will continue to inform how we interpret texts. Like mode, these are contextual factors, **context** being one level of analysis. Frameworks such as **grammar** and **lexis** offer other possibilities.

Language in the real world

Throughout the section you'll be encouraged to think about the language that you use yourself, and that you see and hear around you. One of the side effects of studying language, however, and particularly spoken language, is that you notice your own speech habits, and those of the people around you far more closely.

Key terms

Text: in language study, we call everything we examine a text. A text can be a letter, a book extract, a conversation or the writing on a toothpaste tube!

Mode: the traditional concept of mode focuses on how a text is received, i.e. on whether it is written or spoken.

Linguistic framework: a key set of terminology for Language AS that enables us to look at texts from different perspectives and analyse the language within them.

Context: the context of a text is the set of conditions around that text's production – who is it for? (audience); what is it for? (purpose); what kind of text is it? (genre); how is it received? (mode).

Grammar: used in this book to refer primarily to word class and morphology.

Lexis: the total stock of words in a language; synonymous with 'vocabulary'.

Fig. 1 *Language spotting in the real world*

■ Approaching texts analytically

As is probably clear from the above, learning about and applying the different frameworks to texts will lead you to approach them in a new and more analytical way. It's not unusual for students to say they can't figure out what they ever had to say about texts before learning the frameworks! You will get plenty of practice in analysing texts of many different kinds here. Most importantly for the exam, by the end of this section you will be used to writing analytical sentences. These are the key to analytical writing and enable you to identify a feature, label it accurately and describe its effect.

■ Language analysis

Unit 1 Seeing through language is assessed by an exam. This will be your only AS Language exam, as Unit 2 is a coursework module. The Language and mode section of the exam will require you to analyse and compare two texts. They will be of different modes but have a link (e.g. be on the same topic). This book will therefore also help to prepare you for language analysis work and give you opportunities to practise comparing texts.

What is mode?

In this topic you will:

- ■ learn what mode is
- ■ consider how mode can be conceptualised
- ■ learn about the causes of the key differences in modes

■ Analysing texts from the perspective of mode

This section of Unit 1 is all about analysing texts and text extracts from different modes, so the first thing you need to know is what we mean by mode. By the end of this topic, you should have a clear idea about that, and about some of the basic differences between each mode. The topics that follow this will take you deeper into linguistic analysis, applying the key frameworks to texts from all modes.

■ Spoken versus written text

Throughout your study of English so far, you have probably only considered the written or scripted word. A key difference at AS Level is that you will now also be examining the ways people use language when they talk spontaneously. Although your own spoken language may have been examined before via speaking and listening tasks – presentations, debates and discussions – you are about to embark on your first serious study of spoken English.

■ Conceptualising mode

To conceptualise or to imagine 'mode' as an idea or concept, the traditional approach is to talk about whether a text originally existed (or was intended to exist) as a written or spoken piece of language. There are several channel differences between typical written language and typical spoken language, beginning with those listed in Table 1.

Table 1 *Channel differences between typical written language and typical spoken language*

Written language:	Spoken language:
is received via the **eyes**	is received via the **ears**
is **permanent** – we can check exactly what it says again and again	is **temporary** – we retain what was said to us only in the memory
is **impersonal** – the writer doesn't know exactly who will read it	is **personal** – the speaker is directly addressing an individual or group
is **distant** – it can be read at any time, once written.	is **immediate** – it is heard simultaneously to being said.

Fig. 2 *We use language in all modes all the time*

These are the key traditional differences, because other factors that distinguish written and spoken language are caused by these. Electronic texts do not fit here neatly, and how they are treated is covered later.

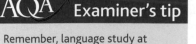

Generalisations and specifics

When we conceptualise these broad differences between the modes, we are always talking in a generalised way – otherwise we just couldn't get started. You'll find that quite a lot of language study is like that. On the one hand, it can be frustrating to figure out these broad issues and then realise they don't always apply, but on the other hand, it can be quite refreshing to argue with these generalities.

If you look back at the original list of differences between written and spoken language (Table 1), you'll realise that these too are very generalised. We might well hear speech via our ears, but our eyes are playing a part too. These differences in how a text is received are known as **channel differences**.

It is an often-quoted cliché that at least 90 per cent of communication is outside of language, and although we have no real way of assessing this, people often say it and accept it as true. We do interpret whether people are being literal or ironic by their facial expression and body language, as well as by their words and tone of voice.

Fig. 3 *Sometimes, body language tells a different story*

There are also large differences between different specific situations of spoken or written language. We sometimes think of these two as opposites, when really they're more like the ends of a **continuum**. The next task should help you to understand this better.

Language around you 3

Where would you place the following situations or contexts on the mode continuum shown in Figure 4? On your own, or in discussion with a partner, try to decide how close to the 'typical' mode features each of these is.

- A political speech.
- A shopping list.
- A textbook.
- A note on the fridge – 'Don't forget to pick me up @ 5.'
- A chat in the pub.
- A class discussion.
- A billboard film advert.

Spoken ——————— Written

Fig. 4 *Mode continuum*

💡 New modes

So far, we've been looking at a traditional view of mode, which assumes that texts are either spoken or written. That is simply no longer true, however, and these days we need a different model that includes newer kinds of communication.

Text messages, internet forums, websites and instant messenger are all new ways of holding conversations. They are neither truly speech nor writing.

Language around you 4

How does electronic communication connect with what you've learned about mode so far? On your own, or in discussion with a partner, consider the following questions:

1. Do you think electronic communication is more like speech, or more like writing? Why?

2. Have a look back at the table of channel differences on page 4 and think about how electronic forms fit into that view of mode. For example, how permanent is a text message?

3. Make a list of the ways that electronic forms can be like/unlike both speech and writing.

Topic revision exercise

Complete the questions on your own, then discuss your ideas with a partner.

1. What do you understand by the term 'mode'?

2. If we conceptualise mode as meaning 'either written or spoken', what is the problem with this?

3. List the following:

   a. Two kinds of written text that are more towards the 'spoken' end of the continuum.

   b. Two kinds of spoken text that belong more towards the 'written' end of the continuum.

   c. Three (as different as possible) electronic texts that belong comfortably in the 'spoken' area of the continuum.

   d. Three (as different as possible) electronic texts that belong firmly in the middle of the continuum.

   e. Three (as different as possible) electronic texts that belong comfortably at the 'written' end of the continuum.

   f. Five features of 'typical' written mode texts.

   g. Five features of 'typical' spoken mode texts.

The written mode

In this topic you will:

- learn about some specific approaches for the written mode
- begin your study of the linguistic frameworks with graphology.

Key terms

Graphology: the framework relating to things we see in a text that aren't actually the words chosen, including: layout; colour; image; and font.

Familiar ground

This is probably quite familiar ground for you – as we have already established, the written mode is what you have spent most time studying so far in English. The key things you need to grasp from this topic are a sense of how broad the written mode can be, and an understanding of the framework of **graphology**.

The typical written mode text

As we established in the previous topic, the stereotype of a written text is that it is permanent, intended for a broad, unknown audience and, therefore, more likely to be formal than a spoken text. As we also established, this is true of only a minority of written texts.

Language around you 5

1. On your own, think of the most formal written text you can. Compare your choice with a partner's.

2. Think about the written texts you've had contact with today. Jot down all that you can think of and categorise them by type if you've read several similar texts.

3. Combining your list with a partner's, try different ways of putting the texts in a rank order, according to the channel or mode features they have (check back in the last topic if you need to). Do you find they end up ordered similarly with different criteria?

AQA Examiner's tip

Although it is useful to discuss graphology in relation to a text as a whole, do not spend too much time on it. It is the most basic way of analysing a text and consequently worth relatively few marks.
Mention it briefly in an introductory paragraph, or save it until the end as reinforcement for some of your more detailed points.

What is graphology?

The word derives from Greek: 'graph' relating to marks, and 'ology' meaning study. In linguistics, we use it to mean the study of those elements of written or printed texts that are visual and contribute to meaning, but are not actually the language chosen. It includes aspects such as how the text is arranged (layout), and whether and how colour is used.

Data response exercise 1

Read the text in Figure 5 on page 8. This is an advert for the Vegan Society that featured in *Natural Health* magazine. Working on your own, make notes on how the text works visually, or discuss it with a partner. What do you think makes it effective?

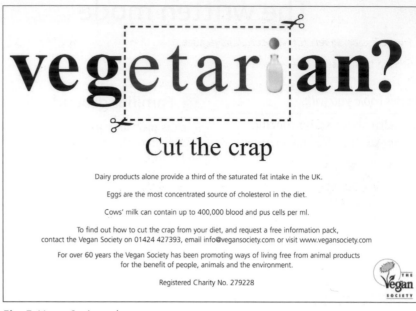

Fig. 5 *Vegan Society advert*

■ Aspects of graphology

Layout

As we've seen with the vegan advert, the way a text is laid out is part of its effect and, in some ways, contributes to its meaning. For example, it is possible to 'draw' a letter, poem or a newspaper article using only lines, and we can still identify the **genre** without any real difficulty (Figure 6).

This is one aspect of the graphological framework. As well as using a standard, accepted layout to help the clarity of a text, it is also possible to use the layout convention of a different genre for a visual pun or clever effect. This is more typical of adverts than other kinds of written text – you would not expect to see it in a non-fiction book, for example.

> ### Key terms
>
> **Genre:** the category a text belongs to, e.g. poem, novel, advert.

Nobody heard him, the dead man,
But still he lay moaning:
I was much further out than you thought
And not waving but drowning.

Poor chap, he always loved larking
And now he's dead
It must have been too cold for him his heart gave way,
They said.

Oh, no no no, it was too cold always
(Still the dead one lay moaning)
I was much too far out all my life
And not waving but drowning.

Fig. 6 *'Not waving but drowning'* by **Stevie Smith**

Data response exercise 2

Figure 7 is an advert for Rubicon Papaya juice.

1 What unrelated genre of text is it copying?

2 How does this add to the meaning of the advert?

New Rubicon Papaya
Exotic superjuice drink

Utterly delicious, and a source of lutein which research suggest can help maintain healthy eyes, helping you see better for longer. Rubicon is working in association with the Eyecare Trust to raise awareness of the important role nutrition plays in maintaining eye health.

Find out more at www.rubiconexotic.com or www.eyecare-trust.org.uk

Fig. 7 *Advert for Rubicon Papaya juice*

Font

It may seem obvious but the choice of font (typeface) does make a difference in a text. Fonts have **connotations** and these need to match with the text's intentions. For more on 'connotations' look in the Lexical-semantic framework in the toolkit on page 214. As a simple illustration, have a look at the next activity.

Colour

Colours, like fonts, have connotations and these are used in texts to create effect and meaning, particularly by advertisers.

Images

Many texts include images – photographs, drawings or diagrams – and for a wide range of reasons. They may be used to convey information, make a text more persuasive or simply to add interest.

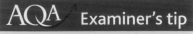
Key terms

Deviant spelling: spelling that is non-standard but used deliberately for effect.

Spelling and punctuation

Deviant spelling is used in some kinds of written texts for a range of effects. For example, in company names or newspaper headlines they can be used to create a pattern or pun. 'Kwik-fit' is a classic example of this, and 'quick' is spelled 'kwik' in several other company names for its connotations of speed. Punctuation may also be used in a non-standard way.

■ Language around you 6

1. Using a telephone directory, see how many company names you can find using deviant spelling or punctuation.

2. Try to decide on reasons for the companies' uses of deviant forms. Can you see any patterns? For example, does there seem to be one main reason or several? Are the same kinds of company using deviant forms?

Fig. 8 *Deviant spelling isn't good for all businesses*

🔍 Written texts as visual texts

The features we have looked at so far relate to the visual aspect of written text, and there are of course plenty of written texts that do not exploit these design possibilities. These tend to be the most formal of texts, like dictionaries and legal statutes, which do not use colour, images or deviant spelling. Dictionaries do, of course, have a distinctive graphological style of their own, varying font to convey different information, and using numbering and columns to organise information clearly. So it is not only the most visually exciting texts that use graphology for meaning – do not make the mistake of saying something doesn't have graphological features just because it lacks colour and pictures.

■ Topic revision exercise

Complete the questions on your own, then discuss your ideas with a partner.

1. What do you understand by the term 'graphology'?

2. Name three aspects of a text you might look at in examining graphological features.

3. Look again at the papaya juice advert (Figure 7). Identify five key graphological features and explain how they help to create meaning in the text.

The spoken mode

The range of spoken language

As noted previously, the spoken mode is the most commonly used. To study it, we look at **transcripts**, which will be introduced in this topic, together with some of the technical terms used in the study of spoken language. As with the written mode, the overall term 'spoken language' covers quite a range and includes planned speech (for example, political speeches), casual spontaneous conversation and a variety of contexts in between. We'll start with some of the features of planned speech before moving into frameworks which relate more specifically to spontaneous speech.

AQA Examiner's tip

We do not always (or even often) speak in full sentences, so do not be too harsh on the participants in transcribed conversations. Expressions like 'incorrect', 'wrong' or 'bad' grammar are unwelcome in analyses and just make it look like you've never seen a transcript before. In speech, people often use **non-standard English**.

Data response exercise 3

The transcript below is from the beginning of an AS English Language lesson. The teacher is introducing the topic, so there is only one speaker in this extract.

1 Read the transcript, trying to 'hear' it in your head as you go. Make sure you check the key first to see what the symbols mean.

2 How do you think the **pauses** and **micropauses** contribute to the meaning of the extract? Are they necessary? What would the text be like without them?

3 Pauses and micropauses, together with some other features, are often called 'non-fluency features' or 'hesitancy features'. Does this label work for all the pauses in this extract?

Key terms

Transcript: an accurate written record of a conversation or monologue, including hesitations and pauses.

Non-standard English: words, phrases and constructions not usually seen in formal texts.

Pause: a gap in the flow of speech, or a period of silence.

Micropause: a gap of less than half a second.

Key
(.) Micropause (less than a second)
(1) Timed pause (number of seconds indicated)
Bold Emphasis

OK (.) today we are going to talk about political correctness (5) for pretty much all the lesson in one way or another (10) now (.) as I've already managed to mention a couple of times (2) it's really crucial that you **don't** subscribe to the *Daily Mail* approach to political correctness (4) OK (.) we need to think more broadly than that (3) the problem with PC is that (2) it is kind of offered as a positive thing to do (2) to show respect and basically to be polite (3) you know (6) you don't run around using (.) using offensive terms (.) because that would not be politically correct (3) the problem with the term is that it was originally conceived as an insult (5) alright (.) so it was first used in the 1960s and 70s (2) in the States (2) to basically mock people who were seen to be taking the party line to a (.) ridiculous extent (3) so it has been an insult term from the very beginning (.) being PC was never seen as being a good thing (4) **but** now (.) it tries now (.) to try and sort of flip itself over and become a positive thing (.) and this is where all the problems stem from (.) and there is still (2) an awful lot of mileage in mocking political correctness (.) isn't there (7)

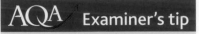
■ Non-fluency and hesitancy: speech features

These features are typical of speech, and are used by all of us in normal conversation. In linguistic study, they fall into the category of speech features, because they are rarely found in the written mode. The Speech framework in the toolkit on page 259 defines and gives examples of these features.

■ Data response exercise 4

The genre of the transcript below is an interview. Tony is being interviewed by Ralph and Colin, having applied to do a bricklaying course, and he is asked about his experience and suitability for the course. Naturally, Tony exhibits some nerves in the transcript as a result of this context.

How many different features can you find which suggest nervousness on Tony's part?

Check terms in the Speech framework in the toolkit again if you need to.

Key:
(.) pause of less than a second
(2) longer pause (number of seconds indicated)
Bold emphasis
[ ] simultaneous speech
[*italics*] selected non-verbal features
(inaudible) inaudible speech

Ralph come in Tony
Tony ⌈hello⌉
Ralph ⌊take⌋ a seat [*sighs*] (.) and I'll introduce Colin an instructor at the centre
Tony ⌈mmm⌉   5
Colin ⌊how⌋ do you do
Ralph I'm from Training Services and you understand that the purpose is to confirm that er (.) you've chosen the **right** ⌈course⌉
Tony ⌊yeah⌋   10
Ralph can I just (.) try and follow one or two things on the form you completed erm you haven't served an apprenticeship
Tony no no (.) no
Ralph no (.) I think you crossed the wrong ones there (.) just ah and you haven't had **any** of these (1) illnesses (.) skin 15 diseases
Tony no no diseases (.) that sort of thing is ⌈alright⌉
Ralph   ⌊ok⌋ eh (1) you can have a chat with Colin ⌈now⌉
Tony   ⌊mmm⌋   20
Colin alright (.) I see from the information that I've got (*inaudible*) you (.) is that you spent er (.) twelve months working for a builder in the south of France
Tony um well (.) yeah I did actually I I spent (1) **two** years over there (.) I worked in a boat yard for some time (.) and 25 [*clears throat*] I worked for a builder as well and (.) you know (.) I did some bricklaying over there (.) I suppose that's what got me interested you know

Colin	yeah (.) erm alright (.) you did some bricklaying over there (1) what kind of things were you [doing]	30
Tony	[well] all sorts of things (.) we would do (.) putting flats up you know and (.) oh just laying bricks (.) that sort of thing you know (.) general building really (.) drain work and that sort of thing	35
Colin	flagging (.) that kind of [thing]	
Tony	[yeah] flagging	
Colin	and then (.) twelve months you spent with (1) Seville isn't it	
Tony	Seville Construction yeah they're a building company as [well]	40
Colin	[yeah]	
Tony	I did some bricklaying er (.) with them too (1) and (1) that was for about er twelve months I think (1) but er the reason I I wanted to do bricklaying was because er I've **always** been interested in it (.) you know	45
Colin	yeah yeah (.) fine [clears throat] er the reason for you coming into training as a bricklayer eh although you've only spent er (1) two years in total full time	
Tony	yeah	50
Colin	yeah (.) erm you don't feel yourself or in yourself (.) competent enough to to take a job as a bricklayer as things stand at the moment	
Tony	no (.) not really well [clears throat] I could do with er practising the bottoms and that sort of thing (.) you know (.) in bricklaying itself that's that's the reason I I want to take the **course** you **know** [interview continues]	55

J.J. Gumperz, 'Discourse Strategies' from P. Drew and J. Heritage (eds.), Talk at Work, 1992

Non-verbal communication

Non-verbal communication (also known as NVC) is a key part of spoken face-to-face interaction. It includes body language, facial expression and **prosodic elements** or **non-verbal aspects of speech**, and is obviously not used in written communication. The written equivalent is the framework of graphology. Graphology similarly contributes to meaning without actually being a linguistic feature (this is also known as **paralinguistics**).

Classroom activity 1

In pairs or small groups, try to communicate with each other silently (and without mouthing words!). You could try:

- expressing how you feel
- explaining what you did last night
- summarising the plot of a book or film.

Language around you 7

Start paying close attention to the way people communicate non-verbally. There are books and websites available about body language, but it is possible to work out quite a lot on your own. This is because we have a kind of shared understanding of the meaning of gestures and signals. This is one aspect of how we cooperate in conversation to ensure we understand one another.

Key terms

Prosodic elements: Paralinguistic vocal elements of spoken language used to provide emphasis or other effects.

Non-verbal aspects of speech (NVAS): a commonly used alternative term for prosodics.

Paralinguistics: the things that add to the meaning of a text that aren't actually language, e.g. graphology, non-verbal communication and prosodics.

Link

For more about how we cooperate in conversation, see Context and mode on pages 20–27.

Fig. 9 *Interaction isn't just with words*

💡 Interaction

A key difference between the spoken and written modes is the element of **interaction**. Although written texts often do address their audience directly, and certainly have to make assumptions about their readers (something to be examined in more detail later), immediate interaction cannot occur in the written mode. Aspects of interaction constitute another group of features that, again, can be examined in more detail in the Interaction framework in the toolkit on page 213.

Key terms

Interaction: the linguistic aspects of how people relate to one another.

Simultaneous speech: two or more participants speaking at the same time.

Interruption: beginning a turn while someone else is talking, in a competitive way.

Overlap: beginning a turn while someone else is talking, in a cooperative way.

Data response exercise 5

Refer back to the transcript from Data response exercise 4 on page 12.

1. Reread the transcript completely.

2. Look at each incidence of **simultaneous speech**. Decide why it occurs, and note whether it is an **interruption** or an **overlap**.

3. Have a look at Tony's use of the phrase 'you know'. What purpose might it serve and how could we label it?

Topic revision exercise

Complete the questions on your own, then discuss your ideas with a partner.

1. How are transcripts different from texts you have looked at before?

2. Name four discourse features.

3. Name and describe three features of interaction.

Blending modes

New modes for changing societies

One of the most interesting things about studying language at this point in time is being able to look at how mode is changing and blending. As society overall becomes less formal, and our language use becomes less formal, this trend combines with the possibilities offered by electronics. There are new and exciting ways of communicating.

This topic will start with planned speech as a kind of hybrid of the spoken and written modes. When we talk about planned speech, we tend to focus on political speeches – not least because they're quite easily available as written (and recorded) data. However, the genre also includes academic lectures, sermons and other public speaking events, such as the best man's speech at a wedding.

Language around you 8

Thinking about a range of planned speech contexts, discuss with a partner or make notes on how planned speech is like writing and how it is like speech. Think about the channel aspects, what speeches are supposed to achieve and what effects these things will have on the language choices made.

Planned speech: the rhetorical framework

You've probably come across some aspects of this framework before in studying persuasive writing at GCSE. **Rhetorical questions** obviously belong here, along with other devices intended to stimulate an audience into thinking or make the speaker's words easily memorable.

Since this is primarily a spoken framework, the sounds of words and phrases can be used for effect, and that is why repetitions of various kinds are included in this framework. **Triads** are particularly effective, whether a straightforward repetition of the same word or phrase three times – e.g. Tony Blair's 'education, education, education' – or a list of three related words or phrases – e.g. Sir Winston Churchill's 'it all do their duty, if nothing is neglected, and if the best arrangements are made'. Three seems to be a particularly powerful number psychologically, and triads help to create the memorability and persuasive power that speeches and many written texts need. Have a look in the toolkit on page 219 for more features in the Rhetorical framework, with explanations and examples.

Key terms

Rhetorical question: a question that is not intended to be answered, or that the speaker/writer answers him/herself.

Triad: a pattern of three words or phrases.

Data response exercise 6

Read the following extract from Emmeline Pankhurst's 'The laws that men have made' speech from 1908, contributing to the Votes for Women campaign. Identify at least one example of the following rhetorical features:

- syntactic parallelism
- triad
- other rhetorical devices.

Check in the Rhetorical framework in the toolkit on page 219 for definitions and examples.

Data extract 1

> Men politicians are in the habit of talking to women as if there were no laws that affect women. 'The fact is,' they say, 'the home is the place for women. Their interests are the rearing and training of children. These are the things that interest women. Politics have nothing to do with these things and therefore politics do not concern women.' Yet the laws decide how women are to live in marriage, how their children are to be trained and educated, and what the future of their children is to be. Let us take a few of these laws, and see what there is to say about them from the women's point of view.
>
> First of all, let us take the marriage laws. They are made by men for women. Let us consider whether they are equal, whether they are just, whether they are wise. What security of maintenance has the married woman? Many a married woman having given up her economic independence in order to marry, how is she compensated for that loss? What security does she get in that marriage for which she gave up her economic independence? Take the case of a woman who has been earning a good income. She is told that she ought to give up her employment when she becomes a wife and mother. What does she get in return? All that a married man is obliged by law to do for his wife is to provide for her shelter of some kind, food of some kind, and clothing of some kind. It is left to his good pleasure to decide what the shelter shall be, what the food shall be, what the clothing shall be. It is left to him to decide what money shall be spent on the home, and how it shall be spent; the wife has no voice legally in deciding any of these things. She has no legal claim upon any definite portion of his income. If he is a good man, a conscientious man, he does the right thing. If he is not, if he chooses almost to starve his wife, she has no remedy. What he thinks sufficient is what she has to be content with.

Emmeline Pankhurst, extract from 'The Laws that men have made', 1908

■ Giving written text a spoken 'feel'

Many written texts make use of features that seem more suited to the spoken mode. Creative writing offers writers more space to play with language than other genres, and we quite often find spoken aspects in novels and poetry. There are many authors writing entirely in **dialect,** or at least using dialect with character voices for authenticity and to add depth to characters. There are also many **first-person narratives** that use **synthetic personalisation** and behave as though the narrator is interacting with the reader. This is true of many adverts as well – we are commonly given commands or addressed like old friends by advertising texts. All of these texts use aspects of the spoken mode deliberately and to achieve an effect. This may be simply to seem less formal, or to involve the audience or to increase the persuasive force of the text, or it may be something much more specific to the text.

■ Key terms

Dialect: the language variety of a geographical region or social subgroup.

First-person narrative: a story or account written from the 'I' position.

Synthetic personalisation: the technique where a writer/speaker uses the second-person pronoun to synthesise or fake a personal relation to the audience.

Data response exercise 7

Examine Figure 10, a label taken from a 'breakfast thickie' bottle. This particular company creates its image using language in a very specific way. At this point, we're looking at how it uses aspects of the spoken mode.

1 Find four phrases that feel more spoken than written, preferably in different sections of the label.

2 Explain the overall effect of the extended piece of text on the right-hand side of the label (above the 'Our new bottle' box).

Check your ideas with the feedback (page 51).

AQA Examiner's tip

When a written text uses spoken features, we still need to define it as 'written' in terms of mode. 'Mixed mode' or 'blended mode' as a category needs to be reserved for electronic texts.

Fig. 10 *A breakfast thickie label*

Speech in literature

Literature allows more creative play with language than many other forms. Even at its least experimental, it tends to use the spoken mode in different ways.

- **Dialogue** represents characters' speech to the audience, and may include some discourse and interaction features. It rarely, if ever, includes the degree of non-fluency that we see in real talk.
- **Interior monologue** is a way of allowing the audience access to the narrator's thoughts. This may replicate some aspects of the spoken mode, although, again, it is unlikely to include much non-fluency.
- **Stream of consciousness** goes a step further than interior monologue and imitates the spoken mode more closely. **Self-repair** and some grammatical features of speech are more to be expected in this kind of writing, although it is still likely to be more fluent than accurate transcripts.

Characterisation can be greatly enhanced by a clear style of speech, so writers do create **idiolects** for their characters. Spoken mode features are also particularly common in first-person narratives, where the narrator may address the audience directly, and interior monologue can be the main type of writing.

Key terms

Self-repair: when a speaker corrects him/herself.

Idiolect: an individual style of speaking, made up of choices in all frameworks.

■ **Data response exercise 8**

Examine the extract below. The narrator is in hospital being treated for anorexia. Look at how the dialogue and the interior monologue have a speech-like 'feel'. What is the overall effect of this use of the spoken mode?

Sure enough, a chirpy little woman (thin, birdlike, but with a turkey's tired wattle) shows up, armed with a rubber mallet. She asks me a few questions about my periods; that's all anyone seems to care about around here.

'I forget. Maybe when I was about seventeen.'

'So you've had no periods for eight years now?'

'No, they come and go. Sometimes I won't have any for a year or two, then they'll come back for a while, then go away again.'

'And how long have they been gone this time?'

'I forget. Maybe a year or so.'

Why do they think I should care, anyway? Who, given the choice, would really opt to menstruate, invite the monthly haemorrhage – a reminder that the body is nothing but a bag of blood, liable to seep or spatter at any moment?

Then I discover what the mallet is for. She asks me to sit on the edge of the bed and starts tapping away at the knees, a sharp, clean crack on the bone. Nothing happens, so I give a little kick to help things along. Then she tickles the soles of my feet and tells me my reflexes are impaired because the electrolytes are out of balance and neurons aren't firing properly, or some such jargon.

Fine with me. I don't want any involuntary responses; soon, in this body, everything will be willed.

J. Shute, Life-Size, 1992

■ **Key terms**

Computer-mediated communication (CMC): communication achieved by means of computer technology.

Synchronous communication: a communication in which both/all participants are present at the same time.

Asynchronous communication: a communication in which participants do not need to be present simultaneously.

Adjacency pair: two utterances by different speakers that have a natural and logical link, and complete an idea together.

■ **Electronic texts and mode**

'Electronic texts' is a massive category, including one-sided texts like e-mails and text messages, more interactive forms like forums and blogs, and conversation-like texts such as chats and MSN. At the moment, since the field is so fluid and many electronic texts can be used in varying ways, we group them together as 'blended' or 'mixed' mode. One helpful way of dividing **computer-mediated communication (CMC)** texts is by separating the **synchronous** from the **asynchronous**. Many features of the written and spoken modes can be found in electronic texts, depending on the context. Obviously, synchronous texts may display features like turns, **adjacency pairs**, and so on, but we can't classify interruptions or overlaps because of the way the software operates. In a spoken conversation, we know what the other speaker is saying (to a degree) when we overlap, but in an online conversation, turns often don't connect in an orderly way, because speaker A may be replying to speaker B's comment from three turns ago. Transcripts of electronic conversations can therefore be quite hard to follow, just like spoken transcripts.

Data response exercise 9

Read the extract below, showing an MSN conversation.

1 Discuss and note down the ways in which the text uses aspects of both spoken and written modes – two aspects for each.

2 Discuss and note down one way in which this kind of communication is different from both spoken and written forms.

3 Decide whether you think it belongs in the middle of the continuum or whether it is closer to the written or spoken mode.

Check your ideas with the feedback (page 52).

1ıℓ Mız ηɑʊɢʜтʏ says:
iyyya!

Steve – 'oh my God, whatever, etc.' says:
alright

1ıℓ Mız ηɑʊɢʜтʏ says:
uk

steve – 'oh my God, whatever, etc.' says:
yeah I'm not too bad, you?

1ıℓ Mız ηɑʊɢʜтʏ says:
yea im wkkid thnks!

1ıℓ Mız ηɑʊɢʜтʏ says:
bit annoyed but ya no lol shit happens!

1ıℓ Mız ηɑʊɢʜтʏ says:
wot ya duin 2nyt

steve – 'oh my God, whatever, etc.' says:
what's up?

1ıℓ Mız ηɑʊɢʜтʏ says:
jus borthers tht I wanna kill lol

1ıℓ Mız ηɑʊɢʜтʏ says:
brothers

steve – 'oh my God, whatever, etc.' says:
ahhh right

steve – 'oh my God, whatever, etc.' says:
tonight? Naff all

Student data

🔍 💡 Noting mode features of texts

These first few topics have been to introduce the main concepts of mode. In the exam, you will be asked to analyse two texts with mode differences. The key things to decide and note are:

- the relation between the writer and audience: personal or unknown
- how fixed the text is: permanent or temporary
- how prepared the text is: planned or spontaneous
- how the text is received: visual or auditory channel.

The language decisions made by the writer(s) or speaker(s) may reflect these mode features, as in the msn conversation above, for example – informal language is used because the participants know each other. On the other hand, the breakfast thickie label shows us that features from the spoken mode can be used in the written to try to create a personal relationship between the writer and audience where one doesn't really exist.

Topic revision exercise

Complete the questions on your own, then discuss your ideas with a partner.

1 Name and describe four rhetorical features.

2 Name two ways a written text might use spoken mode features.

4 Explain why printed adverts often use spoken mode features.

4 Explain why electronic texts are 'mixed mode' or 'blended mode'.

Context and mode

In this topic you will:

- learn about the effect context has on a range of texts

- practise linking features of texts to their context

- examine how the functions of texts can contribute to their meaning

- study some theories about how people relate through language.

Link

The idea of audience and author positioning will be examined in more detail in Unit 2.

The importance of context

As established earlier, the context of a text will be a key factor in how you analyse it, just as it is a key factor in how the text's original audience receives it. When we talk about context, we're concerned with:

- **audience**: the intended or imagined receiver(s) of a text
- **purpose**: again, according to the intention of the author or speaker
- **mode**: the method of delivery and reception of the text
- **genre**: the form the text takes, or the category it belongs to.

Note that these categories are used primarily for written texts. They can be used in reference to spoken and blended mode texts, but their meanings become slightly different. We'll explore each of these in turn here, considering how they interact with the features of the text. Following this, we'll examine some theories and concepts to do with interaction as they relate to texts in different modes.

Audience issues

When defining an audience, it is important to consider a variety of factors. In making assumptions about their audience, the writer is often also saying something about him or herself. The best analyses consider author positioning as well as detailed audience characteristics. For example, if we look back to the Vegan Society advert (Figure 5 on page 8), it is clear that the intended audience is constructed as already vegetarian, health-conscious and concerned about the environment. The author (in this case, the Vegan Society) is positioned or represented as trustworthy and knowledgeable.

For each of the points made about the audience of the Vegan Society advert, select a different relevant quotation from the text that supports the assertion. Use the table below to help you.

Check your ideas with the feedback (page 52).

The audience is:	because the text:
Already vegetarian	
Health-conscious	
Concerned about the environment	

⚙ The purposes of texts

You will be able to make use of the familiar labels from your earlier study here – texts can persuade, inform, review and so on. It is important at this level that you connect these purposes to specific choices made by the writer. You should also recognise that there is rarely a single purpose to any text. Even adverts, those most blatantly persuasive texts, also seek to inform about their product. They can also serve an unintentional purpose of constructing and supporting stereotypes (this will be examined in more detail in Unit 2 Representation and language).

■ Textual form, or genre

Genre is often used as a literary or media term – we can talk about the 'historical romance' genre of novels or the 'buddy cop' genre of films. It's used more broadly here to mean any group or category of texts that can be described as having a set of features or a pattern associated with it. You can consider computer hardware manuals a genre, or job interviews, or family blogs.

Genre can be a useful label when describing the features that meet these criteria, for example, 'The author uses a list of ingredients with precise weights, and numbered instructions to follow the genre features of recipes.'

Look at the Gaggle Blogs homepage on page 22 and identify features of this text that are related to each contextual element:

■ audience
■ purpose
■ mode
■ genre.

Check your ideas with the feedback (page 52).

■ Function and mode

There are four possible functions of texts, but you don't need to see these as four separate 'chunks' in your analysis. This is just another approach to consider and to use if something in a text strikes you as relating to this model.

Gaggle.Net
safe email for students
Gaggle Community >

Welcome to the Gaggle Blogs Home Page

What are Gaggle Blogs?

Gaggle Blogs are a way that students and educators can interface with the rest of the world. Gaggle Blogs are filtered for inappropriate words and phrases. All images are scanned for pornographic content and all URL links are checked for pornographic content. If any rules are violated, the offending blog entry will be blocked and sent to the authors administrator email address pending approval.

About Gaggle

Gaggle is dedicated to providing safe e-mail accounts for students. The tools we provide allow schools to finally feel secure when giving their students e-mail access.

On the Gaggle Network teachers control what can be written and who can correspond with the students. Messages with inappropriate words are automatically re-routed to the teacher's account. This allows the teacher to decide whether or not the student gets to see the message.

In the future Gaggle will provide online tools for the schools of tomorrow. The Gaggle.Net e-mail service is the first of many learning tools we will offer. We invite you to grow with us as we help to prepare schools for the virtual classroom of the future.

How do I sign up?

Students can only get Gaggle accounts through their school. Ask your teacher or the computer lab coordinator to sign you up.

If you're an educator interested in providing Gaggle to your students, please **click** here for our sign up form.

Search Blogs

| | Go |

Browse by Location

1) Select a Country >
United States

2) Select a State/Province >
Select State

Most Popular Blogs

Brad's Silly Jokes Blog

♥Little_Minnie_Me♥

I_LUV_ROCKSTAR_STATUS

my blog

Morgan and Caleb 4ever

Miss Needs A Boyfriend

SKATE IT

The four functions are concerned with:

1 **Writer positioning**: Analysing this function of a text tells us how the writers represent themselves, or the organisation that they are speaking for. The way in which writers reveal their own attitudes and values through the writing is the focus here.

2 **The positioning of others and of ideas**: In examining this function, we can see how others within the text are represented. This will be the focus of your Unit 2 work, as you consider how groups of people, individuals, events and institutions are represented through language.

3 **Audience positioning**: Close analysis of this function brings a clearer view of how the text relates to its audience, allowing us to see how the audience is positioned by the writer and what assumptions are made about the reader.

4 **The text as text**: This function is solely about the text as a unit in itself, and in analysing it we look at how it creates **cohesion** and **coherence**.

Key terms

Cohesion: a measure of how well a text fits together as a whole.

Coherence: a measure of how a text makes sense.

Data response exercise 12

As stated above, the 'function' approach can be used with practically all texts. Look now at the commercial written text below – the 'blurb' from the jacket of a recent book.

1 What attitudes and/or values are revealed through this text? What does the writer give away about him/herself?

2 What impression does the text give of people who use these words?

3 Who does the writer expect the audience to be? What qualities are they presumed to have?

4 What about the text makes it 'hang together' as a complete piece? How does it fit into the genre of blurbs?

Check your ideas with the feedback (page 52).

The pace of modern life can be bewildering: people go **speed dating** but eat **slow food**… It's all very confusing. **Innit**.

For anyone old enough to call themselves a grown-up, *Bling, Blogs and Bluetooth* is the essential guide to these mysteries. This sparkling selection from *The Oldie* magazine's ever-popular 'Modern Life' column combines wit and erudition with a dash of impatience and disdain to explain everything from **Affluenza** and **Chavs** to **Tweenagers** and **Visitor Centres** – oh yes, and far, far more…

R. Ingrams, Bling, Blogs and Bluetooth, 2006

■ Working with the functions of all modes

Although these functions can be usefully applied to any text, they can lead to slightly different questions in more interactive texts. With most written, some electronic and a few spoken texts, the audience is wide and not known to the writer/speaker/author. This means we can analyse assumptions made in the text about the audience as audience positioning. With an interactive text, however, it is more common for the participants to know each other, and therefore some elements of audience positioning are not based on assumption but on shared knowledge and past experience. This function in an interactive text is therefore more useful in revealing and maintaining the participants' existing relationship.

■ Data response exercise 13

This is part of a casual interaction between students. How would you analyse the functions in this text? Follow the stages of the last analysis – decide what each function is doing, then note what linguistic points you can make about it. You should assess the functions of each participant's utterances separately.

Compare your ideas with the feedback (page 53).

Key:
(.) micropause
(1) pause timed in seconds
[ ] simultaneous speech

Kristy	and he tries really hard (.) and I think that's sweet and I really like him (1) I can't stand people who can't be arsed
Tom	otherwise know as a chav
Kristy	yea (.) um (.) but they ⌈blame other students ⌉
Tom B	⌊well, no (.) then again⌋ (1) yea (1) Hannah, your (.) your argument doesn't fit because you look at (1) my family an (.) John Michael and Andrew all dropped out of education but I'm still tryin
Kristy	no
Hannah	no (.) I mean like (.) young offenders that (.) like (.) do crimes and that
Tom B	do you're on about people (.) violent peop (0.5) people who commit crimes (1) are you on bout in education or in real life
Hannah	I mean in life
Tom B	oh (.) all right ⌈then ⌉
Hannah	⌊I'm ⌋ on bout I didn't even (1) I'm not on bout education
Kristy	that was ⌈me ⌉
Hannah	⌊it was Kristy who brought⌋ ⌈up education ⌉
Tom B	⌊I knew I heard it⌋

■ Theory

Accommodation

According to H. Giles, when we speak to another person, we *adapt* our speech to *accommodate* them. This is not generally considered something we do deliberately, but subconsciously. We may accommodate by making our speech more like theirs, in terms of the strength of our accent, or the fillers and expressions that we choose. This reduction of social distance is known as **convergence**. Making our speech less like someone else's, by hanging on to and exaggerating our individual traits such as preferred fillers or accent features, is known as **divergence**. Divergence increases social distance and can be used to exclude people. It is possible to converge or diverge either **upwards** or **downwards**.

■ Key terms

Accommodation: the process of adapting one's speech to make it more or less similar to that of other participants in a conversation.

Face: the persona or role a person projects or acts out in a conversation.

Convergence: when a person's speech patterns become more like those of the other person in a conversation.

Divergence: when a person's speech patterns become more individualised and less like those of the other person in a conversation.

Upwards: when applied to convergence/divergence, movement towards Standard English.

Downwards: when applied to convergence/divergence, movement away from Standard English.

Received pronunciation (RP): the 'poshest' UK accent.

Standard English (SE): a universally accepted dialect of English that carries a degree of prestige.

	somewhere (0.5) I was only half listenin (.) to be honest (3)
Tom	course
Tom B	I was looking at my phone (1) I was looking at my phone (.) and tried to join the conversation. (2) well no (.) yea, w w what I hate is when (.) err (.) job seekers' allowance (.) it's unemployed (.) allowance (.) or unemployed benefits because (1) ⌈ fine
Kristy	⌊ I don't ⌋ think we should give it to people
Tom B	yea, but it's alright if you're actually looking for a job, but there are ⌈ people
Hannah	⌊ no ⌋ Well I (.) I ⌈ disagree with that
Kristy	⌊ no, if you can't ⌋ work,
	fair enough. Well I ⌈ don't understand
Tom B	⌊ no, but, you'd get disability allowance ⌋
Kristy	people who can't be arsed

Tom Ball, Kristy Harding, Tom Page and *Hannah Spencer*

■ Blended mode texts and function

The key factor that changes how to approach a functional analysis is interactivity. Blended mode texts that are not interactive, or are one-way only, e.g. websites and individual e-mails, can be approached in the same way as written texts. Texts with more interactivity, such as msn conversations or e-mail exchanges, need to be examined in the same way as spoken interactions.

💡 Interrelation and language

As well as examining features of language use, linguistic study also allows us to consider how people use language to relate to one another. The theories of **accommodation** and **face** are very useful in the analysis of direct interaction in the spoken mode, but also in the new blended modes, as people negotiate and try to manage relationships in interaction that is not face-to-face.

■ Language around you 9

Speaker A is a man with a **received pronunciation (RP)** accent who speaks **Standard English** and sounds rather formal overall. Speaker B is a man with a strong local accent and dialect, who frequently swears and uses slang. Describe the movement each makes in the following scenarios (i.e. upwards/downwards convergence or divergence).

Check your answers with the feedback (page 53).

1 Speaker A reduces the formality of his speech when speaking to Speaker B, by making his RP accent less pronounced and using 'mate'.

2 Speaker A makes his RP accent very distinct and addresses Speaker B as 'good sir'.

3 Speaker B increases the strength of his accent, addresses Speaker A as ''tha' and curses every other word.

4 Speaker B lessens the strength of his accent when speaking to Speaker A, addresses him as 'you', swears less, and uses fewer slang terms.

■ Extension activity

Describe the situations that might lead to the above behaviours – what genre of conversation might each be?

Face theory

Goffman stated that we all present a face in each conversation we have. This may be a clear role, like 'customer' or it may be related to our purpose in that conversation, like 'listening friend'. He surmised that we all protect each other's faces by playing along, sometimes even explicitly making statements like 'you're such a good listener'. The ways in which speakers protect, support or challenge each other's faces is described as **facework**.

Face theory developed

Brown and Levinson extended Goffman's original theory by suggesting that, apart from the specific role played in a particular conversation, we all have two basic face needs that are constantly in tension. Our **positive face need** is to be accepted and liked, while our **negative face need** is to be independent, and not to be imposed upon.

A **face-threatening act (FTA)** either directly challenges someone's face/persona – 'you don't know what you're talking about!' – or threatens their positive or negative face needs, or both. A command threatens positive face needs, as it doesn't make the receiver feel liked, accepted or equal to the speaker. A command also threatens negative face needs by imposing on the receiver's freedom. Anything that lessens an FTA is a politeness strategy; or an FTA can be made **off-record** (i.e. by not saying it at all). 'Isn't it hot in here?' may be an off-record request for a drink, for example.

Politeness, according to Brown and Levinson, is the way we handle having to compromise or threaten people's positive or negative face needs. They theorised that **positive politeness** is used to appeal to someone's positive face need, and **negative politeness** is used to appeal to someone's negative face need. In theory, either kind of politeness can be used for any kind of FTA – a threat to negative face can be countered with positive or negative politeness. Broadly speaking, positive politeness reduces the distance between participants, while negative politeness respects and upholds social distance. It can be argued that negative politeness is more polite than positive politeness. Most of us have preferred strategies, but good communicators seem instinctively to know when to use which kind of politeness.

Positive politeness includes strategies such as:

- using slang/dialect/non-standard forms: 'Give us a cuppa.'
- using terms of endearment: 'Give us a cuppa, love/mate.'

Typically, positive politeness can be used between people of equal social standing, or from people of higher status to those of lower status – for example, a boss might call someone 'mate' to get a favour. Used the other way around, however, it would seem weird or rude.

Negative politeness includes strategies such as:

- expressing pessimism: 'I don't suppose I could have a drink?'
- acknowledging the imposition: 'Sorry to trouble you, but could I have a drink?'

Facework: the way people work together to protect and support each other's 'faces' in conversation.

Positive face need: our need to be liked and to feel part of a group.

Negative face need: our need to be allowed independence and to do our own thing.

Face-threatening act: a communicative act that threatens someone's positive or negative face needs.

Off-record: dropping a hint, saying something without really saying it.

Positive politeness: strategies that emphasise social closeness.

Negative politeness: strategies that recognise the independence or the status of the person you are speaking to.

Negative politeness can be used to people of a higher status. It is supposed to be typically British to use more negative politeness, sometimes with many extra phrases: 'I know I'm a pain, but would you mind terribly...'

Fig. 11 *Politeness strategies in action*

Thinking points

Can you think of ways that you tend to use politeness strategies? It's useful to think of different situations, as the context you are in is key here.

Language around you 10

Write down the exact words you would use if you had to make the following FTAs:

1 Asking a friend to lend you a pen for the third time this week.

2 Asking a parent for money to go out.

3 Getting a relative you don't see very often to open the window.

Language around you 11

1 Next to your answers to Language around you 10, note whether they were positive, negative or off-record.

2 For each scenario, script other approaches, so that you have a full set of positive, negative and off-record strategies for each.

Using theories in analysis

These relation theories are most obviously relevant when examining texts with an element of interaction. Although they were conceived with speech in mind, they can usefully be used in analysing some electronic texts.

Data response exercise 14

Read the e-mail below, sent from a student to a teacher.

How is politeness used here?

Check your ideas with the feedback (page 54).

> Blatantly already gave us loads, but practice poetry q's please!
>
> Thankyooooou
>
> Jake

Another angle to consider: pragmatics

Pragmatics refers to the gap that sometimes exists between what is meant and the words actually used.

Language around you 12

Explain the pragmatic meaning of each of the following, and comment on the strategies being used. Check your ideas with the feedback (page 54).

1. *Mum*: And what time do you call this, then, lady?

2. *Stranger*: Excuse me, but have you got the time at all?

3. *Teacher*: Decided to join us, have you, Rob? Would you happen to have the time on you?

Pragmatics and paralinguistics

We usually interpret the pragmatic meaning of things from their context, and the paralinguistic features used help us in the interpretation. The sentence 'he's happy today', if meant literally, has a neutral **intonation**, but it can also be said ironically with a more exaggerated intonation that starts and ends high. In written and blended mode texts, this can be harder to detect. This is one of the reasons emoticons (smileys) and abbreviations such as j/k (just kidding) are used in the blended mode.

Topic revision exercise

Complete the questions on your own, then discuss your ideas with a partner.

1. Name the four aspects that make up the concept of 'context'.

2. a Explain the difference between convergence and divergence.
   b How would you upwardly converge?
   c How would you upwardly diverge?

3. a Define 'face'.
   b What are your positive face needs?
   c What are your negative face needs?
   d Describe a positive politeness strategy.
   e Give an example of a negative politeness strategy.

Key terms

Pragmatics: the 'real' meaning of a text or message, the idea we understand when 'reading between the lines'.

Intonation: the way the pitch of our voices goes up and down as we speak.

Lexis, semantics and mode

In this topic you will:

- learn about the frameworks of lexis and semantics
- study some lexical-semantic features of different modes
- practise commenting on lexical-semantic features of a range of texts.

Key terms

Semantics: relating to the meanings of words or a text.

Synonym: a word meaning the same as another word.

Register: the level or degree of formality of a text or word.

Slang: informal vocabulary more usual in spoken than written language, often associated with a particular group or context.

Semantic field: a group of words related by their meaning, e.g. the words novel, play, poem belong to the semantic field of literature.

Secondary semantic field: a semantic field not directly related to the subject matter of the text.

Extension activity

Repeat the exercise with new words, or compare notes with another group and see if you can add to each other's ideas.

The words we choose to use

Both **lexis** and **semantics** are concerned with the words we choose to use. For each, there is a section in the Lexical-semantic framework in the toolkit on page 214, which you will need to refer to as you work through this section. For now, we'll start with the concept of lexis.

Lexical choices

The English language has a complex history and over the centuries has borrowed words from many sources – Latin, Greek, German, French – as well as adapting Anglo-Saxon and Norse words. This means we have a vast choice of words at our disposal, often with several ways of saying the same thing. One of the ways we can distinguish between these various **synonyms** is by their **register** or degree of formality and complexity. As with many things in language, the decision about which word to use is bound up with context.

An obvious example here is the use of **slang** – words you use with your friends that are not necessarily appropriate when talking to your parents, and would most likely be even less appropriate with your grandparents. Your casual speech register is likely to be quite different to that of other generations.

You'll need to make far finer distinctions that this, however, but as a competent user of English already, you instinctively know that 'estimate' is a more formal lexical choice than 'guess'.

Language around you 13

1. In a group, find several synonyms for the following in a thesaurus: house; food; kill. For each synonym listed, think about factors like:
   - the kind of person who might use that word
   - the context it could appear in
   - any contexts where it wouldn't be appropriate.

2. Rank the synonyms from most formal to most informal (you may not be able to do this precisely and might end up with some ties).

Check your ideas with the feedback (page 54).

The basics of semantics: field

We often identify the **semantic field** of a text when analysing it, because it can be a quick way of summing up its focus. Semantic fields get more interesting, however, when you look at secondary ones, or fields used as metaphors. For example, in some sporting texts, there is a kind of extended metaphor of battle: the winning team 'triumphs', players are 'heroes' and they 'fight bravely'. This kind of **secondary semantic field** tells us much more about the 'flavour' of the text than if you just comment on the main semantic field of the sport involved. A similar field is also often used when writing about serious illness and death:

people 'fight' cancer, they die 'after a long battle'. To an extent, this reveals our underlying attitude to death and illness as something to be fought against, an enemy. This approach of noting related words to find secondary semantic fields tells us a lot about the connotations of a text and will also be useful in Unit 2.

Data response exercise 15

Using the Lexical-semantic framework in the toolkit on page 253 to help you, find examples of the following in the extract below:

■ main semantic field

■ secondary semantic field

■ jargon

■ informal lexis

■ cliché.

Try connecting the features you've identified to their effect. How do they connect to the context of this text?

Check your ideas with the feedback (page 54).

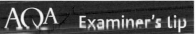

■ Key terms

Cliché: an overused expression.

Well, now you've found out how amazing your body is, I bet you're itching to take a peep at the working bits inside. Don't worry, this is quite normal. *But DON'T do it!* The body isn't designed to be opened by non-experts and this can result in serious body breakdowns!

For example, in 1994 a French postman cut open his body to check that the body mechanics (also called surgeons) had removed a body bit called the appendix. The poor old postman's body broke down for ever.

What that postie needed was a body-bit checklist with details of what each body part is designed to do. Then he might have found out what was going on inside his body without looking inside. Well, as luck would have it, this handbook features just such a checklist and it's coming up next ...

Nick Arnold and Tony DeSaulles, The Body Owner's Handbook, 2002

AQA Examiner's tip

When you are writing full analyses of texts, you'll always need to connect *features* you identify with their *effect* and/or *meaning*. In the feedback to Data response exercise 15 (page 65), you have examples of how labelled features are explained by reference to the *context* of the text.

Figurative language: language that is not used in a literal way; features like metaphor, simile and personification.

Metaphor: a figure of speech or figurative usage where an object is described as being or as though it were something else.

Simile: a comparison between two things using 'like' or 'as' (e.g. 'the boy jumps like a frog').

■ Lexis, semantics and the written mode

As a general rule, the written mode uses a higher register than the spoken, although there are of course exceptions. There are no lexical or semantic features that are specific to the written mode, but it could be said that we use a fuller range of registers in writing than in speaking, and are more likely to use jargon. **Figurative language** is often more obvious in the written mode, and is more likely to be used in a deliberate way.

■ Data response exercise 16

Read the first stanza of the poem *Crush* by Carol Ann Duffy below.

1 In this extract, identify:

   a a metaphor

   b a simile

2 Make some notes on effects the imagery has here.

Check your ideas with the feedback (page 54).

> The older she gets,
> the more she awakes
> with somebody's face strewn in her head
> like petals which once made a flower.

■ Lexis, semantics and the spoken mode

One particularly interesting lexical feature of speech is vague language. This can take various forms and is widely used in casual conversations.

Non-specific names that are made up are used for things we can't identify, or have forgotten the name for – *thingummy, whatsit, whojamaflip*. People often have preferred vague labels that they use, so they can make up part of our idiolect.

The interesting thing is that we sometimes use these vague, non-specific names even when we do know the name for something. It may be that we don't want to seem like a know-it-all, or maybe we've only just

Fig. 12 *Does vague language work here?*

Fig. 13 *Should we always be precise?*

learned that word and feel awkward about using it, or perhaps the context is just too casual for jargon-laden language to be used.

Vague **tails** are often used when we've run out of things to say and want to mark the end of our turn, or when we don't want to appear too clever or over-confident. These are phrases like 'and that', 'or something', 'and stuff' and 'or whatever'.

Vague times and measurements are also often used in speech. We often arrange to see someone 'about seven', 'nineish' or 'around half-eight'. Again, being precise about time may seem, in some contexts, to be excessively picky. Sizes of things that we can't see in the conversation are often described by reference to something we can see, 'about the size of that chair', for example.

We've already seen -*ish* used for time, but the vague **suffixes** -*ish* and -*y* can be used in many situations: bluey/bluish, 'the sky's all aeroplaney'.

Fixed expressions

Another key lexical feature of speech is the use of fixed expressions. These may take the forms of **idioms** or clichés, such as 'at the end of the day', or **collocational** pairs and triplets, like 'this and that' or 'hook, line and sinker'. Popular phrases from the media are also often borrowed in everyday speech.

Other lexical features of speech

Broadly speaking, the spoken mode is likely to use a more restricted lexical range than the written, and to make more use of colloquialisms. The overall register may well be lower, and the lexis less complex.

Fillers are encountered primarily in the spoken mode and are generally used unconsciously. Often it is part of a person's idiolect whether they tend to say 'like', 'ok' or something else when hesitating.

Discourse markers are used to indicate a change of topic, or a return to an earlier topic. They may be a single word: 'well', 'so', 'anyway'; or a whole phrase: 'as I was saying', 'going back to what I said before'. They act as attention getters and are commonly found in classroom talk as well as casual conversation.

Hedges are very commonly used in speech to soften what we are saying. They include phrases like 'sort of', words like 'maybe', and politeness strategies like 'could you possibly'. They are important in everyday conversation as they prevent things from seeming too blunt.

Key terms

Tail: a word or phrase added on to the end of a sentence.

Suffix: an ending that adapts the original word in some way.

Idiom: metaphorical or non-literal sayings common in their cultural context.

Collocation: a set of words, often a pair or a phrase, which has become strongly associated.

Filler: a word, phrase or sound used to fill a gap.

Discourse marker: a word or phrase used to gain attention and to show the topic is being changed.

Hedge: a word or phrase used to pad out and soften what's being said.

Data response exercise 17

Using the Lexical-semantic and Interaction frameworks in the toolkit (pages 213 and 214), check the meaning of the following and find examples of them in the transcript on page 32. Some are from previous topics.

- colloquialism
- reformulation
- discourse marker
- hedge
- three-part exchange.

Check your answers against the feedback (page 54), bearing in mind that there are more examples of these features to be found.

Transcript

Tim	and what's the idea obout the earth (.) Yin was earth (.) dark weak cold more like a **wo**man (.) what do **you** think (.) do you **agree** with it
Matt	**I** do
Tim	you do (1) hand **on** (.) let's have a girl (.) Sylvia come on (.) 5 you seem to be willing to talk
Sylvia	**ru**bbish
Tim	do **you** think it's rubbish (1) what's it saying about women
Clare	they're ⌈weak⌉
Tim	⌊right⌋ (.) yeah it's saying they're weak (.) now (.) 10 would you agree
Boys	yes sir
Tim	no (.) not the lads (1) that all women are weak
Girls	⌈**no no no**⌉
Boys	⌊**yes yes**⌋ 15
Tim	well (.) **some** of the boys think yes (.) **all** of the girls obviously think no (.) who do you think made the myth up (.) a woman or a man
All	**a man**
Tim	why do you say it was a man 20
Sylvia	coz he's saying **horrible** things about women
Tim	well I bet it was a ma who first thought of it as well (.) what do you think it would have been **like** for a woman living at the time (1) from what's been said int he story so far (.) how do you think women were **treated** 25
Clare	**terrible**
Tim	why do you think it would have been terrible
Clare	because they had to **work**
Tim	they had to work (.) yes (.) I bet they did
Jenny	they got **whipped** 30
Tim	they **might** have got whipped (.) they might have done (.) I don't know (1) and who's the **gaffer** (.) who's in **charge**
Clare	**stupid** men
Tim	stupid men eh [*student laugh*] right do you notice what we've done (.) we started off saying we're going to look at 35 ideas around the world (.) how important (.) what **else** have we also done
Jenny	saw how men looked at women
Tim	we say how mean looked at women (.) you're **nearly** there (.) what **exactly** do you mean (.) can you say (.) tell us a bit 40 more (.) go on
Jenny	how he doesn't like her (.) how he thinks she's weak
Tim	yet but what else have we looked at here
Clare	how they lived
Tim	how they **lived** (.) in other words the ideas they had about 45 themselves and the **way** they **lived** (.) so (.) from a story long ago we've used that story to work out how people thought about themselves (.) how they lived

A.D. Edwards and V.J. Furlong, The Language of Teaching, *1978*

■ Lexis, semantics and blended modes

Depending on the context involved, blended mode texts can use features of speech and of writing. E-mails, online chat and blogs are often written in a more speech-like style and may use some of the features identified here, while commercial e-mails and websites are likely to use more standard English, even if the style and lexis overall is quite informal.

■ Electronic communication and lexis

There is a great deal of controversy over the use of 'txt' or 'textese' or 'text message language', but it remains a key feature of some kinds of electronic text. Frequently used in text messages, it is also seen in chat rooms, bulletin boards and some e-mails. The main features of txt and 'netspeak' are shown in Table 2.

There are also whole semantic fields of internet-related terms. 'Blogging', 'netiquette' and 'surfing' are a few examples of hundreds of new words in this area. There is also 'techie' jargon – which only computer experts understand, but many new computer-related words of the last 20 years began as jargon words known only to a few, e.g. RAM, defrag, FAQ.

These lexical features of electronic texts are genre and mode features, as they are bound intrinsically with the electronic mode and the specific genre of the text – the BBC News website, for example, rarely uses txt, unless it's a story about txt.

Table 2 *Main features of txt and 'netspeak'*

Feature	Description	Examples
Deletion	Missing letters out, often vowels	gd (good) ppl (people)
Clipping	Missing off start or end letters	goin (going)
Letter homophones	Using a single letter that sounds like the word	u (you) r (are)
Number homophones	Using a number that sounds like the word, or part of a word	4 (for) 2moro (tomorrow)
Phonetic spelling	Spelling the word the way it sounds	fone (phone)
Acronym	Using initial letters only – can be pronounced as a word	lol (laughing out loud)
Initialism	Using initial letters only – is read as letter names, not a word	btw (by the way)
Blend	Combining two or more words or part words (at least one word must not be complete)	blogorrhea (the disease of blogging to excess)
Deviant spelling	Using a non-standard spelling for effect, often not reducing the number of letters	boi (boy) woz (was)

■ Data response exercise 18

Refer back to the MSN conversation on page 19. Make five points describing the features of the text, using as wide a range of terms as you can at this point. You should include the effects, purposes or meanings of features with your answer.

■ Topic revision exercise

Complete the questions on your own, then discuss your ideas with a partner.

1 Name five features from the frameworks of lexis and semantics.

2 Create a semantic field of animals with five terms.

3 Define and/or give examples of the following:
   a hedging
   b discourse marker
   c acronym
   d personification
   e vague language.

Phonology and mode

In this topic you will:

- learn about the framework of phonology
- study some phonological features of different modes
- practise commenting on phonological features of a range of texts.

Key terms

Phonology: the study of the sounds used in a particular language.

Link

Basic phonetic terms will also be needed in Section B Language development, and in studying accents at A2.

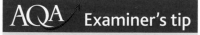

AQA Examiner's tip

Note that you are *not* expected to use or learn the IPA for your exams. It is important, however, that you understand that letters do not directly relate to sounds in English, and that you learn some basic phonetic terms.

The study of sound

Phonology is the study of sound, so in this section we'll be looking at how sound is used and manipulated in texts of various kinds. This phonological framework clearly is used differently in speech than in written or electronic modes – you actually hear speech, whereas phonological effects in written texts are often 'heard' only in the mind.

Some of these features will be familiar to you, but there will also be new terms here. Some of the ways in which sound is described will be relevant also in Section B Language development, later in this unit.

The International Phonetic Alphabet (IPA) is used to describe sounds more precisely than letters. For example, the 'a' in 'hat' and 'cart' do not sound the same, and the 'a' in 'grass' may be like either, depending on your accent. The IPA was created to enable linguists to describe sounds more accurately, making these fine distinctions. Dictionaries give pronunciations of words using the IPA, as it allows far more precision than using letters.

Data response exercise 19

Examine the two brief extracts below, and note which consonant sound group is dominant in each. Refer to the Phonological framework in the toolkit on page 217 for the labels.

It was drowsily warm,
with dozens of bees
lazily buzzing
through flowers and trees.
Hairy Maclary decided to choose
a space in the shade
for his afternoon
snooze.

L. Dodd, Hairy Maclary and Zachary Quack, *2004*

Peter Piper picked a peck of pickled peppers.

Puns

Because puns play with sound and meaning, they can be considered semantic or phonological effects. Most puns rely on a word sounding like another word or words. Have a look at the pun explanations in the Phonological framework in the toolkit on page 217, and complete the activity below.

Language around you 14

1. Collect examples of shop and business names that use puns, e.g. hairdressers like 'A Cut Above' or fish and chip shops like 'The Codfather'. You should aim to find at least two examples of each kind of pun.

2. Share and compare your findings within the class.

3. Is one type of pun more common than others?

4. Do the types of pun line up with the types of business?

Phonology and the written mode

Phonological features in the written mode are usually literary effects like **alliteration**, **assonance**, rhythm and rhyme. Although we tend to think of these as poetic devices, they occur in many types of text, including headlines and advertising slogans.

Data response exercise 20

Write a short paragraph describing the phonological effects of the extract below.

Check your ideas with the feedback (page 55).

> The Great Ouse. Ouse. Say it. Ouse. Slowly. How else can you say it? A sound which exudes slowness. A sound which suggests the slow, sluggish, forever oozing thing it is. A sound which invokes quiet flux, minimum tempo; cool, impassive, unmoved motion. A sound which will calm even the hot blood racing in your veins. Ouse, Ouse, Oooooouse…

G. Swift, Waterland, *1983*

Phonology and the spoken mode

An obvious thing to note here is that people speak with **accents,** and this is occasionally reflected in a transcript. More common, though, are features like **elision**, **emphatic stress** and the use of non-verbal sounds, especially non-verbal fillers or voiced pauses.

Data response exercise 21

In the following short utterances below, describe and comment on phonological and other features.

1. so (.) well (.) um ( ) I've er decided that It ah really would be best if uh you stepped back from this project (.) for a while

2. an' like she's losin' int'rest (.) y'know (.) 'cos 'er mam won't let 'er do **nothin'**

Key terms

Alliteration: the repetition of consonant sounds at the beginning of words or stressed syllables.

Assonance: the repetition of vowel sounds, or of similar vowel sounds.

Accent: the specific way words are pronounced according to geographical region.

Elision: the missing out of sounds or parts of words.

Emphatic stress: emphasising a word or phrase in speech (usually indicated by bold type).

■ Phonology and blended modes

There are several ways in which blended mode texts may make use of phonology, depending on their context. Some written texts may use phonology to evoke speech, thus blending modes creatively. The representation of accent in dialogue or even an entire novel is a good example of this, as in the *Wuthering Heights* extract below.

■ Data response exercise 22

Read the brief extract from *Wuthering Heights* by Emily Brontë and note down your first impressions of the passage. What does it make you think? How is your reaction to it affected or created by the representation of accent?

'T' maister nobbut just buried, and Sabbath nut o'ered, und t' sahnd uh t' gospel still i' yer lugs, and yah darr be laiking! Shame on ye! Sit ye dahn, ill childer! They's good books enough if ye'll read 'em; sit ye dahn, and think uh yer sowls!

E. Brontë, Wuthering Heights, *1847*

So phonology can be a helpful way for writers to evoke the spoken mode and create character and atmosphere. Bringing an accent to the page can help the audience to 'place' the action more clearly in a real location, and some writers are often described as writing about 'real' people because they use accent and dialect in their work. This description comes from an assumption that working-class people have stronger accents and that they are somehow more 'real'.

Link

Accent and dialect are explored in more detail at A2 in Unit 3.

■ Phonology in electronic texts

There are two aspects to sound in electronic texts. There are actual sounds included, for example background music on a website, and there is also the representation of sound visually. We'll focus on the latter, but you should acknowledge that the possibility of including audio is another way in which electronic texts are different.

Creativity and phonetic spelling

As noted in Lexis, semantics and mode (pages 28–33), phonetic spelling is used in many informal electronic texts. On social networking sites, forums and bulletin boards, as well as in chat, msn and e-mail, a range of phonetic effects can be found. This may just be simplified spelling based on sound, like the use of 'coz' for 'because' to save time, but often it is used in a creative way to represent the writer/speaker more clearly, for example elongated sounds like 'Noooooo!' This can't be claimed to save time or space in typing, so it must have a different purpose, and it seems to be similar to the purpose of smileys or emoticons – to try to make up for the lack of non-verbal communication (NVC) in on-screen communication.

People can choose how to represent themselves more freely online than in 'real life', and spelling choices can be an important part of projecting an on-screen identity.

Topic revision exercise

Complete the questions on your own, then discuss your ideas with a partner.

1 Explain why the IPA is necessary.

2 Name two sound groups and give examples.

3 Name five phonological devices or features.

4 Identify a phonological feature or group of features you could look for in each mode.

Grammar, syntax and mode

In this topic you will:

- begin to develop your grammatical knowledge
- learn about the framework of syntax
- study some grammatical and syntactical features of different modes
- learn how to use grammatical and syntactical features in meaningful analysis.

Key terms

Grammar: the word framework concerned primarily with word class and morphology. It deals with patterns of usage rather than punctuation or rules.

Grammar and syntax – the key to successful analysis

If you want to achieve a good grade at AS and A2, it is vital that you engage with **grammar** and **syntax** in the analysis questions. There are exercises in this topic to help you practise this, and you will find explanations and examples in the relevant frameworks in the toolkit on page 206.

Remembering word classes

You will not be asked about **word class** in isolation (no exam consists of a list of words for you to classify), nor will you be directed to particular words in a text to categorise. In the course of your analysis, however, you are expected to identify word classes used frequently or unusually. You might comment, for example, that most of the nouns used in a text are abstract and why that is, or what effect it has. You could also comment that a certain word class is unusual in this genre and explore why the writer has chosen to use it.

In starting out, you'll need to go back to the Grammatical and morphological framework in the toolkit (page 207) many times to become familiar with the terminology, and it may help you to use frames to remember the classes of words. For example, 'a little ___' is likely only to be followed by a common noun.

■ Key terms

Syntax: the linguistic framework dealing with word order and sentence structure.

Word class: words that have the same formal properties.

Proper noun: the name of a specific individual, place or work: John, Fluffy, Halifax, the Mona Lisa, Frankfurter.

Common noun: the name of an object, type of animal, person or idea.

Abstract noun: the name of an abstract idea or concept, e.g. peace.

Concrete noun: a subcategory of common nouns – the name of a tangible, physical object.

■ Word class: types of noun

You already know that a noun is a 'naming word', and you may well be comfortable distinguishing **proper nouns** from **common nouns**. The next activity will help develop your understanding of nouns by introducing another pair of possibilities: **abstract** and **concrete**.

■ Language around you 16

Look at these two sets of nouns. Each set represents a different category. Explain in your own words, and as clearly as possible, what the difference is between the two sets. Check your ideas with the feedback (page 55).

Set A: peace; hypocrisy; terrorism.

Set B: elephant; lung; shop.

■ Data response exercise 23

Compare the two extracts below, taken from webpages, in their use of nouns.

1 Identify which is the most common noun type in each text.

2 Explain how this relates to their context.

Check your ideas with the feedback (page 55).

Lemon Chicken with Rosemary – Serves 4

Ingredients
4 boneless chicken breasts, skinned
1 lemon, sliced
2 tbsp olive oil
120ml/4fl.oz. lemon juice
1 tbsp dried rosemary

Instructions
1. Place the chicken, sliced lemon, olive oil, lemon juice and rosemary in a shallow dish and mix well. Cover and marinate overnight in the fridge.
2. Grill over medium coals for 15–20 minutes, turning 3 or 4 times and basting with any remaining marinade, or until cooked through. Serve hot.

www.recipes4us.co.uk

AQA Examiner's tip

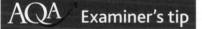

The grammatical and syntactical frameworks are the key to success in English Language and it is often students' knowledge of these frameworks that has the most effect on their final grade.

Word classes (e.g. noun, adjective) are very important from now on. To analyse a text well, you need to be able to accurately identify the key word classes within it.

ⓘ **Friends of the Earth Trust** 80,655 searches

Friends of the Earth Trust works to inspire and educate the public to become more personally involved in improving their local environment. We achieve this by responding to public concern and providing reliable, well informed and researched solutions to environmental problems. Our vision is of a world where everyone's needs are met in a way which values our quality of life an safeguards the future of the environment.

Friends of the Earth wants a world where protection of the environment and meeting everyone's needs go hand-in-hand.

How you can support Friends of the Earth Trust through everyclick.

Everyclick.com works just like any other search engine but it also enables you to raise money for Friends of the Earth Trust every time you search the web.

There are a number of ways in which you can make sure every search you make benefits Friends of the Earth – to see full details just put your mouse over the icons below. The amounts raised are updated monthly.

£1,521.80   293   2   0

www.everyclick.com (October 2007)

■ Word class: pronouns

If you look in the Grammatical and morphological framework in the toolkit on page 207, you'll find various types of pronoun. The first group to get to grips with is the personal pronouns, as these are the ones you must know if you are to succeed. Check what they are and how they are labelled before attempting the next activity.

■ Data response exercise 24

Identify the underlined pronoun in each sentence.

1 If you ask <u>me</u>, that Laura's gone way too far this time.

2 Is your washing all dingy and grey? <u>You</u> need sparkle-white!

3 <u>We're</u> looking for Little Lane, can you help us?

4 By the age of only three, <u>he</u> could already play several scales on the trumpet.

■ Word class: verbs

Verbs have different types, just as nouns do. **Dynamic verbs** are what you expect verbs to be – they are the ones that describe an activity or process. **Stative verbs**, on the other hand, are often overlooked as verbs, as they describe a state rather than anything active. The most common of these is 'to be'. There are also ways of classifying verbs based on the job they are doing at that time – their **tense and aspect**. An interesting category of verbs is the **modal auxiliaries**, which have a range of effects on the main verbs they appear with. The following activity will help you to explore this.

■ Language around you 17

Rewrite the following sentence from the register of school reports three times, using a different modal auxiliary each time. Check whether you need to change anything else in the sentence and comment on how your choice changes the meaning.

'Andrew will achieve well this summer, if he improves his attendance and behaviour.'

■ Sentence function: what does the sentence do?

This way of categorising sentences is relatively simple to deal with and can be applied to texts in all modes. There are four categories: **declarative; imperative; interrogative;** and **exclamatory.** Essentially, they tell us what the sentence is supposed to be doing in the text.

Most sentences are declaratives, but certain types of text will feature a lot of imperatives or interrogatives. Some texts include interrogatives that appear to be declaratives, and that's always worth mentioning. Exclamatories are the least common and therefore often worth commenting on when they appear.

■ Data response exercise 25

In the transcript on page 40 (which is part of the interview you looked at on pages 12–13), Colin – one of the interviewers – tends to phrase several of his questions to Tony as declaratives. Note which lines these appear in and suggest why he might do this.

■ Extension activity

Spot and label the other pronouns in Data response exercise 24.

AQA Examiner's tip

A good test for stative/dynamic verbs is that stative verbs are not used in the continuous aspect in Standard English. For example, we do not say 'I am believing in ghosts', but we would say 'I am contemplating ghosts' or 'I am thinking about ghosts'. Thus 'believe' is stative, but 'contemplate' and 'think' are dynamic.

■ Key terms

Dynamic verb: a verb of action or movement, e.g. jump, eat.

Stative verb: a verb describing a state, e.g. be, know.

Tense: relating to where we locate a verb's action in time.

Aspect: relating to the duration of an event. Verbs can be in either the perfective or the progressive aspect.

Modal auxiliaries: will, would, can, could, shall, should, may, might, ought.

Declarative: a statement.

Imperative: a command.

Interrogative: a question.

Exclamatory: an exclamation not in any other category.

Key:
(.) pause of less than a second
(2) longer pause (number of seconds indicated)
Bold emphasis
[ ] simultaneous speech
[*italics*] selected non-verbal features
(inaudible) inaudible speech

Colin alright (.) I see from the information that I've got
(*inaudible*) you (.) is that you spent er (.) twelve months
working for a builder in the south of France

Tony um well (.) yeah I did actually I I spent (1) **two** years over
there (.) I worked in a boat yard for some time (.) and   5
[*clears throat*] I worked for a builder as well and (.) you
know (.) I did some bricklaying over there (.) I suppose
that's what got me interested you know

Colin yeah (.) erm alright (.) you did some bricklaying over
there (1) what kind of things were you [doing]   10
Tony [well] all sorts
of things (.) we would do (.) putting flats up you know
and (.) oh just laying bricks (.) that sort of thing you
know (.) general building really (.) drain work and that
sort of thing   15

Colin flagging (.) that kind of [thing]
Tony [yeah] flagging

Colin and then (.) twelve months you spent with (1) Seville
isn't it

Tony Seville Construction yeah they're a building company as   20
[well]
Colin [yeah]

Tony I did some bricklaying er (.) with them too (1) and (1)
that was for about er twelve months I think (1) but er the
reason I I wanted to do bricklaying was because er I've   25
always been interested in it (.) you know

Colin yeah yeah (.) fine [*clears throat*] er the reason for you
coming into training as a bricklayer eh although you've
only spent er (1) two years in total full time

Tony yeah   30

Colin yeah (.) erm you don't feel yourself or in yourself (.)
competent enough to to take a job as a bricklayer as
things stand at the moment

Tony no (.) not really well [*clears throat*] I could do with er
practising the bottoms and that sort of thing (.) you   35
know (.) in bricklaying itself that's that's the reason I I
want to take the **course** you **know**
[*interview continues*]

J.J. Gumperz, 'Discourse Strategies' from P. Drew and J. Heritage (eds.),
Talk at Work, *1992*

■ Adding descriptive detail: adjectives, adverbs and adverbials

These three categories add extra detail to a text and can reveal a lot about
the attitude of the writer or speaker towards the subject, as well as about
the subject itself. **Evaluative adjectives** are often worth commenting on
as they can drastically change the connotations of a text and influence
the audience.

Language around you 18

Describe the effect of changing the evaluative adjective in the sentence below. How does the girl appear in each version?

1 'She was tall and slim, and appeared to be trying to avoid my gaze.'

2 'She was tall and scrawny, and appeared to be trying to avoid my gaze.'

3 'She was tall and toned, and appeared to be trying to avoid my gaze.'

Data response exercise 26

Read the extract below and comment on the underlined descriptive elements, labelling them in as much linguistic detail as possible. Note that some are two-word phrases – if the underline continues between the words, treat them as one unit.

Check your ideas with the feedback (page 56).

The Best Driving Tours:

The Gorges of the Ardeche (the Rhone Valley): The river that carved these canyons (the Ardeche, a tributary of the Rhone) is the most temperamental French waterway: Its ebbs and flows have created the Grand Canyon of France. Riddled with alluvial deposits, grottoes, caves and canyons more than 285m (935 ft) deep, the valley is one of France's most unusual geological spectacles. A panoramic road (D290) runs along one rim of the canyons, providing views over a striking, arid landscape. Plan to park and walk a little on some of the well-marked paths. The drive, which you can do in a day even if you make frequent stops, stretches between Vallon-Pont-d'Arc and Pont St-Esprit.

D. Porter and D. Prince, Frommer's France, 2007

Fig. 14 *The Gorges of the Ardeche*

Grammar, syntax and the written mode

Our understanding of syntax as a system is based entirely on the written mode since it is only relatively recently that other forms of language have been considered worthy of study. So, although we can talk about the 'syntax of speech', most of the labels under the syntax framework heading were devised by looking at written text.

■ Key terms

Minor sentence: a grammatically incomplete sentence.

Simple sentence: a sentence consisting of a single main clause.

Compound sentence: a sentence consisting of two or more main clauses.

Complex sentence: a sentence consisting of a main clause with one or more dependent clauses.

Compound-complex sentence: a sentence consisting of two or more main clauses and at least one dependent clause.

Clause: a unit of meaning containing a verb.

Ellipsis: the missing out of a word or words in a sentence.

Head: a repetition of part of a sentence at the start of it.

Tail: a word or phrase added on to the end of a sentence.

Tag question: a brief ending tagged on to a statement that turns it into a question.

The types of sentence – **minor**, **simple**, **compound** and **complex** – are explained in more detail in the Syntactical framework in the toolkit on page 221. These are the key syntactical terms that you need, but, to make sense of them, you must first understand clauses, which are also defined more thoroughly in the toolkit.

■ Data response exercise 27

Comment on the effect of the syntax choices in the following.

1 I'd had enough that day. Really. One more thing was certain to send me crashing over that cliff and on to the rocks beneath.

2 With incredible self-restraint, Sarah explained that she was not able to carry out that task just at that minute as she had quite a lot of work of her own to do. The nerve of that man!

3 Measure out 100g of flour and rub in 50g butter. When the mixture resembles fine breadcrumbs, add a little of the water.

■ Grammar, syntax and the spoken mode

Spoken language does not follow the same syntax as written language, and units of sense in speech are labelled as 'utterances' rather than 'sentences'. True complex sentences are relatively unusual in speech, but where **clauses** or sentences are connected, it is usually with a coordinating conjunction. This follows the general trend of speech being less formal and less complex than writing.

We also more commonly use **ellipsis** in speech, especially when supporting words with gestures. Pronouns especially are often omitted (e.g. 'going out tonight?') and many more words are contracted than might be in some written texts (e.g. 'he could've gone').

Oddly, as well as missing things out in speech, doubling grammatical elements is not uncommon. People often add **heads** or **tails** for emphasis or clarity: 'She's dead nice, her' or 'Clare, I really like her.'

It's worth looking at the types of question asked in transcripts. For example, direct questions are more commonly used in speaking – when we can expect an instant response – than in writing. **Tag questions** rarely feature in writing but are common in speech, as are other forms used as tag questions, such as 'yeah' ('You're coming, yeah?'). Be careful about labelling all questions that follow a statement as tag questions. Tag questions must use either the original verb or an auxiliary, or reverse the original statement from positive to negative (or vice versa).

It was you, wasn't it?

You are coming, aren't you?

He didn't leave, did he?

■ Grammar, syntax and blended modes

Some blended forms, like text messages and bulletin board messages, use speech-like grammar. An elliptical style is often associated with e-mail and most electronic communication, which, again, is speech-like. More formal e-mails and websites are likely to use the more formal written style, and this will be clear in their grammatical variety and syntactical construction. There are no grammatical features that are specifically blended mode.

■ Topic revision exercise

Since the grammar and syntax topic is vast, the revision activity is correspondingly large. The text below is an extract from an article originally published in *The Guardian* newspaper. It displays a range of features that contribute to its meanings. Answer the questions and check your answers on page 203.

1. Identify and comment on the sentence functions in the first paragraph.

2. Identify and comment on the pronoun used in the second paragraph.

3. Identify and comment on the tense used in the second paragraph.

4. Comment on the clause placement in the last sentence of the second paragraph.

5. Identify and comment on the nouns used in the third paragraph.

6. Comment on the effects of the adjectives used.

Use the other frameworks also to analyse the text 'Wear your ethics with pride'. There are semantic and rhetorical effects worth commenting on.

Step into a changing room and try on that latest shirt. It suits your aesthetics. But does it fit your ethics?

You want to know how it was made, so you scan its barcode into the changing room wall and a webcam screen displays rows of exhausted workers sewing the next batch in a factory in Indonesia – or Bulgaria, Morocco or China. Will this ever happen? The technology is simple, but most retailers would rather focus your attention on the washing instructions.

Globalisation has created employment for millions of people, especially women, in poor countries. They desperately need these jobs but often face appalling conditions. Their right to join trade unions is frequently violated, preventing workers from securing decent conditions.

Retailers claim to be stamping out so-called sweatshops but many are actually turning up the heat. Their demands for faster, cheaper and more flexible production undermine the very labour standards they claim to promote. Last minute orders create excessive overtime for workers forced to meet a deadline.

K. Raworth, '*Wear your ethics with pride*', The Guardian, *Monday 23 February, 2004*

Exam preparation

In this topic you will:

■ learn strategies for approaching and structuring a comparative analysis

■ consider how to pull everything together

■ see a sample analysis question and answer.

Examiner's tip

The question features a list of points explaining what to look for in the texts ('In your answer you should consider...'). These are specifically written for the texts on this paper and will help you in your analysis. Producing an answer by using these points to give it structure is a safe approach to take.

💡 Analysis skills

Now that you've been introduced to the key information you'll require for this part of Unit 1, it is time to focus on the skills you need to demonstrate. The assessment for this part of the course is an exam question, in which you will be asked to compare two texts of different modes. You will be expected to analyse how the texts' language is affected by their mode and context, and to explore how the texts convey meanings. This question carries 30 per cent of the AS marks. One-third of the marks are for AO1 and two-thirds for AO3.

The assessment objectives

AO1 Select and apply a range of linguistic methods, to communicate relevant knowledge using appropriate terminology and coherent, accurate written expression.

AO3 Analyse and evaluate the influence of contextual factors on the production and reception of spoken and written language, showing knowledge of the key constituents of language.

💡 Approaching a question

Below is a sample question from Unit 1.

Examination-style question

1   *Text A* is an internet dialogue conducted via MSN Messenger. The participants are Pam and her son Max, who is in Rome visiting a friend's family before returning to Britain.

      Text B is the introduction to the Lonely Planet tourist guide to Rome.

      (a) Identify and describe the main mode characteristics of the texts.

      (b) Examine how the participants in Text A and the writer of Text B use language to achieve their purposes and create meanings.

      In your answer you should consider:

      ■ vocabulary and meanings

      ■ grammatical features and their effects

      ■ topics and how they are structured

      ■ interactive features of language in Text A

      ■ how the language of Text B addresses the reader and shapes their response.   *(45 marks)*

AQA specimen paper

Text A

ie	From	To	Message	
18:29:27	Pam	Max	Pam sent the wink 'Bouncy Ball' (1) just wondering if you are online?	
18:29:30	Max	Pam	I am	
18:29:48	Max	Pam	I was just writing you an email	
18:29:55	Max	Pam	but I can talk to you on here now	5
18:30:07	Pam	Max	Brill, I have never done this before. Have you got a room for the weekend?	
18:30:24	Max	Pam	I am going to be ok for accommodation in Rome	
18:30:59	Max	Pam	did I tell you that I am going to watch Milan-Rome in the San Siro on Sunday?	10
18:31:03	Pam	Max	Are you flying straight back to Manchester?	
18:31:41	Max	Pam	via Amsterdam, i fly from Rome to there and then to Manchester	
18:32:00	Pam	Max	Your dad will be mighty jealous. i will tell him. I suppose you want roma to win?	15
18:32:19	Max	Pam	of course	
18:32:54	Max	Pam	also i am going on a ski-ing excursion in France at Easter which should be a laugh eh	
18:34:38	Pam	Max	In rome it is very difficult to cross the road because the green men only last for two secs and it is best to have a nun with you	20
18:35:27	Pam	Max	Brill about the skiing. Where abouts?	
18:35:49	Max	Pam	ok, thank you for that. i remember it was quite tricky when we were there this summer but luckily we will have a roman with us so it should be alright	25
18:36:00	Max	Pam	Risoul	
18:36:14	Max	Pam	type it into google and you can see a panoramic view	30
18:37:10	Pam	Max	Never heard of it. Sure it isn't Tamworth (2) in disguise?	
18:37:26	Max	Pam	lol. No	
18:37:40	Max	Pam	by the way mum, LOL means Laugh Out Loud	35
18:39:15	Pam	Max	OK, will load up google earth!	
18:40:08	Pam	Max	Glad you told me about LOL Julie sent it to me in a text	
18:43:01	Pam	Max	going now to cook tea. lovely to talk to you like this. I will try again! Take care. I love thinking about you doing all these exciting things x	40
18:44:13	Max	Pam	me too	
18:44:17	Max	Pam	speak to you soon	
18:44:30	Max	Pam	much love to you and dad and girls and boys	45
18:44:32	Max	Pam	x	

Line 1: The wink 'Bouncy Ball' is an animation sent to the screen of the other participant.
Line 31: There is an indoor skiing centre in Tamworth.

Steve Cooper

Text B

Rome

'I now realise all the dreams of my youth,' wrote German poet Goethe on his arrival in Rome in 1786. Perhaps Rome today is more chaotic, but certainly no less romantic or fascinating. In this city a phenomenal concentration of history, legends and monuments coexist with an equally phenomenal concentration of people going about everyday life. It is easy to pick the tourists, because they are the only ones who turn their heads as the bus passes the Coliseum.

Modern-day Rome is a busy city of about four million residents and, as the capital of Italy, it is the centre of national government. Tourists usually spend their time in the historic centre, thereby avoiding the sprawling, architecturally anonymous suburbs. While the look of central Rome is most obviously defined by the Baroque style of the many fountains, churches and palaces, there are also ancient monuments, beautiful churches and buildings of medieval, Gothic and Renaissance periods.

Realistically, a week is probably a reasonable amount of time to explore the city. Whatever time you devote to Rome, put on your walking shoes, buy a good map and plan your time carefully, and the city will seem less overwhelming than it first appears. It is best to avoid Rome during August, when the weather is suffocatingly hot and humid, making sightseeing an unpleasant pastime. Most Romans head for the beaches or mountains at this time, leaving half the city closed down.

Lonely Planet Guide to Italy, *2003*

■ Guidelines in the question

You will notice that the guidelines help you to remember to use the language frameworks and functions you have met in this section. The points to consider will be different according to features of interest in the particular texts chosen each year, and one way of approaching the answer is to work systematically through them. There are other possibilities, however. You may prefer to take a more contextual route, examining how language is used according to the subject, audience, purpose and genre of each text. You might feel that using the frameworks to guide and structure your answer is the best way of remembering them all. You might choose to put the functions at the centre of your analysis and consider these in order as a way of organising the answer.

■ Language around you 19

To give yourself some practice, try collecting a selection of four to six texts that can be paired up for practice analyses. In the exam the two will be of different modes but will be connected in some way to help you compare them, so make sure you collect texts on related topics or with similar contexts that are of different modes. Try working to a time limit of 15 minutes and list the features that are most interesting in that time. Then, take a further 10 minutes to plan a structured, ordered response. This exercise is good for trying out different ways of approaching texts. It is best if you find a structure that works for you rather than your class all working from the same mental checklist in the same order. You could try structures based around:

- frameworks (e.g. look at lexis-semantics, then grammar, etc.)
- context (e.g. look at audience-related features, then purpose, etc.)
- function (e.g. look at each in turn)
- compare and contrast (e.g. deal with similarities first, then differences)
- anything else that makes sense to you (and enables you to examine the right kinds of feature, of course!).

This method of preparation helps to train you to find the key features quickly, and is an efficient way of determining the approach that is best for you. To extend it, try setting comparative analyses for your classmates and create a list of guidelines, similar to those in the sample paper, to guide their response. You will also need to practise writing several full answers before the exam.

However you approach writing a full comparative analysis, there are three key things to bear in mind:

1 It is a *comparative* analysis and you should not be writing a full analysis of one text and then the other. Compare and contrast as you go along.

2 No one could produce an analysis including everything possible in the time available. Be selective in the features you include. Ask yourself: 'Is this interesting? Is it meaningful? Does this feature enhance the text's effectiveness?'

3 Part of the assessment is about the accuracy of your writing. Spell and punctuate correctly and express yourself clearly.

A sample response

Here is a sample student response to the sample exam question above. Comments in the margin relate specifically to the underlined sections:

The function of both texts is to inform the audience about Rome and activities affiliated with the city. To do this both sources contain many linguistic features. In the MSN conversation it is Max who is informing his mother Pam of his experiences whilst in Text B the writer is informing his audience of what one can expect in Rome. However whilst Text A is an interaction between family members, Text B is written in the view that the reader has possibly purchased the *Lonely Planet Guide* and is therefore interested in visiting Italy. Hence text B is written for that purpose.

The lexis in Text A is of a high frequency, colloquial nature, for example 'should be a laugh'. As Max and Pam are familiar with one another using high frequency language is acceptable in the relationship. Furthermore pronoun usage is frequent i.e. 'you...I'. These devices give a familiar feel to the conversation and make the text informal and inclusive in nature. Like Text A, Text B is also informal in tenor. Pronouns are used here too as the writer looks to address the reader through the writing. For example, 'whatever time you devote to Rome'. This gives the text a feeling of warmth and recognition of interests and allows the text to seem written in light of the readers' needs fulfilling the expected language usage between the two to get views across. However unlike Text A, words are often lower in frequency. For example 'sprawling' and 'thereby' are used. This allows for a professional feel despite the informality of other aspects of the text and gives the opinion that the writer is sophisticated and therefore trustworthy. In this way Text B is accomplishing its purpose

> The candidate could have increased the amount of detail here by being more precise, e.g. 'second-person pronouns are used...'

> The candidate continually refers to both texts to produce a thorough comparison.

of informing the reader of the city in a way that connects to the audience.

Grammatically Text A has a variety of devices which help meanings to be achieved. The text is based within mixed tense, between the present and future. An example of these tenses are, 'I can talk to you on here now' and **'I am going to watch'**. These frequent changes in tense give a view between the two speakers of how life is for one another. Furthermore the majority of sentences are in a question and answer format.

'Have you got a room for the weekend?'

'I am going to be ok for accommodation.'

This format allows the flow of conversation to remain cohesive and inclusive whilst remaining in its informative state. When talking of Rome Max uses negative connotations such as 'difficult' and 'tricky'. This is in a direct contrast to Text B which uses adjectives of a positive nature, for example, 'romantic' and 'fascinating', these are seen as hyponyms of wondrous. Furthermore Text B uses modifiers such as 'phenomenal' to further appeal to the reader by glorifying the city of Rome. A further contrast between the grammatical uses is that Text B uses poetry to emphasise the beauty of the city. Therefore it is apparent that while Text A is concentrated more on the practicality of the city and the difficulty it can cause, Text B is focused upon the picturesque aspects of Rome. In this way both texts accomplish their intended purposes.

Topic shifts in both texts are loose in structure, Text A, being a spontaneous mode, at points has sudden topic shifts, for example after telling his mother of his accommodation being ready, Max shifts to talking about a football match he is going to. This spontaneous nature is carried throughout the conversation and at points impedes on a full cohesive interaction. Topics are largely based upon what is happening in the present and future activities. **This use of tense** keeps the textual purpose as informative. Text B is in contrast to this spontaneous mode as the text is planned out and therefore is specifically structured for topic changes. Changes in topic occur with a new paragraph. This structure was possibly done to aid cohesion and seems more professional. Topics in Text B are chosen in a way that has a clear beginning, middle and end to the source which makes the text easy to follow. Although the topic layouts differ in the two texts, both reach their intended purpose. As Text A is spontaneous full cohesion isn't necessary and the topics used are able to accomplish the informative aims. Likewise Text B achieves its aims as it is reader friendly and set up in a way that shows planning and thought whilst also remaining informative throughout.

Text A includes many interactive features which aid purpose and meaning. Open questions are used frequently throughout. For example, 'where abouts?' these open questions invite an extended reply giving both speakers equal chance to respond and allowing both writers choice of reply. At the beginning of the text Pam initiates a graphological feature using the bouncy ball wink. This shows playfulness giving the text a warm feel before anything is said and setting the tone for the conversation. Pam also tells a joke with 'sure it isn't Tamworth in disguise?' which keeps the manner friendly. Another interactive feature of the text is the use of an acronym 'lol' to show

This is an error – the candidate is mixing grammatical tense and actual time.

This reference to tense is vague, so the candidate cannot get any credit for it. What is needed are examples with all labels used, to provide evidence the candidate actually understands the label.

laughter in response to a joke, creating a sense of acknowledgement and understanding as a spoken conversation between the two would. These features keep the text friendly and warm, indicating and maintaining a good relationship between mother and son in the text.

The language of Text B addresses the reader directly with its **use of imperatives** whilst acting as a guideline, 'avoid Rome during August' thus shaping the response of the reader into thinking over what the writer has told them due to its friendly nature. In addition Text B is helpful and gives good information such as advising holiday makers to 'buy a good map' meaning the reader will respond warmly to the text as intended by the writer. Additionally by using positive adjectives and intensifiers, the audience will gain a feeling of fondness and awe about Rome which ultimately the writer wants and is successful in doing so.

The two texts have a clear structure suited to the occasion for which they are being written. The use of inclusive address in the two texts is probably the most effective single feature but for different reasons. In Text A it draws information from Max about Rome whilst in Text B it is used to include the audience and allow the text to appear helpful. Overall both texts are effective as pieces of informative works because they use strong features from a range of frameworks to convey their specific meanings.

> The candidate has used ideas from a range of frameworks to analyse these texts. This is essential to meeting the assessment objectives.

Examiner's comment

This is a solid response to the question set and it would probably achieve a B or C grade.

Its strengths are that it:

- considers aspects of all frameworks
- constantly refers to both texts, comparing and contrasting
- makes some complex comparisons, for example that both use inclusive address but differently
- makes some good points about the effect of features.

To improve the answer, it needs:

- to be much more precise in identifying features, with examples
- to more clearly consider the functions, especially how the audience is positioned in Text B
- to look at more complex features, especially grammatical ones (these are always the key differentiator)
- to explore more interactive features
- to more explicitly describe mode features of both texts and how these lead to differences.

■ Where next?

The way that texts are analysed and compared in this section of Unit 1 will be developed to an extent in Unit 2, where you will be looking at how texts represent people and ideas. Texts remain, unsurprisingly, a central part of A2 English Language study, and you will have the opportunity to examine historical texts and texts using different varieties of English, and to develop your own linguistic interests via a small-scale research project.

■ Further reading

Crystal, D. *Making Sense of Grammar*, Pearson Education, 2004

Crystal, D. *Rediscover Grammar*, 3rd edn, Pearson Education, 2004

Feedback

This part of the book provides all the feedback for the Language around you and Classroom activities in Unit 1, Section A, as well as the Data response exercises. For the answers to the Topic revision exercises, please go to pages 202–205.

What is mode?

Language around you 1

It's a fairly safe bet that you have used the spoken word more than you have the written word. In studying both now, you are finally going to study the mode of English actually used by most people most of the time.

Language around you 2

You probably felt, as most people do, that speech is more informal and more interactive, while writing is more planned, logical and purposeful. There are exceptions of course – it would be nonsense to claim that speech is always informal (think about a job interview, or meeting the Queen, for example).

Language around you 3

There's no real right or wrong here, but it's likely you placed the chat in the pub close to the typical spoken end of the line, the textbook close to the typical written end of the line, with the others closer to the middle.

Language around you 4

There are many possible answers to question 1 and probably no single correct one. As with speech and writing, the key answer is perhaps 'it depends'. If by electronic mode you're thinking of the BBC News website, it's pretty close to written language, except in the key difference of permanence. You can bookmark a site and find it's changed when you come back to it. That never happens when you put a bookmark into a book!

For question 3, again, there is a wide range of possible answers. For example, electronic forms can be like speech in that they can have an informal tone. That is true of all electronic forms – web, txt, chat, and so on. On the other hand, they can have a visual element that speech does not, either through web design or the use of emoticons/smileys. They share this visual element with written texts to an extent, but their spontaneity and informality can make them completely unlike written forms.

The written mode

Language around you 5

The most formal texts are probably legal statutes or sacred texts. Their language is quite difficult for many people, and they remain in use for a long time.

As for texts you have encountered today, there is probably quite a range. You may have consulted textbooks, noticed some billboard or magazine advertising and perhaps read a newspaper. There are several ways you could have organised your lists – by formality, immediacy, permanence, breadth of audience – and with varying results. Possibly you found a similar rank occurred with different criteria, especially if your list was quite long.

Data response exercise 1

The advert mainly works on a kind of visual pun, implying that removing the letters 'etari' is the same as 'cutting the crap' – in other words, that vegetarians should become vegan if they hope to have a healthy diet. There are other features that contribute to the overall effect, of course, but this visual play is a key part of the advert's impact.

Data response exercise 2

1 The text uses the genre of an eyetest chart.

2 The text claims that the juice contains a substance that helps maintain healthy eyes, so the eyetest chart supports this by making the reader think of eye tests and of eye health. The way the text is slightly out of focus until it is seen through the glass also supports the idea that the juice could help eyesight.

Other layout features include devices like text boxes, bulleted or numbered lists and, especially in newspapers and magazines, satellite and inset articles, pull quotes, subheadings and headlines.

Language around you 6

Text message-type spelling is becoming more popular in company names and adverts, mostly in a bid to seem 'cool' and 'in touch' with younger consumers. You may also have seen non-standard 'k's used, and maybe some exclamation marks to suggest speed or informality. It tends to be companies who trade on friendliness and want to seem approachable who play with spelling in their names – you don't see many banks or solicitors advertising themselves in this way!

The spoken mode

Data response exercise 3

If you read the extract without the pauses, it's really hard to make sense of it all. In spoken text, pauses frequently act in a similar way to punctuation in written text, dividing up the units of sense and allowing the audience to see which words belong together. This isn't true for every pause, of course. Some are there to allow the possibility of response and perhaps the teacher is scanning the room for signs that show the students understand, such as nods. It's also possible that in some of the longer pauses, he or she was hoping for a verbal response from a student, then carried on speaking when no one answered.

The labels 'non-fluency' or 'hesitancy feature' are not very helpful as overall terms, since the punctuation-type pauses do actually aid fluency, making spoken text easier to follow. There are times in the extract, as in many examples of spontaneous speech, when the pauses are non-fluent or indicate hesitancy, but this is not the function of the majority of them.

Data response exercise 4

Tony uses:

- non-fluent repetition (e.g. line 13)
- non-verbal fillers/voice-filled pauses (e.g. line 26), and the throat-clearing could be described as a non-verbal filler in this transcript too)
- pauses and micropauses (e.g. line 26–27 before 'you know').

Classroom activity 1

We tend to have an instinctive understanding of body language, so this activity was probably not very difficult. It depends on what you chose to communicate, however – feelings are somehow easier to explain in gesture than specific events.

Language around you 7

No feedback for this activity.

Data response exercise 5

All the simultaneous speech in this transcript can be described as overlap, since it always has a cooperative or supportive purpose – one speaker is simply encouraging the other (as in line 33) or beginning their turn with a slight overlap (as in line 26).

Tony's use of 'you know' is one of the many clues in the transcript that he is nervous and seeking approval or reassurance. It can be described as a monitoring feature in that he is using it to provoke a response, mainly from Colin.

Blending modes

Language around you 8

Like writing, planned speech is:

- likely to be formal
- well-organised and structured
- for a wide audience, not personally known to the speaker.

Like casual speech, planned speech is:

- able to use non-verbal communication (rather than graphology)
- not available to be experienced again, unless recorded
- experienced via the ears, as an auditory rather than a visual phenomenon.

Data response exercise 6

Syntactic parallelism: 'whether they are + positive evaluative adjective x3'

Triads: 'how women are to live in marriage, how their children are to be trained and educated, and what the future of their children is to be'; equal/just/wise; shelter/food/clothing.

Other rhetorical devices:

- Rhetorical questions are used: 'What security of maintenance has the married woman?'
- Men and women are presented as contrasting opposites (like a 'them and us' scenario).
- Inclusion of the audience: by using 'Let us…' (rather than 'I shall'), Pankhurst is presenting the assumption that the audience is with her, thus strengthening her position.

Data response exercise 7

1 Possibilities include:

- 'a chunk of mashed banana' in the ingredients listing
- 'Please keep me cold' next to the barcode
- 'Pop round to Fruit Towers' at the bottom right.

2 Most of the examples of a spoken mode 'feel' are due to informality and often a kind of vagueness – 'a chunk' of mashed banana is very non-specific and feels like something you would say in describing a recipe, whereas a written recipe would need to say precisely how much banana. 'Please keep me cold' is much friendlier than the usual 'store below 4°C' of most drinks bottles, and the first-person pronoun 'me' personifies the product, creating a relationship between it and the consumer. 'Pop round' has similar connotations of something you would say to a friend.

Addressing the reader directly and in a casual, 'chatty' tone makes the text very informal as a whole. It has a friendly feel to it, which is intended to convey the idea that the company is trustworthy and reliable, like a friend.

Many aspects of the label's design have a 'small company' feel, which makes the producer seem more reliable than a big corporation; it is easy to believe that they are interested in the audience's wellbeing, that they are not concerned only with making money.

■ Data response exercise 8

The dialogue seems authentic, which helps us to get lost in the story. If readers are not able to 'hear' speech as genuine, this getting lost is impossible, and then the novel simply can't work as a novel.

The main way Shute achieves this is through the grammatical feature of ellipsis – neither character says more than is necessary, just as we don't in normal speech. How jarring and unnatural the following would seem:

■ 'And how long have they been gone this time?'

■ 'I forget how long they have been gone this time.'

The author uses exactly the same technique in the interior monologue. For example, in the last paragraph of the extract: 'Fine with me' is a grammatically incomplete sentence (a minor sentence – check the Syntactical framework in the toolkit for more detail), but it is entirely typical of the spoken mode and helps to create the character's voice as genuine. Using speech-like language in the narrative as well as the dialogue helps us as readers to engage with characters and to care about what happens to them.

■ Data response exercise 9

1 Some suggestions:

  a *Spoken mode*: Conversation begins with greetings.

  b Adjacency pairs are used (although sometimes they are disjointed, e.g. line 12 replies to line 7. This gap is due to the timing of turns appearing on the screen).

  c *Written mode*: Colours are used as part of the on-screen identity.

  d Deviant spelling is used, sometimes for speed but not always (e.g. iyyya – clearly no quicker to type than 'hiya').

2 There is some interaction but it's less immediate than when speaking to someone, so there are gaps between adjacency pair utterances, like lines 7 and 12 – but notice that Steve repeats part of the question at the start of line 12 to make it clear.

3 It's probably closer to the spoken mode. Although there are graphological features (colour, font, deviant spelling), the discourse and interaction features are more obvious. Turns are observed in a particular way, the participants respond to each other, they self-repair, and the overall informality is much more speech-like. It's also worth noting here that most of the metaphors we use for CMC relate to speech – chatrooms, msn conversations, webchat, and so on.

■ Context and mode

■ Data response exercise 10

The audience is:	because the text:
Already vegetarian	asks directly, using ellipsis 'vegetarian?' (implying 'are you...?').
Health-conscious	offers facts about 'saturated fat' and 'cholesterol'.
Concerned about the environment	states that veganism is 'for the benefit of ... the environment'.

■ Data response exercise 11

■ *Audience*: The insistence on the blogging environment being 'safe', with lots of protection from inappropriate content, tells us that this is aimed at teachers, not pupils. The clean layout with the simplest of images also supports this adult audience.

■ *Purpose*: The repetition of ideas about safety and appropriateness helps to persuade the reader, as does the impersonal tone: URLs and e-mails 'are scanned', rather than the friendlier 'we scan'. The phrase 'schools of tomorrow' is also persuasive and has a rhetorical force – it sounds like something from a speech.

■ *Mode*: The single image and the uncluttered layout create a no-nonsense feel, while the search box and links are typical mode features.

■ *Genre*: Some of the mode features are also linked to the genre in this case. The page could be classified as broadly commercial, since it is in effect promoting a product. The features that are persuasive, therefore, can be considered genre features, and the search box and links are also typical of blogs.

■ Data response exercise 12

1 The writer's attitude towards the book's topic is that these words are 'bewildering', and they are treated with 'disdain' and 'impatience'. The writer represents him or herself as being like the reader, in need of this book to explain these 'confusing' words.

2 There is a clear assumption that anyone using these words is not 'a grown-up'.

3 The writer assumes that the audience is 'a grown-up' and will not understand the words.

4 The text explains clearly what the book is about, using examples of the words explained within. The way the writing is described is typical of a review, or blurb.

■ Data response exercise 13

Self positioning:

■ Tom B presents himself as keen to join in, openly admitting that he began speaking before really knowing what the topic was. This acknowledgement may be what causes his hesitation in his next turn, shown by fillers (err), repetition of sounds (w w what) and recycling (job seekers' allowance/ unemployment allowance/ unemployment benefit).

■ Kristy and Hannah show themselves to be keen to participate in the conversation, and present an assumption that they are different to the people they're discussing, largely through the 3rd person plural pronoun "they", and the common noun "people". The use of a generalised and more inclusive "you" only occurs later when Tom introduces it.

■ Tom appears to mainly add comments to others' turns. He extends Kristy's first utterance by linking it with the idea of a "chav", and comments on Tom B's partial attention with a possibly sarcastic "course".

Positioning others and ideas:

■ People on benefits are presented as mostly lazy by most of the participants, although Tom B shows he's not really willing to accept that broad idea with his general hesitancy on that topic and the qualification of those 'actually' looking for a job.

■ Education is interestingly presented as being separate to 'real life'.

Relationships:

■ The high degree of overlap and interaction between these participants shows their close relationship.

■ All the students appear comfortable and familiar with each other. The use of mildly taboo language (arsed) supports this informal and friendly tenor.

Text:

■ The topic of people being on benefits is fairly constant throughout the extract, with other sub and side topics present. There is an interesting explicit shuffle to return to the 'real' topic when Tom B admits he didn't really know what was being discussed.

■ There is a topic loop, or perhaps an example of recycling when Kristy returns to the idea of people 'not being arsed' at the end of the extract.

■ Language around you 9

1 Speaker A is converging downwards to Speaker B.

2 Speaker A is diverging upwards from Speaker B.

3 Speaker B is diverging downwards from Speaker A.

4 Speaker B is converging upwards to Speaker A.

■ Language around you 10 and 11

There are no right or wrong answers here, but most people would use a positive politeness strategy for 1, and negative strategies for 2 and 3.

These are possible strategies. Compare with others if possible, to see a range of approaches.

The pen	
Positive politeness.	You know how you're so well organised and always have the right stuff? Well, lend us a pen, mate?
Comment:	*Uses flattery and a term of endearment to stress closeness*
Negative politeness:	I don't suppose you'd lend me a pen again, would you?
Comment:	*Expresses pessimism, allowing choice (in theory, a friend can say 'no')*
Off-record:	Oh no, I don't seem to have my pen…
Comment:	*Not-so-subtle hint, but still not actually asking for a pen*
Money	
Positive politeness:	You'll give me some money, won't you, oh bountiful Dad?
Comment:	*Expresses certainty – implying that Dad is generous, and uses humour effectively*
Negative politeness:	You couldn't possibly let me have some money, could you?
Comment:	*Super-polite, pessimistic and allowing choice*
Off record:	Shame I can't go out tonight.
Comment:	*Again an indirect request via hint*
Window	
Positive politeness:	Hey Auntie Daphne, open the window, will you?
Comment:	*Clear acknowledgement of imposition, and choice clear*
Comment:	*Slangy approach implies closeness. (NB: this is the hardest one to come up with, because a relative you don't know very well isn't someone you'd really use positive politeness with.)*
Negative politeness:	I'm sorry to bother you, but could we have the window open please?
Off-record:	Warm in here, isn't it?
Comment:	*Again, a hint. This time the question invites a response, making it harder to ignore.*

■ Data response exercise 14

Although a very informal text as a whole, negative politeness is used in that Jake expresses awareness at disturbing his teacher. 'blatantly already gave us loads, but' in this example can be seen as a highly informal version of 'I'm sorry to bother you, but'. Note also the electronic mode features of deviant spelling – both for speed ('q's' for questions) and for effect ('thankyooooou'), and the non-use of capitals.

■ Language around you 12

1 The implication is clearly that she is late. By being asked the time, she is perhaps being given a means to escape (perhaps her watch has stopped), but she is also being put on the spot to explain herself. The 'And' starting the sentence acts as a discourse marker and there are no politeness features here – the 'lady' is sarcastic. It's clearly a question asked by someone of higher status in the conversation.

2 This is a simple request for the time, using markers of negative politeness because the speaker is asking someone they don't know for a favour – clearly an FTA. The 'excuse me' is a discourse marker to begin the subject, and the tail 'at all' emphasises the possibility that the addressee may not have the time – it allows him/her to say 'no' quite easily, thus acknowledging and reducing the stranger's imposition.

3 This is quite sarcastic, although it does make use of politeness strategies. The first part uses positive politeness, as it is colloquial in register using chatty syntax and Rob's first name is used. The second sentence with its hedging and pessimism seems to use negative politeness, but is actually quite sharply sarcastic and invites Rob to explain himself.

■ Lexis, semantics and mode

■ Language around you 13

Here are some examples for 'house', in rank order:

Abode – this is quite an old-fashioned word, so it would probably appear in a written context in something quite formal or dated. Unlikely to be spoken very often.

Dwelling – this is a formal word and also quite old-fashioned, but its connotations are different from abode. It is used in legal documents but could also be used about a rustic house (like Grandmother's cottage in Red Riding Hood). Again, unlikely to be spoken very often.

Home – this word is commonly used and has warm connotations of comfort, safety and family. It's spoken frequently but might not be found in some very formal or technical registers.

■ Data response exercise 15

- *Main semantic field*: the body – body, appendix, body bits. This is natural, as the main topic of the text is the body.
- *Secondary semantic field*: machinery – 'the working bits inside', breakdown, mechanics. This field operates as a metaphor comparing the body to a machine.
- *Jargon*: appendix. Jargon use is limited in this text as its intended audience is children who don't have any specialist knowledge in the field, i.e. a child non-specialist audience.
- *Informal lexis*: peep, postie. This is related to the child audience as well, but also to the purpose of informing in an accessible way.
- *Cliché*: as luck would have it. The use of cliché fits into the dominantly informal and non-threatening style of the text as a whole.

■ Data response exercise 16

The idea of somebody's face strewn in her head is a metaphor, while 'like petals' introduces the simile that follows it. The overall impression here is of something unwanted, because the face is 'strewn' and the petals described are no longer part of a flower. The imagery contributes to the stanza's sense of sadness at cast-away flowers and past loves.

■ Data response exercise 17

- *Colloquialism*: gaffer.
- *Reformulation*: what exactly do you mean (.) can you say (.) tell us a bit more.
- *Discourse marker*: well.
- *Hedge*: they might have got whipped.
- *Three-part exchange*: why do you think it would have been terrible/ because they had to work/ they had to work (.) yes (.) I bet they did.

■ Data response exercise 18

There are many things to comment on in this text. The suggestions here are just some of the possibilities.

Reduced forms are frequent in the text, e.g. 'uk' for 'are you ok?', used for speed in this synchronous online interaction.

Colloquialisms and lexis that might be taboo in other contexts are also common: 'arsed', 'shit', 'wanna'. This is due partially to the mode, and also to the audience – the participants are familiar with each other.

Deviant spelling is used for effect: 'wkkid', 'kwl', and as a feature of MSN conversation.

Self-repair (borthers/brothers) is used to clarify meaning and to correct a previous line already sent. (Once sent, lines can't be taken back to correct, just as spoken words can't be retrieved.)

Turn-taking is observed, even though sometimes a participant will seem to have two or three turns together. This is typical of the MSN genre, as participants can't hear each other start to talk as they would in a spoken conversation. This is why questions are often not answered immediately.

Phonology and mode

Data response exercise 19

1 *Fricative* (mainly z and s sounds). Note the long vowels too – ow, ee, oo – they also add to the 'drowsy' atmosphere created

2 *Plosive*. Tongue-twisters work by using sounds from the same group to make it easy to mix them up, e.g. p, t, k.

Language around you 14

No feedback for this activity.

Data response exercise 20

You may have noted some of the following:

- Assonance – repeated use of the 'oo' sound: 'ouse'; 'oozing'; 'exudes'; 'unmoved'.
- Alliteration – repeated 's' sounds: 'say'; 'sound'; 'slowness'; 'sluggish'; etc. Notice how this is supported by the other fricatives, notably 'z' in 'ouse' and 'ooze', etc.
- The sounds used in the passage support what it says about sounds – i.e. Swift uses phonological features to back up the content of the text.
- The long vowel sounds and fricatives together slow the text down (as Swift says), evoking the slow movement of the river, which is the topic of the passage.

Data response exercise 21

1 The frequent micropauses, combined with the non-verbal fillers and the use of two different discourse markers at the start, suggest that the speaker doesn't really want to say these words. The uncomfortable subject is reflected in the speaker's use of non-fluency features.

2 This is clearly from a highly informal context, as we can see in the frequent use of elision, e.g. 'an'' and the use of the fillers 'like' and 'y'know'. The speaker's accent is also represented in the use of 'mam' and the elision of the 'h' on 'her'.

Data response exercise 22

For many people, this extract is challenging. The accent represented is broad, and rather old-fashioned (the first edition is from 1847), and you may not have understood what Joseph was saying. If you did find it hard to understand, you probably felt quite uncomfortable with it. This distance from the text – and therefore the character – may well be part of Brontë's intended effect. Joseph, the servant, is the only character to speak like this and it is a key part of his characterisation, making him difficult to understand and therefore hard to empathise with.

Language around you 15

No feedback for this activity.

Grammar, syntax and mode

Language around you 16

Set A contains abstract nouns, while Set B consists of concrete nouns. The names do help explain the difference. Abstract nouns are sometimes described as 'things you can't touch', and this does mostly cover it – abstract nouns can't usually be perceived with the senses. Abstract nouns include emotions, concepts and beliefs. Concrete nouns can be 'touched' and are objects and living things. Another distinction is that we all (largely) share the same perception of concrete nouns, whereas the experience of an abstract noun is highly individual. Asked to draw a cow or a table, most people's pictures would be similar, but if asked to draw anger or truth, the range would be wide.

Data response exercise 23

The recipe uses mostly concrete nouns, e.g. chicken, lemon, oil, dish. The Friends of the Earth text uses mainly abstract nouns, e.g. public, environment, solutions, needs. It is natural that recipes should use many concrete nouns in their listing of ingredients and their references to equipment to be used in preparing dishes. Charity texts like the Friends of the Earth explanation, however, are concerned with ideals and concepts, and therefore rely on abstract nouns to express their principles.

Data response exercise 24

1 First-person singular object pronoun.

2 Second-person singular subject pronoun.

3 First-person plural subject pronoun.

4 Third-person singular subject pronoun.

Language around you 17

Here are some possibilities, with comment.

- 'Andrew could achieve well this summer, if he improves his attendance and behaviour.'

This version expresses Andrew's achievement as a possibility – it could happen, on condition that he improves things. It is far less definite than the original 'will improve', which implies that improvement will automatically lead to achievement.

- 'Andrew would achieve well this summer, if he improved his attendance and behaviour.'

This version is more like the original version, in that the possibility of achievement seems more definitely linked to improvement. It also sounds more pessimistic overall. The implication is that the writer doesn't think it likely that Andrew will make the necessary improvements.

- 'Andrew may achieve well this summer, if he improves his attendance and behaviour.'

This version is a lot less definite than the original, offering less hope to poor old Andrew. Although there isn't the pessimism of the second example, there is less certainty of the effect changes in his attendance and behaviour would have.

Modal verbs often carry really useful information in analysing a text. They can indicate the attitude of the writer/speaker (but not always – as the 'can' in this sentence implies!), and they can allow a writer or speaker to express uncertainty or doubt, or to hedge. Modality can also be conveyed by other words and phrases, such as 'maybe' or 'perhaps', but modal verbs achieve this neatly and subtly.

■ Data response exercise 25

Lines 2–3; 18–19; 28–29.

It seems to be a kind of politeness strategy on Colin's part to avoid asking too many direct questions. It could be seen as a negative politeness strategy because he's avoiding using commands like 'tell me about it' and giving Tony more options by making it more open-ended.

■ Language around you 18

'Slim' is a relatively neutral adjective, suggesting a factual description. The girl here is not characterised very strongly – she may be avoiding the gaze through nervousness, arrogance or for any number of reasons.

'Scrawny' is a far more negative choice, and contains a judgement on the part of the writer – the girl is portrayed as excessively thin. In this case, you may see her avoidance of the gaze as nervousness.

'Toned' implies a healthiness that 'scrawny' does not, and she may in this case appear haughty and arrogant in her behaviour, since we may read her appearance as being fashionable and desirable.

Interestingly, how we respond to evaluative adjectives can vary dramatically depending on our personal and cultural context. The suggestions here regarding why the girl is avoiding the gaze reflect this – your interpretation may be very different to these. For example, the reading of 'toned' above is quite negative – you may have read this description as relating to a healthy and therefore friendly person, who must be avoiding the gaze for a valid reason. The 'scrawny' description, on the other hand, may have led you to see the girl as fearful, more than simply nervous.

■ Data response exercise 26

There are a few superlatives in this extract: 'Best'; 'most temperamental'; 'most unusual'. These strengthen and heighten the description and are a common feature of the genre of travel guidebooks. The adjectives chosen to combine into superlatives are interesting: 'temperamental' personifies the river and contributes to a view of this landscape as somehow hard, unpredictable. 'Unusual' supports the idea that this tour is worth following as a special experience, a sense also conveyed by 'striking'. 'Arid' supports 'temperamental' in implying a toughness to the landscape, something extreme. 'a little' is an adverbial reducing the intensity of 'walk', while 'well-marked' is a compound adjective made up of the adverb 'well' and the verb 'marked', used as an adjective in this case to describe the paths favourably.

■ Data response exercise 27

1 The short, simple sentence opens the extract sharply, and following this with the minor sentence 'Really' creates a spoken mode feel. The longer, more detailed sentence following this choppy start varies the rhythm and prevents the piece being overtaken by short sentences.

2 This initial complex sentence allows a considerable amount of detail to be shared with the audience. Shifting the adverbial 'With incredible self-restraint' to the start makes it the focal point of the sentence and leads us to see the request for Sarah to 'carry out that task' as unreasonable, as we start the extract seeing things through Sarah's eyes. The exclamatory following this complex sentence offers a change in rhythm and pace, and allows further characterisation of both Sarah and 'that man'.

3 The imperatives in this opening compound sentence are equal in importance, so are coordinated with the conjunction 'and'. In the second sentence, the first half is actually dependent on the second half, indicated by the subordinating conjunction 'when'. This technique is typical of recipes and prevents an over-keen cook adding water before the mixture is ready.

■ Exam preparation

■ Language around you 19

No feedback for this activity.

Introduction

What do we mean by language development?

Children are born unable to speak or to understand the words spoken around them, but within five to six years most of them will be speaking fluently in their mother tongue. Some of them will be speaking more than one language and, even within a matter of a few weeks from birth, many children will respond in different ways to different types of language used around them.

Something has clearly developed in that time, and linguists generally believe that language is *acquired*, not *learned*. Acquisition is not the same as learning. Some linguists say that language is 'caught not taught', and this simple distinction goes to the heart of one of the biggest debates about how most children become fluent speakers by about the age of five. Do they have some kind of inbuilt tendency to tune into language, some kind of ability to grasp its rules system, or do they pick up language from that used around them? As you work your way through this section, many of these ideas will be explored, and the ideas and theories of others assessed. You will have the opportunity to reach your own conclusions.

In this section you will look at the first sounds children make, the first words they speak, and how the meanings of these words are understood. You will also look at how children put these words and parts of words together into meaningful patterns and combinations, as well as how they come to understand how language is used around them to achieve different things.

You will then move on to explore the transition children make from spoken language to written language. This includes how they read and how they start to write (or even use word-processing software), and how they use other blended modes of communication, such as e-mail.

To do this you will need to be clear about the linguistic frameworks you have already studied in Section A Language and mode. You must be prepared to develop your understanding of many of these areas with reference to the language children use and that which is used towards them.

Making a start

Have a look at the data on page 58. All of these are things children have said between the ages of one and five.

Note: in Section A Language and mode you will have learned that one of the differences between written and spoken language is that speech doesn't occur in sentences. Strictly speaking, therefore, all the examples in this section should be written down as a string of words. This could be confusing, however, so for the sake of clarity, punctuation has been used throughout.

Data response exercise 1

1 What do you notice about the **utterances** spoken?

2 What else do you think you need to know to help you make more sense of the data?

Check your ideas against the feedback (page 123).

a	'Dat.'
b	'Horsey!'
c	'Me want one.'
d	'There's a band of mouses.'
e	'What you doing?'
f	'Not eat that daddy.'
g	'Doctor made my ear better.'
h	'I just putting her back.'
i	'The goodies are going on their ship cos they've caught a baddie.'
j	'Don't do that because you'll hit the men and they'll fall over.'
k	'Ruby goes down the stairs backwards, but when she's more older she'll be able to go forwards.'

Key terms

Utterance: a stretch or continuous unit of speech.

Morphology: the study of word structure, especially in terms of morphemes.

Pre-verbal: the stages before actual words are uttered.

This exercise allows you to start thinking about what happens as children acquire language, and to start looking at some of the different factors that might influence what they say and understand. Many of these utterances will be looked at in more depth as this section on language development progresses.

As context is so important, for each of the data sets given in this section we have tried to include a brief reference to what the child was doing and the age the child was at, but this is by no means the full picture.

■ The basics of language development

Each topic will give you more information about how children develop one or part of the linguistic frameworks. For example, there are topics on children's acquisition of new words (lexis) and their meanings (semantics); their acquisition of grammar (syntax and **morphology**), sounds (phonology) and the ways they appreciate the subtle and indirect styles of adult communication (pragmatics). Key terms relevant to the frameworks are defined as they appear in the topics, and then appear again in the appropriate framework in the toolkit on page 206.

Table 1 *Stages in language development*

	Stage	Main features	Approximate timings
Pre-verbal	Vegetative	Reflex crying noises	0–4 months
	Cooing	Open-mouthed vowel sounds	3–6 months
	Babbling	Repeated consonant–vowel sounds and combinations of these	6–12 months
	Proto-word	Babbling sounds that seem to match actual word sounds. A 'fuzzy area' between pre-verbal and grammatical stages.	9–12 months
Grammatical	One word/holophrastic	Single recognisable words	9–18 months
	Two word	Two-word combinations	18–24 months
	Telegraphic	Three, four, five and six-word combinations, gradually expanding as the child grows older	24–40 months
	Post-telegraphic	As telegraphic, but grammatically complete utterances	36 months onwards

Lexical and semantic development

Key terms

Referent: the object or person in the real world to which a sound consistently relates.

Plural: the marking of a noun to indicate how many are being talked about.

Possession: the marking of a word to indicate that it possesses or owns something.

What do we mean by 'lexical' and 'semantic' development?

When we talk about lexical and semantic development, we mean the ways in which a child develops his or her understanding and use of words and their meanings. *Lexis* (words) and *semantics* (meanings) are quite difficult concepts to separate, so here we will look at them together.

What is a 'word'?

Before you can say that a child has spoken his or her first word, it is important to explore what a word really is. Then you can work out if that cry of 'dada' actually means 'daddy' or if it's just a sound that is produced any time someone – or something – enters the room.

Words are often defined using the written mode as a frame of reference (i.e. by referring to a word as being made up of letters and being linked to form sentences). This, however, is not a particularly helpful definition when dealing with children's language. As the focus of this section on language development is mostly on children's spoken language, and because children develop their understanding and use of spoken language long before they start to read and write, a more useful definition of a word might be one that relates more to sounds and meanings.

The linguist Steven Pinker refers to a word as 'a stretch of sound that expresses a concept', so a word can be a sound that relates to an object in the world. But it is only when the sound is related directly and consistently to that object (what some linguists call the **referent**) that we can really call it a genuine word. So, that cry of 'dada' probably means 'daddy' (or something like 'look there's daddy' or 'it's daddy' or 'hello, daddy') if it appears only when the child's father appears – rather than the child's mother, aunt, pet cat or Teletubbies doll.

Words have meanings

Pinker also – and more importantly from our perspective – defines a word as 'a stretch of sound that has to be memorised because it cannot be generated by rules'. Words are therefore not simply sounds that relate to objects in the world, but part of a system of language that uses rules and memory to create meanings. On one hand, words just have to be learned from scratch because there is no obvious link between most words and their referents. (Why does the word 'dog' relate to a four-legged furry animal that goes 'woof', for example?) But on the other hand, as you will see from the topics on morphology and syntax, language consists of rules that govern areas such as tense, **plurals** and **possession**, and word meanings also have something like a rule-governed system underlying them.

Much of this is to do with links between meanings of words. Some word meanings are learned because they are part of a category that a child has already established in his or her own mind (Figure 1). Other meanings are learned because the child has been able to make a leap of understanding about contrasts between objects and their properties (big/small, happy/sad), or about the comparisons between different objects (big/bigger/biggest, dog/cat/sheep/cow).

Cooing: open-mouthed vowel sounds made by babies of about 3 to 6 months old.

Babbling: repeated consonant–vowel sounds and a combination of these made by babies of about 6 to 12 months old.

Proto-words: sounds that resemble actual words but that are not consistently applied to their referents.

Productive vocabulary: the words a child can actually speak.

As you will see during the topic on phonology, the sounds children produce develop from **cooing** to **babbling** and then into the **proto-word** stage. Whatever our definition of 'word', it seems clear that children understand a great deal about what words mean and what they can do before they actually start to produce them themselves.

💡 First words

A child's first recognisable word usually appears at about 12 months of age, but this varies depending on the child. Some children will not utter a single word at all, but instead will start speaking using two- or three-word utterances at a later date.

Once children reach 18 months, they will often have a **productive vocabulary** of around 50 words: that is 50 words that they can say. They will understand many more than 50 words, but this is harder to test. By the age of 24 months, most children will have reached a 200-word productive vocabulary, and by 36 months it will be around 2,000 words. Learning new words is something most people do all their lives, but the speed of children's acquisition of lexis is staggering; most linguists put the figure at something close to 10 words a day.

The first words children produce tend to fall into quite similar categories, and many researchers (including Brown, Nelson and Gentner), along with many parents, have logged the early language of children. Katherine Nelson placed the early words of children into four categories: naming; action; social; and modifying. She found that far and away the largest category was naming words, with around 60 per cent of a child's first 50 words being nouns.

📋 Data response exercise 2

Analyse the following data and place the words into the relevant categories: naming; action; social; and modifying.

Check your ideas against the feedback (page 123).

Rachel's first words

Jasper	no	my	cuddle
socks	yes	toast	biscuits
Daddy	yeah	Marmite	cat
shoes	ta	jam	wassat?
juice	poo	ball	bubbles
bye bye	book	hot	Laa-Laa
more	duck	cup	jump
hello	quack quack	spoon	nice
hiya	woof	bowl	two
Nana	please	Mummy	eyes
Grandad	bot-bot	bang	weeble

Jane Hale

As you can see from the research and the previous exercise, the vast majority of early words are nouns. There is a logic to this as nouns are a word class that usually relates to tangible objects in the real world. (The language researcher Elizabeth Spelke notes that children tend to prefer objects that are solid, still, continuous and well-defined in shape.) Social words, such as 'hello', 'yes', 'bye bye' and 'night night', also have a significant role to play in young children's lives and in the interaction they share with their parents and carers, and these appear quite frequently in children's early vocabularies. It is also apparent from Data response exercise 2 that not all words are easily placed into a single category; depending on context, certain words might mean different things and function as different word classes. Context is absolutely vital, which is why it is always a good idea to explore child language data in its context.

Influences on language acquisition

One important point to note is that while the word classes different children acquire in the early stages are often very similar, the words themselves may differ considerably. A child brought up in the countryside might be likely to use nouns such as 'cow', 'tractor' and 'tree', while a child brought up in an inner-city area would be more familiar with 'car', 'shop' and 'park'. This variation depends largely on environment and could be used to offer support for theories of language acquisition that place input at their centre.

There is also a degree of personal variation found in the types of word that children use in the early stages. Some linguists have identified what they call 'referential' children, whose early words are largely made up of nouns (rather like in Nelson's research mentioned above), while other children, referred to as 'expressive', prefer to use action and social words.

Early meanings

Even before children start to say recognisable words, their proto-word utterances carry interesting meanings. Expressions such as 'joo' or 'doo' (presumably linked to the word 'juice') often accompany actions that the children themselves, or people around them, are carrying out: drinking a mug of juice; filling a cup with water; laying out plates on a table; or putting a carton of milk back in the fridge. While the proto-word might sound like a simple label, it is more likely to be a form of **holophrase**, the meaning of which is more like a short utterance along the lines of 'look there's some juice' or 'it's dinner time'. As children's language develops, these holophrases start to die out and more recognisable words begin to appear. But they don't always mean what they seem to…

Extension of children's early words

Children's early words are often **overextended** to cover more things that have similar properties or similar functions to the actual object. An example is a child referring to any kind of round fruit as an 'apple', or labelling rats, squirrels and rabbits as 'mouse', presumably because they share similar characteristics. On other occasions, words have their meanings **underextended** to cover a narrower definition of a word's meanings. In this case, a child may have a clear idea what a banana is, and use the word when faced with a real banana on their plate, but will not be able to see that a picture of a banana in a book or a photograph of

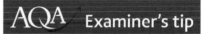

AQA Examiner's tip

Be careful when you talk about children's vocabulary. They usually understand many more words than they can produce.

■ Link

For more on theories of language acquisition, see Language development theories on pp101–110.

■ Key terms

Holophrase: a one-word utterance that is used to communicate more than the one word on its own.

Overextend: to stretch the meaning of a word.

Underextend: to contract the meaning of a word.

■ **Key terms**

Overextension: a feature of a child's language where the word used to label something is 'stretched' to include things that aren't normally part of that word's meaning.

Hyponym: a word within a hypernym's category.

Hypernym: a category into which other words fit.

a bunch of bananas can be labelled in the same way. Children often have quite specific meanings for objects around them, and the mislabelling they apply sheds some light on how they learn to link words and their meanings to objects around them.

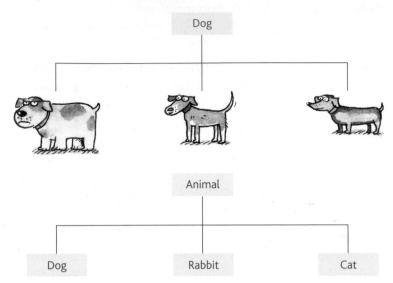

Fig. 1 *Categorising word meanings is part of semantic development*

There is a variety of theories about extension. The linguist Leslie Rescorla noted three forms of **overextension** in her 1980 study.

Categorical overextension is the most common form, and best exemplified by looking at the example of the apple above: the label of 'apple' is stretched to include other types of fruit within a similar, larger category. The same type of extension might relate to the word 'mouse', where the other animals are similar in appearance. In this form of overextension, the **hyponym** 'apple' is perhaps taken to stand for the **hypernym** 'fruit', and it is only when a child has picked up other hyponyms within the same category (such as 'orange', 'pear', 'melon') that these overextensions start to disappear.

Analogical overextension is found in about 15 per cent of Rescorla's cases, and is related more to the function or perception of the object: a scarf might be called 'cat' when a child strokes it, or a cement mixer might be termed a 'football' because of its apparently similar shape and rolling action.

Mismatch or predicate statements are a third form of overextension noted by Rescorla and account for about 25 per cent of the overextensions in her study. These are statements that convey some form of abstract information. An example quoted in Rescorla's research is a child using the word 'doll' when referring to an empty cot. This may appear to be a complete mislabelling of the item, but appeared to be linked to the fact that the doll could usually be found in the cot, but wasn't there on this occasion.

■ **Data response exercise 3**

Analyse the following examples of children's language and the contexts that gave rise to them. Try to explain which form of extension is taking place within each example.

Check your ideas against the feedback (page 123).

Child's words	Context to utterance
Tiger	Used when looking at pictures of tigers, lions and leopards in a picture book
Socks	Used when referring to gloves
Duck	Used when talking about feeding ducks, pigeons and other birds in a park
Cat	Used when pointing at door where cat normally waits
Shoes	Used when referring to own pair of shoes but not when talking about any other type of shoe

While it is fairly clear that labels like proper and concrete nouns can be linked easily to their referents (the objects or people they refer to), other word classes are not quite so simple. Adjectives and adverbs of manner, for example, that relate to feelings and judgements, are often acquired later on in a child's development. Prepositions, determiners and auxiliary verbs tend to appear later for other reasons, largely because they have no clear-cut semantic meaning that can be understood by looking at a 'thing' in the real world. As you will see in the topic on syntax (page 66), these words gradually start to appear in the **telegraphic** and **post-telegraphic** stages.

■ Developing meanings

Children's own *use* of overextensions is one thing, but what of their *understanding* of words' meanings? Do children use overextensions because they genuinely think the objects they are naming are the same thing (i.e. that the pear really is an apple), or are they using overextensions to plug a gap in their vocabulary, knowing full well what the difference is?

■ Research point

Research carried out by Thomson and Chapman (1977), and Hoek, Ingram and Gibson (1986), suggests that children know and understand far more words than they produce.

> In one experiment, five children (twenty-one to twenty-five months old) who were overextending words were first given a naming task in which they were shown pictures and asked to name them. Overextensions were identified and then used to design a comprehension test. For example, if the child overextended dog on the naming test to include cows, horses, cats or sheep, the comprehension test would include pictures of these animals as well as a picture of a dog. The child would then be asked, "Show me the dog".
>
> The results were quite dramatic. Overextensions in comprehension were much less frequent than in naming.

W. O'Grady, How Children Learn Language, 2005

Thinking point

What might such experiments tell us about the nature of overextension? Do children use overextensions because they genuinely believe a dog is a cat, or are they using terms they know are wrong until a more accurate term is acquired?

■ Key terms

Telegraphic: the stage during which children use three or more words, usually omitting grammatical words (i.e. determiners, auxiliary verbs and prepositions) but keeping lexical words (i.e. nouns, verbs and adjectives).

Post-telegraphic: the stage after telegraphic during which many of the omitted words from the stage before start to appear.

It also seems clear from studies carried out, and observation of children's language, that children make sense of new words they encounter by working out what they *don't* mean. They often apply their cognitive skills to make distinctions between words they already know and words that appear to have opposite meanings. So, while reading a Teletubbies book, a two-year-old might be able to identify the 'small teletubby' on the page, even though she doesn't fully grasp the meaning of the word 'small', by realising that it's not the 'big teletubby' she has just correctly identified on the same page. She may not know what either adjective actually means, but is able, through a process of elimination, to work out that if one is 'big' then the other one, which looks different, probably doesn't have the same label.

Similarly, a child can logically assume that, given the choice between an object with whose label they are familiar and another object that they have no label for, the new word they hear will probably apply to the new object. For example, if a child understands the word 'mouse' and is presented with a picture of a mouse and a rabbit, when asked 'Where's the rabbit?', the child will probably be able to identify it correctly. After all, if it's not the mouse, it's probably the other one.

■ Building meanings

The linguist Jean Aitchison has identified a model of three stages in children's acquisition of words and their meanings (Table 2). This offers a useful overview of the processes outlined so far in this topic.

Table 2 *Aitchison's model showing the three stages of children's acquisition of words and their meanings*

Labelling	Associating sounds with objects in the world around the child
	Linking words to things
	Understanding the concept of labels
Packaging	Starting to explore the extent of the label
	Often the stage during which over- and underextensions occur most frequently
Network building	Making connections between the labels they have developed
	Understanding opposites and similarities, relationships and contrasts

As an example, labelling might mean attaching the label 'cat' to a particular animal. Packaging would consist of establishing what makes this animal a cat as opposed to a bird or a snail, e.g. four legs, size, fur. Network building would consist of the child making connections between cat as a label and the cat as a type of animal.

As Aitchison's model makes clear, children's acquisition of words and their meanings is not simply a question of remembering labels they have been taught. It is an active and deductive process that involves the child making sense of his or her surroundings and then mapping out connections between words and the world. The competing theories behind child language are explored later in this section, but much of what you have read here will be useful in looking at whether children learn language through imitation or if certain processes are inbuilt.

Extension activity

Recording (or otherwise obtaining) your own child language data is one way of exploring and analysing what children actually say. If you do not have access to younger brothers, sisters, nieces or nephews, or even children of your own, then don't panic! There are many reality TV programmes featuring young children (*Supernanny* and *House of Tiny Tearaways*, for example), while Teachers' TV often features lessons from Reception and Year 1 classes. Elsewhere, you will find audio and video online that you can use. Approaching local schools and nurseries is something that you can also consider, but be aware that you must seek written permission from parents and institutions, as well as making sure your recordings are conducted safely and ethically.

When you have some data, try the following:

1. Examine some of the early words used by different children and explore the different word classes used.

2. Look at any examples of over- or underextension and try to group them into the relevant categories.

3. Study the range of different semantic fields covered by children in their early words.

4. Compare the lexis used by children of different genders to see if there are any noticeable patterns between girls and boys.

Topic revision exercise

Complete the questions on your own, then discuss your ideas with a partner.

1. What is a proto-word?

2. Why are so many of most children's early words nouns?

3. What is overextension and what types are there?

4. How do children start to 'map out' connections between the different words they acquire?

Grammatical development – syntax

In this topic you will:

- learn how children's early language develops through different identifiable stages

- see how children build up longer and more complicated utterances as they get older

- study the patterns in children's early grammatical development.

What do we mean by 'syntax'?

Syntax is another name for *word order*. When we talk about a child's development of syntax, we are referring to how he or she starts to put words together into patterns, and how he or she develops an understanding of the ways in which word order can control meaning. As you will have seen from the Introduction, as children get older they produce longer and more sophisticated utterances. For more on the ins and outs of syntax, consult the Syntactical framework in the toolkit on page 221.

A growing language

As children grow older, their language skills develop and they begin to piece together longer utterances. Typically, a child of 18 months would be able to put together two-word phrases such as those below, while a child of 24 months or older might be producing some of the utterances seen in the Data response exercises 4 and 5.

a	'Sit chair.'
b	'Mummy pushchair.'
c	'My cup.'
d	'Shut door.'

However, length of utterance – in other words, how many words a child strings together – is not the only factor you need to consider when studying child language.

Linguists use the term **mean length of utterance (MLU)** when analysing what children say. MLU is used to work out the average length of a child's utterances across a sample of data and takes into account not just the individual words but the **morphemes** as well. In an expression such as 'I eating', the child is using two words but three morphemes. 'Eating' can be split into two morphemes: *eat* and *-ing*, where the **free morpheme** *eat* carries the main meaning, and the *-ing* **bound morpheme** indicates the progressive aspect, showing that the child can talk about their action as continuous and ongoing.

The same pattern can be seen in other examples.

- I runned = three morphemes: *I* + *run* + *ed*.
- There was three mans = five morphemes: *There* + *was* + *three* + *man* + *s*.

So you can see that the complexity of what a child is saying is not just based on how many words they use, but also the grammatical units within those words. It is children's use of these morphemes that can often help us grasp what is going on inside their minds.

Key terms

Mean length of utterance (MLU): a calculation based on the average number of morphemes used across a number of utterances.

Morpheme: the smallest unit of grammatical meaning.

Free morpheme: a morpheme that can stand independently and act as a meaningful unit on its own.

Bound morpheme: a morpheme that can only have meaning when attached to a free morpheme.

Link

For more on morphemes, see Grammatical development – morphology, pages 76–80.

Data response exercise 4

Look at the utterances opposite. Count up the number of morphemes used in each one. Check your ideas against the feedback on page 124.

a	'What you doing?'
b	'Not eat that daddy.'
c	'Where's man going?'
d	'The cavemans are laughing'
e	'The soldiers falled over when they got hitted.'

Stages in a child's acquisition of language

One of the most noticeable developments with child language is the progression from proto-words to the one-word stage, and then from the one-word stage towards two, three, four and more words in an utterance. Basically, as children get older they produce longer and more complicated utterances. In fact, most linguists use the numbers of words as the names of the stages themselves: proto-word; one word/holophrastic; two word; telegraphic; post-telegraphic (Table 3).

It's important to realise that these stages should only be seen as a loose framework and not a straitjacket for every utterance from every child. It is not uncommon for some children to bypass the one-word and even two-word stages and go on to produce telegraphic utterances as their first words. Meanwhile, many children do not limit their utterances to just one stage at a time: many will vary their utterances depending on context. It's therefore a good idea to look at as much data as possible – and to consider the context fully – before making judgements about children's abilities.

Table 3 *Stages in a child's acquisition of language*

Stage	Main features	Example
Proto-word	Consonant–vowel–consonant–vowel sounds that are similar to actual words, but applied inconsistently to referents	*Goggie* – this could mean 'dog' but would have to be applied consistently for this to be clear
One word/ holophrastic	Single words that relate consistently to identifiable referents	*Daddy*
Two word	Utterances consisting of two words in a range of patterns	*Daddy go.* *Where mummy?* *Drink allgone.*
Telegraphic	Utterances consisting of three or more words, in which key content words are used while grammatical function words are omitted	*Where daddy gone?* *That my doll.* *Give doggie biscuit.*
Post- telegraphic	Utterances where grammatical words missing from the telegraphic stage start to appear, and clauses begin to be linked into longer sentences	*We went to the park and played on the swings.* *That's my dolly cos granny bought it for me.* *That baddy got eaten by the dragon.*

One-word/holophrastic stage

At the one-word stage, it's very difficult to talk about syntax as the child doesn't have any options: they either say the word or they don't. As you have seen from Lexical and semantic development (pages 59–65), first words tend to fall into four main categories, with nouns being the most common word class. One part of grammar that might be relevant to the one-word stage is morphology, but that will be covered in the next topic.

As the child gets older, he or she will start to combine words into short utterances and this is known as the two-word stage. But before we look at this, it's worth commenting on the holophrastic stage and some of the differences between this and the one-word stage.

Holophrastic means 'whole phrase' and it's a stage during which children use what sound like one-word utterances to convey more than one word's meaning. For example, if a child says 'doggie' when the family dog enters the room, the child might be just labelling the animal with a word, but it's equally likely that the child is trying to convey something like 'look, there's the dog' or 'the dog's come in'. It's quite possible that most one word utterances are in fact holophrases, one notable exception being when parents sit with young children and ask them to name and label objects in picture books, as below:

> *Parent*: What's that?
>
> *Child*: Dog.
>
> *Parent*: That's right. Now, what's that?
>
> *Child*: Sheep.

Phrases can also consist of two words that the child has 'chunked together' after hearing them spoken around them. Utterances like 'inthere' or 'wassat' can be termed **gestalt expressions**: they sound like one word and almost function as short sentences ('put it in there' or 'what is that?'). The most likely explanation for these gestalt expressions is that the child has yet to **segment** the sounds into separate words, so some elements of adult speech such as 'Shall we put your top on?' or 'Have you got your shoes on?' become 'topon' or 'shoeson'.

▣ Two-word stage

At the two-word stage, syntax comes into play and the child is likely to combine words into a range of patterns to create mini-sentences. The word order of these two-word expressions is often very close to adult syntax. In 1973, Roger Brown noted that many of the patterns these expressions fall into are linked to the semantic relationships between the words; or, to put it another way, the words' meanings fit together into patterns.

■ Research point

Roger Brown, one of the most influential child language researchers, put together a table of the main two-word combinations spoken by children at this stage. A slightly simplified version of this is printed here.

Table 4 *Two-word combinations*

Child's utterance	Two-word combination and meaning expressed
I walk/daddy go	Doer + action (often takes the grammatical form of subject + verb)
Eat dinner	Action + undergoer (often takes the grammatical form of verb + object)
Baby medicine/dolly dinner	Doer + undergoer (often an early form of a subject + object where the verb is missed out, i.e. *baby takes medicine/dolly eats dinner*)
My shoe/mummy hat	Possessor + thing (where the possessor and thing will generally be nouns)
Naughty cat/big car	Property + thing (with the property usually being an adjective)
Go away/come here	Action + location

W. O'Grady, How Children Learn Language, *2005*

■ Key terms

Gestalt expressions: expressions which group words together into unsegmented 'chunks'.

Segment: to break down the stream of speech into understandable units of meaning.

■ Link

For more on segmentation, see Phonological development on pages 81–85.

Thinking point

What reasons might there be for children following these patterns of use? Can you link these patterns to any of the theories of language development later in this section?

Data response exercise 5

Using the research point above, try to identify the patterns in the two-word utterances below. Compare your answers with the feedback (page 124).

a 'Daddy go.'

b 'Mummy bag.'

c 'Ball gone.'

d 'Get drink.'

e 'Cup inthere.'

f 'Lion sad.'

As with the holophrastic stage, many of these two-word utterances may have wider or more detailed meanings that the child cannot yet express. It is when they move into the next stage – telegraphic speech – that a more varied pattern of grammatical structures starts to emerge.

Another child language researcher, George Braine, noted that at the two-word stage, children use patterns of two-word utterances that seem to revolve around certain keywords. He called these 'pivot words'. These pivots combined with what he called 'open words', which were less frequent but much more varied. So, a word like 'allgone' would act as a pivot and be combined with a range of other words to create two-word expressions, such as '*allgone* dinner', '*allgone* milk', '*allgone* Daddy'.

It is perhaps important to say here, however, that when you look at child language data, you should not necessarily view what a child says as an incorrect or underdeveloped form of adult speech, but as an example of early language showing signs of rule-governed behaviour.

Telegraphic stage

Beyond the two-word stage, children move into what is known as the telegraphic stage, adding more words to their utterances, but often omitting apparently less meaningful grammatical words such as auxiliary verbs, determiners and prepositions.

Data extract 1

(Telegraphic stage)

Context: girl watching train go by a few minutes after her mother has left for work.

Age: 2 years 4 months.

Ruby: Mummy go work on train.

Link

The significance of children's language patterns will be discussed further in Language development theories on pages 101–110.

Data extract 2

> (Telegraphic stage)
>
> **Context**: imaginative play with teddy bears and figures.
>
> **Age**: 2 years 8 months.
>
> *Adult*: What are you doing?
>
> *Stan*: I giving blanket to monkey.

Data extract 3

> (Telegraphic stage)
>
> **Context**: looking over balcony and finding fisherman who's been there for last three mornings isn't there.
>
> **Age**: 1 year 10 months.
>
> *Mattie*: Where man gone?

Data extract 4

> (Telegraphic stage)
>
> **Context**: watching TV with father and asking question about girl on CBeebies.
>
> **Age**: 2 years 6 months.
>
> *Liam*: What her doing?

Data extract 1 from the telegraphic stage shows how the child's increased sophistication in grammatical structure can now lead to more precise meanings. We call this stage 'telegraphic' because it resembles the language used in old-fashioned telegrams (where you paid by the word and omitted unimportant lexical items, perhaps similar to parts of today's text-speak). The main content, or **lexical words**, are there, but **grammatical words** are missing. The auxiliary verb *'is* going' is missing, as is the preposition *'to* work', along with the determiner *'the* train', and on the level of morphology (the way words themselves are made up of smaller units) the *-ing* inflection on *'going'* is lacking. But having said all that, the meaning of the child's words is clear. This type of running commentary is also fairly typical of children at this age and above.

In Data extract 2, a slightly different grammatical structure is used by the child. A subject + verb + direct object + indirect object is clear from this utterance: the direct object is the thing being given ('blanket') and the indirect object is the recipient of the blanket ('monkey'). This is part of the wider range of grammatical structures employed by children in the telegraphic stage, more of which can be found in Jean Peccei's *Child language: a resource book for students*.

A slightly different example of a child at the telegraphic stage can be seen in Data extract 3. In this example, the child has constructed a question but has omitted the non-essential grammatical items: in this case the auxiliary verb 'has' and the determiner 'the'. Syntactically, this is more advanced than Data extract 2, as the child has created a question structure.

In Data extract 4, a similar question structure has been used to that in Data extract 3, but again the auxiliary verb 'What *is* her doing?' is missing. On this occasion, the correct person pronoun has been used ('her' is a third-person pronoun), but the wrong form (object *her* rather than subject *she*).

Key terms

Lexical words: words that have meaning on their own – usually nouns, main verbs, adjectives and adverbs.

Grammatical words: words that carry meaning as part of longer grammatical constructions, e.g. prepositions, determiners and auxiliary verbs.

While we might be tempted to concentrate on what's missing from these utterances, we should be careful not to miss what is there and how capable the children seem to be of describing the world around them in a variety of ways, asking questions and expressing how they feel. While the telegraphic stage is characterised by what is missing, in terms of communication these utterances are very clear within their contexts and reflect a rapid development in the children's understanding and production of language.

Questions and negatives

The two-word and telegraphic stages are a time in which the typical sentence structure used in declaratives starts to be manipulated by children as they explore the world around them and the language that describes it.

An important aspect of syntax is the way in which it can be altered to create questions and negatives, and children quickly make use of a range of methods to either ask who, where, when, what or why, or to say no. Linguists Ursula Bellugi and David McNeill carried out many observations on children during the 1960s and 1970s. They theorised that there are distinct stages that children progress through as they develop and apply rules to the creation of negatives and questions.

Stages in question development

David Crystal, in *Listen To Your Child*, summarises Bellugi and McNeill's three stages of question development as follows (adapted with new examples):

1   The use of intonation to signal that a question is being asked. For example, 'Allgone' said in a rising intonation might show that the child is asking if the drink has been finished.
2   The use of question words such as 'what', 'why', 'where' and 'when'. For example, 'What dat?', 'Where mummy?', 'When dinner ready?'
3   The manipulation of word order (syntax) to create longer and more detailed questions. For example, 'Where is mummy going?', 'When is dinner ready?', 'What are you doing?'

From this you can see that as the child develops, his or her questions become longer and more sophisticated. Even at the two-word stage, though, there is a basic understanding of syntax, with the child realising that the question word ('what', 'where', etc.) must come at the front of the phrase being spoken. As they get older they have to use more complicated word classes, such as auxiliary verbs, to create more detailed questions. So, 'Where is mummy going?' consists of: *wh-* question word + auxiliary verb + subject + main verb.

Stages in negative formation

There are similar developments for negative formation, and David Crystal points to six stages:

1   The use of a negative word on its own ('no' or 'not').
2   Combining a negative word with other words in the two-word and telegraphic stages, usually at the beginning of the utterance ('No bed' or 'not eat it').
3   Using the negative word in the middle of the utterance ('Me *no* like that' or 'I *not* want apple').

■ Link

For more on pragmatics, see
Pragmatics development on pages
85–89.

4 Increased accuracy of negative words within the utterances, often in the form of contractions being used with the auxiliary verbs ('She *isn't* going' or 'I *don't* want another').

5 Increased complexity and range of negative words ('I haven't got any' and 'I hardly spoke to him').

6 Saying no without saying no (a trick adults often use with children and that they gradually pick up themselves.

As with many patterns in children's language development, the more complicated the expression, the longer it takes to master. Some of these later stages only appear consistently at four or five years old.

■ Beyond the telegraphic stage

As children pass through the telegraphic stage, the missing words – the determiners, the auxiliary verbs and the prepositions – start to appear in the right places, and a range of more complex grammatical features is used. The post-telegraphic stage sees the appearance of more confident use of forms such as the passive voice, different tenses and aspects, and a wider range of clause structures. Noun phrases are also built up into more detailed structures.

Beyond the telegraphic stage, the post-telegraphic utterances of children start to resemble the patterns of adult speech. Clauses are linked with conjunctions to create complex and compound sentences, while different types of clause crop up to serve different functions.

For an explanation of the grammatical and syntactical terms used in this topic, look at their frameworks in the toolkit on pages 207–212 and 221–222.

Data extract 5

(Post-telegraphic stage)

Context: imaginative conversation with father.

Age: 2 years 9 months.

Stan: My head falled off and rolled around but I put it back on again.

Data extract 6

(Post-telegraphic stage)

Context: talking while playing.

Age: 3 years 6 months.

Liam: The goodies are going on their ship cos they've caught a baddie.

Data extract 7

(Post-telegraphic stage)

Context: conversation with father about baby sister.

Age: 4 years 9 months.

Stan: Ruby walks down stairs backwards, but when she's more older she can walk down them forwards.

Data extract 8

(Post-telegraphic stage)

Context: talking while playing.

Age: 4 years 6 months.

Stan: Don't do that because you'll hit the men and they'll fall over.

In Data extract 5, the child uses a compound sentence containing three clauses linked by coordinating conjunctions (*and* and *but*). Within a few months, however, he and his brother are regularly using complex sentence structures with subordinating conjunctions such as *because* ('cos') and *when*, as seen in Data extracts 6 and 7. This added complexity allows the children to express a more developed sense of the world around them, with issues such as cause and effect, as seen in Data extract 8 ('*because* you'll hit the men and they'll fall over'); condition (e.g. *if* I don't eat my dinner); and result (e.g. *so* it fell over) all emerging.

Data extract 9

(Post-telegraphic stage)

Context: conversation in car with father.

Age: 4 years 10 months.

Liam: If the baddies attacked the castle and the goodies weren't there, what would happen, daddy?

Data extract 10

(Post-telegraphic stage)

Context: conversation with father.

Age: 4 years 11 months.

Stan: The other game which Liam was playing was really tough.

Clauses of condition appear too, as seen in Data extract 9 ('if the baddies attacked'), while a **relative clause** ('which Liam was playing') is added in Data extract 10, to offer more information about the subject of the whole sentence. In many ways this is almost adult speech, with a variety of structures being used to explain and describe the world in more detail and with more precision. But there is still some way to go before children become expert communicators, and one particular element of their understanding – pragmatics – still needs some development.

Tense and aspect

Another feature of the post-telegraphic stage is children's increased skill at marking tense and aspect. Some elements of tense are covered in the morphology topic (pages 76–80), but one word class that children seem to use with increased sophistication at this stage is the auxiliary verb. As you have seen from the examples above, auxiliaries are often left out at the two-word stage, but become increasingly important when questions, negatives and accounts of past events need to be formed.

Looking back at Data extract 2, it is clear that the child is trying to create the present progressive 'I am giving', which uses an auxiliary verb to mark the present tense, and an *-ing* inflection to mark the progressive aspect. Even without the auxiliary verb, the meaning is still fairly clear, but when slightly more complicated sequences of events need to be

Key terms

relative clause: a subordinate clause that is used to add more information about another clause element. It acts like an adjective.

recounted, the auxiliary verb is more necessary. Take, for example, the difference between 'I have found it' and 'I found it'. In the first example, the auxiliary verb marks this as a present tense construction, while the use of the main verb in the past participle form *found* shows that this is a present perfect construction. The action of finding has been completed but is still relevant to what the child is doing now ('I have found it and now I'm digging with it'). The second example, 'I found it', is a simple past tense construction, recounting that the event has finished and is perhaps no longer relevant. The use of an auxiliary verb allows the child a subtler palette from which to draw his or her descriptions of what is happening and what has been done.

It's not all plain sailing, however. Auxiliary verbs can be troublesome, as Data extracts 11 and 12 demonstrate.

Data extract 11

(Post-telegraphic stage)

Context: talking while playing.

Ages: 2 years 8 months to 2 years 9 months.

Liam: Did you hid it in my castle?

Stan: Yes, I hid it in the dungeons.

Data extract 12

(Post-telegraphic stage)

Context: talking while playing.

Ages: 2 years 8 months to 2 years 9 months.

Liam: I couldn't found it.

In Data extract 11, Liam's attempt to form a question about an action in the past using an auxiliary (*did*) is hampered by the fact that he attempts to mark the past tense on both the auxiliary and main verbs. In fact the 'correct' adult version ('Did you hide it?') only requires the past tense to be marked on the auxiliary verb.

Likewise, a doubling up of tense marking is clear in Data extract 12, where Liam's statement uses two verbs (*could* and *found*) when only one is required to be in the past tense.

Data extract 13

(Post-telegraphic stage)

Context: talking to father about TV programme.

Age: 5 years 7 months.

Liam: Look at what some people have did.

In Data extract 13, Liam has correctly used the present tense *have* but has added the past tense *did* rather than the past participle *done,* which would have created the present perfect.

Passive voice

Another grammatical structure that appears as the child develops is the passive voice, a construction that children often understand from a fairly early age, but whose structure makes it more difficult to actually construct.

Data extract 14

(Post-telegraphic stage)

Context: talking while playing with toy soldiers.

Age: 4 years 2 months.

Stan: The baddy's been got by the goody leader.

In Data extract 14, Stan successfully forms a passive construction by applying the action of the verb (*to get*) to the subject of his sentence (*the baddy*), and adding the agent of the verb (*the goody leader* – the person who has performed the 'getting') at the end.

Fig. 2 *Grammar: the building blocks of language*

Data response exercise 6

Analyse the Data below and, for each statement, suggest which stage you think the child has reached and why. Suggest what the adult target might be, and explain linguistically the differences between what the child has said and the adult version.

Check your answers with the feedback (page 124).

a   'I sit daddy lap.'

b   'Cat gone.'

c   'I done.'

d   'Doctor made my ear better.'

e   'How long is it till my birthday?'

Extension activities

Using your own child language data, try to do the following:

1.   Work out the MLU in a number of different examples of children's talk at different ages.

2.   Study the two-word patterns used by the children you have data for and establish which of Brown's two semantic roles the children's language fits into.

3.   Examine the formation of negatives and questions.

4.   Explore the uses of tense and aspect. Is there a pattern to the uses of them at particular ages?

5.   What kinds of clauses are used at different ages and how are these clauses linked?

Topic revision exercise

Complete the questions on your own, then discuss your ideas with a partner.

1.   What is syntax?

2.   What stages do most children go through as they develop syntax?

3.   Why are questions and negatives harder for children to acquire than statements?

4.   How can tense and aspect be problematic for children to acquire?

Grammatical development – morphology

In this topic you will:

- learn how children's early language makes use of morphemes

- study how children apply morphological rules, often creating 'virtuous errors' and new words

- learn about the patterns in children's early morphological development.

Link

There is more on the importance of word endings in the English language in Unit 3, Section A of the A2 Student Book).

Key terms

Inflectional morphology: the study of how morphemes are used to create different grammatical functions.

Derivational morphology: the study of how morphemes are used to help create new words.

Virtuous error: a mistake that is logical and that sheds light on a child's processes of language development.

What is 'morphology'?

As has already been outlined in the topic on syntax, children's early language development is characterised by an increasing length of utterance as time goes on. In simple terms, the older a child is, the longer the utterance they can produce. But this is only part of the picture.

Morphology is an aspect of grammar that becomes increasingly important as children's language develops.

Word endings mark important distinctions between things like singular and plural, present and past tense, comparatives and superlatives, and many other concepts. These are all examples of what is called **inflectional morphology**, where words are altered to create new grammatical forms. Another form is **derivational morphology**, in which prefixes and suffixes are added to create entirely new words. This will be discussed later in this topic.

Making words do different things – inflectional morphology

Data response exercise 7

Look at the bold examples in the following data. Look at the number of morphemes used in each example and study their different functions. Use your knowledge of morphemes from the topic on syntax to help you with this.

When you have finished, check your answers against the feedback (page 124).

a 'I **walked**.'

b 'He has two **dogs**.'

c 'I am **eating**.'

d 'I am the **tallest** person in my class.'

e 'He used the **steamer** to cook lunch.'

f 'The **doctor's** surgery.'

Once you are comfortable with these ideas, read on to consider some of the ways in which children's early uses of morphology fit into certain patterns, and how children gradually build up longer and more morphologically sophisticated language.

'Virtuous' errors and new words

When studying the early utterances of young children, you may come across some or all of the features in the data below. These **virtuous errors** are not mistakes as such, because they have an underlying logic to them. They can tell us a great deal about what a child is picking up and understanding from the language around them, and how they are trying to apply rules to their own language.

a	'I runned.'
b	'There was three mans.'
c	'I eating.'
d	'This goody is braver than that one.'
e	'That baddy got a shooter.'
f	'They shotted their arrows at the baddies.'
g	'Daddy go work.'

It is unlikely that a child would have heard an adult say 'I runned away' or 'There was two mans', although we do have to be careful not to make sweeping assumptions: a child might hear and use non-standard varieties of English such as Jamaican creole or multi-cultural London English, which often use plurals such as 'mans' or 'mans dem'. Likewise, a child may well have heard an older sibling using a form such as 'runned'. This is one reason why the context of children's utterances is so important.

Overgeneralisation

So, if the child hasn't heard these expressions, where do they come from? One answer seems to be that children start to apply rules to their own language that they have observed in action in other people's language. If a child has heard the -ed sound being used to tell a story about events that have already taken place – in the past tense – they might start applying the -ed ending to all the verbs they use. Of course, most of the time this will produce perfectly acceptable past tense verbs, such as *walked*, *pushed* or *opened*, but English grammar isn't always so simple and many of the most widely used verbs tend to have irregular past tense forms. Hence, a child saying 'runned', 'seed', 'eated', 'holded' is not just creating nonsense but rigidly applying rules: what linguists call **overgeneralisation**. They may be errors but they're logical errors.

■ Link

There is further discussion of non-standard English in Unit 3, Section A.

■ Link

Exploring children's spoken Language and the influence of siblings and parents could make an interesting Language investigation for Unit 4.

■ Key terms

Overgeneralisation: the over-application of a grammatical rule; a form of virtuous error.

■ Link

Theories that account for such virtuous errors are covered in more detail in Language development theories on pages 101–110.

Research point

Jean Berko carried out an experiment in the 1950s to test children's use of the -s plural. She found that when faced with a picture of an imaginary animal called a 'wug', children tended to create the plural 'wugs' when asked to complete the statement: 'This is a wug. Now there is another one. There are two of them. There are two…'

Of the four to five-years-olds tested, 76 per cent formed the regular -s plural, and 97 per cent of the five to seven-year-olds did the same. Berko also used other nonsense words, such as *heaf*, *cra*, *tor* and *lun*, with broadly similar results.

Thinking points

1   Why did the wug have to be a made up creature? Why couldn't Berko have used a picture of a cat or a dog?

2   What does this research suggest about the nature of children's acquisition of grammar?

3   What other tests could you devise to test children's use of morphemes?

Fig. 3 *The wugs test*

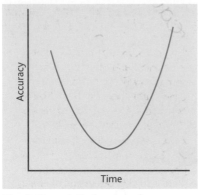

Fig. 3 *Brown's U-shape graph*

■ **Link**

See Language development theories on pages 101–110 for more on theories about imitation and deduction.

Regression

Bizarrely, as children grow older, these errors seem to increase. Take, for example, an utterance spoken by a three-year-old: 'I holded the plane and it flied.' Three months previous to this, the child had been able to say 'I held' and 'It flew' – the correct past tense forms of the verbs – but here he is using an overgeneralised -*ed* ending. So has he regressed? Not really. What seems to be the case (and this is an area researched by Roger Brown in the early 1970s) is that his early use of the correct form was probably down to a simple repetition of the correct adult form he heard around him. Once his deductive processes have started to fathom out that most verbs take -*ed* in the past tense, he starts to apply this rule more actively, leading to virtuous errors like that above. So on one level he appears to have slipped back, but on another conceptual level he has progressed. As Roger Brown discovered, it's only a matter of time before the correct endings for verbs start to reappear, this time with a more solid grasp of which verbs take which endings. This takes the form of a U-shape when charted on a graph.

Along with verb endings, children learn to apply other endings to different types of words. Nouns often take the -*s* ending in the plural form; adjectives take -*er* and -*est* to form comparatives and superlatives; a possessive -*'s* inflection can be added to signify ownership; and new words can be created by adding -*er* endings, as seen later in this topic.

Brown noted a pattern to the acquisition of inflections (and other grammatical morphemes, such as short words like *in* and *on*, *a* and *the*). He drew them up into a seven-point chart, as seen in Table 5.

Table 5

	Feature	Example of morpheme as part of child's utterance
1	Progressive aspect verb endings	I walk**ing** She is eat**ing**
2	Prepositions	Put nappy **on** Drink **in** cup
3	Plural noun endings	Two boy**s**
4	Possessive	Baby**'s** dummy Mummy**'s** bag
5	Determiners	Give me **the** milk I want **a** drink He ate **my** biscuit
6	Regular past tense ending	I walk**ed** I runn**ed**
7	3rd person singular regular present tense	She see**s** me Shrek like**s** mud

*Adapted from **J.S. Peccei**, Child Language: a resource book for students, 2005*

In addition to this, by the time most children are 24 months old, they are starting to use what is called telegraphic speech: they happily use content words but miss out grammatical words. When a child says something like

'I walking', they have managed to employ a noun phrase (the pronoun *I*) and a verb phrase (*walking*), but have missed out the auxiliary verb (*am*) that is required to make the utterance grammatically complete. When you start to unravel the details of what children are saying, many different processes seem to be at work.

Data response exercise 8

Have another look at the data on page 77. Analyse the virtuous errors and new words in each example, and try to identify the nature of each, e.g. *the child has applied an overgeneralised plural ending*.

Once you have finished, check your ideas against the feedback (page 124).

Making up new words – derivational morphology

Beyond the inflectional morphology discussed above, children also show an ability to manipulate derivational morphology, creating new words and applying patterns they hear around them. Three main patterns have been noted in the table below.

Table 6

Process	Explanation	Example
Conversion	Using a word as a different word class	'I jammed the bread.'
Affixation	Applying endings to words to create new ones	'It's crowdy in here.' 'This bread is very jammy.' 'He's shooting his shooter.'
Compounding	Joining existing words together into new combinations	'Horsey-man.' 'Tractor-man.'

In many cases, these processes lead to the formation of perfectly acceptable standard forms of words, but in other cases new words or nonsense words are created. In the examples above, the conversion of the noun *jam* to the verb *jammed* is certainly logical when you think of *butter* as both noun and verb ('There's the butter.' 'I'm buttering my toast.'), while the adjectives *crowdy* and *jammy* both follow the pattern of adding -*y* endings to nouns like *rain/rainy*, *cloud/cloudy* and *sun/sunny*. The noun *shooter* is already used in cockney as a slang term for a gun, but (assuming that the child hasn't been subjected to a diet of Vinny Jones films) seems to come from a perfectly logical affixation of the -*er* suffix that has the meaning of someone or something that shoots. The process of compounding often creates more charming expressions: 'Horsey-man' might be someone who rides a horse, and 'Tractor-man' someone who drives a tractor.

Data response exercise 9

Using the expressions in the table below, label the process at work in each of the words in bold. Use the terms 'conversion', 'affixation' and 'compounding' in your answers.

When you have finished, check your ideas against the feedback (page 125).

AQA Examiner's tip

It's helpful to remember individual researchers and case studies for when you write answers in the exam. But if the names don't come to you, don't worry: examiners are also interested in your ability to make sense of children's language development in your own terms, not just to produce encyclopaedic lists of names and case studies. Examples of child language data from your own family, from transcripts studied in class or taken from unscripted TV programmes are all as valid as recognised case studies, if you have something interesting to say about them.

Expression	Context
'It's very **nighty**.'	Driving home in the dark
'**plant-man**'	Talking about a gardener
'I **sharped** them.'	Talking about two pencils
'There's a **cycler**.'	Talking about someone riding a bike

W. O'Grady, How Children Learn Language, *2005*

🔍 Extension activities

Using your own data, consider the following questions:

1 Does the MLU increase gradually as children get older or does it go through particular 'leaps'?

2 Does the use of overgeneralisation occur on particular types of word but not on others?

3 Which theories of language development might be supported or challenged by the patterns you observe in your data?

Topic revision exercise

Complete the questions on your own, then discuss your ideas with a partner.

1 What is a morpheme?

2 What's the difference between inflectional morphology and derivational morphology?

3 What is overgeneralisation?

4 What are 'wugs'?

Phonological development

What do we mean by 'phonological' development?

Phonology is a term used to describe the sounds within a particular language. When we refer to phonological development we are talking about the ways in which children develop their understanding and use of the sounds of English.

Early phonological development

One of the main characteristics of children's speech to the lay observer is its 'baby-like' sound. Sounds such as 'gaga', 'choochoo' and 'wabbit' might spring to mind when you think of a child's early words. As you study examples of child language in more detail, you will see that – like many other aspects of children's early language development – the phonology of child language has distinct patterns and a logical structure.

Children use different types of sound at different stages in their development, but, as you have already seen with lexis, semantics and grammar, it's important to look at what children *understand* as well as what they *produce*. For example, children may be clearly able to differentiate between the different sounds used by adults, but be unable themselves to produce all these sounds. And from a very early age – some argue from before birth itself – children seem to tune into familiar voices and languages, and this apparently primes them for the acquisition of their mother tongue.

Research point

Studies on infants have shown that newborns have a natural preference to attend to the human voice above all environmental sounds. When listening to the human voice they show a distinct preference for listening to speech over non-speech sounds like laughing and coughing. DeCasper and Fifer (1980) demonstrated that 3-day old babies can identify their mothers' voices, while Mehler *et al.*, (1988) showed that 4-day old babies can distinguish between utterances in their mothers' language and those in another language.

J. S. Peccei, Child Language: a resource book for students, 2005

Thinking points

 1 How might these findings be used to support different theoretical positions on language development?

2 How might a child's predisposition towards the sounds of speech in their mother tongue assist them in their acquisition of language?

Children are born universal, in the sense that they are capable of producing any sound in any human language, be they the clicks of the southern African Xhosa or the *ch* sounds of Scots. However, they soon narrow their range through a process called phonemic contraction to concentrate on the **phonemes** of the language/s most in use around them. So, while a child born in England to English-speaking parents could theoretically produce the sounds of Cantonese, Urdu or French, they would generally contract their range by the age of 12 months to the sounds of English.

Children also need to be able to break down or segment the streams of sounds that they hear into meaningful units. They will quickly pick out the most frequently used sound units from the language around them and start to realise that certain sounds relate to particular objects and actions.

Cooing and babbling

Pre-verbal stages of child language such as cooing and babbling are characterised by different uses of consonants and vowels: cooing consists of openmouth vowel sounds such as *oo* and *aah*, while babbling starts to combine consonants and vowels into CVCV patterns (i.e. a consonant followed by a vowel, then a consonant followed by a vowel) such as 'gaga', 'baba' and 'woowoo'. Babbling itself can be split into two categories: reduplicated and variegated. Reduplicated babbling consists of the same CV structure repeated (as in the examples above), while variegated babbling consists of combinations of different CV structures, such as 'baboo' or 'gaba'.

Proto-words

As you have already seen with the development of early words, there are 'fuzzy areas' between the stages. It is no different when considering phonological development, and one such area is between the babbling and the one-word stages: the sounds children make may sound like real words but do not actually refer consistently to objects around them. These are known as proto-words and can include examples such as 'mama', 'dada', 'baba'.

To understand children's early phonological development, it is important to have at least a basic understanding of the processes behind the creation of different sounds. *Place of* **articulation** refers to the place in the mouth where the sound originates. *Manner of articulation* refers to the way in which the sound is produced.

Intonation and meaning

Children's use of phonology is particularly helpful to them when they are at the one- and two-word stages, as it can offer another level of meaning to utterances they make. A child who says 'my car' may use different strengths of intonation to express different ideas with the same phrase. A stress placed on the noun *car*, might indicate that the child is labelling the item or pointing at one of their toys, but a stress placed on the possessive determiner *my* could suggest that she is pointing out it's her car and not someone else's.

Like many things in a child's early development of language, intonation is often an imprecise means of creating meaning in English. Children therefore soon move on to more complex grammatical and semantic means of expressing what they really want. In many world languages, however, it is possible to change the meaning of a word just by changing the **pitch** level at which it is spoken. Mandarin Chinese is the best known of these, and one sound can have as many as four different meanings depending on the intonation used.

Early mistakes in sounding words

A number of processes are involved in the ways young children make 'mistakes' with their sounds. It's worth pointing out that we're not dealing with how words are *spelled* but how they are *sounded*.

Some of the main processes, their explanations and examples for each process are shown in Table 7.

Table 7 *Sounding words*

Process	Explanation	Example
Addition	Adding an extra vowel sound to create a CVCV structure	*horse* becomes *horsey* *dog* becomes *doggie*
Deletion	Leaving out the last consonant of a word, so a word like mouse becomes mou (mow)	*cat* would be pronounced *ca* *pig* would be *pi*
Reduplication	The repetition of particular sounds and structures	*choochoo* *weewee*
Substitution	One sound is swapped for another, easier sound	*rabbit* becomes *wabbit* *sing* becomes *ting*
Consonant cluster reduction	Children find it difficult to produce consonant clusters – groups of two or more consonants – so will reduce them to smaller units	*dry* becomes *dai* *frog* becomes *fog*
Deletion of unstressed syllables	The removal of an entire unstressed syllable from a word	*banana* becomes *nana* *pyjamas* becomes *jamas* *pretending* becomes *tending*
Assimilation	Assimilation is a process in which substitution occurs but the sound changes because of other sounds around it, e.g. a sound is substituted with one that is closer to others in the word	*doggie* becomes *goggie*

Data response exercise 10

Look at the following examples of child language. Try to identify which processes are at work in the **bold** words. The adult target word is given in brackets next to each example. In some cases, there might be more than one process in each extract.

Once you've completed this, check your ideas against the feedback (page 125).

a   **Mou** (mouse).

b   Can I play on the **puter** (computer), daddy?

c   The bunny eated the **cawwot** (carrot).

d   We went on a **orsey** (horse) ride.

e   I want my **banket** (blanket).

f   My **boot** (book).

g   It's a **babbit** (rabbit).

Patterns in the mistakes

You should be able to see from this brief exercise that, in early child language, what might appear to be random sounds made by children actually follow clear, regular patterns. Many of the errors are the result of the child trying to produce a sound, but actually producing one that is either made in a nearby place of articulation or through a slightly different manner of articulation.

Take some examples of substitution for instance:

■ sing – ting

■ zebra – debra

■ thing – ting.

The pattern for all of these is similar: a fricative sound is replaced by a stop sound in roughly the same area of the mouth. **Fricatives** and **stops** are different manners of articulation.

Children find fricatives harder to produce than stops, which occur in roughly the same area of the mouth. So a fricative *z* is replaced by a stop *d*, and a fricative *s* by a stop *t*. It's not essential that you know these different terms for places and manners of articulation – and this is only scratching the surface of what is a very technical area of linguistics. It is useful, however, to understand the overarching reasons for children's early production of sounds and to be able to link the labels to actual examples.

But is it simply a matter of production? Do children actually hear the same things as adults or have the same internal representation of the sounds? In a well-known case study, Berko and Brown looked at how children failed to pronounce certain sounds but could recognise when someone else got them wrong. For example, a child couldn't say 'fish' and instead said 'fis' (substituting the *s* for *sh*) but noticed when an adult got it wrong. This situation is sometimes termed 'the fis phenomenon'.

As with many other areas of child language, most children gradually grow out of these mistakes. According to William O'Grady, by the time most children are four they have probably mastered most sounds, perhaps with the exception of *r/w* and *th(ink)/th(is)*.

Key terms

Fricative: a sound that is created by the slow and controlled release of air through the mouth, creating friction.

Stops: sounds where the air flow is completely stopped. They are created in the throat (e.g. glottal stop), at the back of the mouth (e.g. *ck*), at the alveolar ridge (e.g. *t*) or by the lips (e.g. *p*).

Fig. 5 *Early words often display common phonological patterns*

It's also important to look at context. In the speech of many teenage Black British speakers, for example, it's fairly common to find *d* used instead of *th*, and among Cockney or Estuary speakers, it's normal to drop initial *h* sounds in words like 'horse' or 'house'.

 Extension activities

1 How could you test to see if a child can tell if a word is pronounced incorrectly by a parent or carer if they themselves cannot actually say it properly?

2 Using your own examples of child language data, look at the phonological patterns in children's pronunciation of particular words.

Topic revision exercise

Complete the questions on your own, then discuss your ideas with a partner.

1 What is phonemic contraction?

2 What patterns are there to children's early pronunciation 'errors'?

3 What is the 'fis phenomenon'?

Pragmatic development

In this topic you will:

- explore how children learn to understand the unspoken rules of communication

- learn how children start to grasp what they should and shouldn't say

- explore how children use humour, implicature and inference when communicating

- look at how children make the leap to near-adult communication.

Key terms

Implicature: expressing meaning indirectly.

Inference: drawing out these meanings from others' speech

What do we mean by 'pragmatics'?

Pragmatics is an area of language study linked to the things people *mean* rather than what they actually *say*. When we talk about pragmatics, we are usually referring to things like **implicature** and **inference**, politeness, humour and awareness of context. We can also include within pragmatics, however, the unspoken rules of communication, such as knowing when to take a turn in a conversation, when not to speak, and when expressing agreement is the best option (even if you really disagree).

How pragmatic awareness develops

As we grow older, our understanding of the way the world works and how people use language to get what they want grows too. But for a child, pragmatics can be a more problematic and less clear-cut area of language development.

Take some of the following examples:

1 A woman asks where the post office is and is told in reply, 'It's a Sunday.'

2 A teacher says to a student who has just dropped a crisp packet on the floor, 'There's a bin over there, you know.'

3 A person walks into a room and says 'Is it me, or is it cold in here?' and someone else in the room shuts the window.

4 A father says to his daughter who has just dropped his mobile phone in the paddling pool, 'Thanks very much, that makes life a lot easier.'

5 A student says to her friend, 'Mmm, nice jacket. Are there lots of charity shops in Peckham?'

In each of these cases, it should be fairly clear to a fluent adult speaker that something more than just the semantic meaning of the words is being conveyed, and in some cases almost the exact opposite meaning is intended. To a child of four or five years, however, who is competent in grammar, phonology, lexis and semantics, the pragmatics of these utterances might seem completely alien.

💡 The functions of children's early language

If pragmatics is all to do with what you mean rather than what you say, then it's undoubtedly important to look at what children might mean in some of their earliest utterances. The linguist Michael Halliday broke down children's early language functions into what he termed a 'taxonomy of language'.

- Instrumental: This is when the child uses language to express their needs (e.g. 'Want juice').
- Regulatory: This is where language is used to tell others what to do (e.g. 'Go away').
- Interactional: Here language is used to make contact with others and form relationships (e.g. 'Love you, mummy').
- Personal: This is the use of language to express feelings, opinions and individual identity (e.g. 'Me good girl').

The next three functions all help the child to come to terms with his or her environment.

- Heuristic: This is when language is used to gain knowledge about the environment (e.g. 'What the tractor doing?')
- Imaginative: Here language is used to tell stories and jokes, and to create an imaginary environment.
- Representational: This is the use of language to convey facts and information.

http://en.wikipedia.org

Data response exercise 11

Study the examples in the table below. Try to identify which of Halliday's functions might be at work in each utterance.

Suggested answers are given in the feedback (page 125).

Utterance	Context
'Put me down!'	Child talking to father who's lifted her up
'Biscuit!'	Child pointing at biscuit tin
'Why, daddy?'	Child asking father a question about why the biscuits are all gone
'I walking.'	Child giving commentary as she shows how she can walk without help
'Look at me, I'm a fairy.'	Child in dressing-up clothes draws attention to the game she is playing

Extending the repertoire

One way in which children develop pragmatics is by seeing what works and what doesn't in their interactions with adults. While much of the acquisition of syntax and morphology can be linked to **nativist theories**, such as those of Noam Chomsky and Steven Pinker, **social interaction** plays quite a large part in the development of communicative skill in this field.

Data response exercise 12

The exchanges in the following data centre around three children's requests for biscuits (a morning ritual that could often descend into tantrums if the required number or type of biscuits wasn't forthcoming). The requests become more indirect as the children get older. Analyse the exchanges for the children's use or grasp of pragmatics and then check your ideas against the feedback (page 125). (You will need to use technical terms to do this. Refer to the Lexical-semantic and Grammatical and morphological frameworks in the toolkit on pages 207–212 if you need reminders.)

Context: different conversations with parents shortly after breakfast, over a three-year period.

a   *Ruby*: dat (pointing at biscuit tin, age: 1 year 6 months).
b   *Ruby*: biscuit, daddy (age: 2 years).
c   *Stan*: I want a biscuit, daddy (age: 3 years 6 months).
d   *Stan*: Can I have a biscuit, daddy? (age: 3 years 9 months).
e   *Stan*: Please can I have a biscuit, daddy? (age: 4 years 2 months).
f   *Liam*: I'm hungry, daddy (age: 4 years 9 months).
g   *Liam*: Stan's had a biscuit (age: 4 years 9 months).

As you can see, the words themselves remain largely the same (*biscuit, daddy, I*), but the pragmatics become more sophisticated. Why is this? Perhaps it has something to do with the fact that as children get older, their parents and caregivers are less prepared to respond to blunt and often apparently rude demands or requests. They expect children to recognise the usually unspoken (although sometimes very explicit – 'you're not getting a biscuit until you say please') rules of politeness. This is something children have to develop through interacting with others: there are no genes for politeness or sarcasm!

Along with a growing awareness of indirect ways of getting what you need comes an appreciation of the importance of context. If pragmatics is to do with extracting intended meanings from what is said, and using indirect means to get what you want, it is also about drawing meanings from the contexts in which they are uttered. In Example 1 on page 85, the response 'It's a Sunday' might appear to be completely irrelevant to the question asked, 'Where's the post office?', but the reply relies on the shared understanding that post offices don't normally open on a Sunday. In the extract below, a similar process is at work.

Key terms

Nativist theories: these suggest that language acquisition is 'built in' to or 'innate' in all humans.

Social interaction theories: these suggest that verbal and social interaction will help a child's language development.

Link

For more on nativist theories, see Language development theories on pages 101–110.

Data extract 15

Context: conversation with father on holiday.

Age: 4 years 9 months.

Liam: Daddy, when can I go outside?

Father: Have you got your shoes and socks on?

Liam: No.

On the surface, the father's response appears to have nothing to do with Liam's question, but he understands it to be a condition to be met before he can go outside. Again, this type of understanding is not something that appears to happen overnight, but one that comes with exposure to language in use and interaction with other speakers.

■ Learning the ropes: taking turns and using politeness

While children's acquisition of words, meanings, morphology and grammatical structures is impressively rapid, language acquisition is much more than just understanding words and putting them in the right order.

As adults, most of our communication takes place using spoken conversation, and conversation has its own rules and structures (see Section A Language and mode for more about this). Children are often quite capable of conducting two-way conversations, and indeed have been trained for this since they were little with ritualised games such as *Peek-a-boo* and *Walkie round the garden*. (This is according to Catherine Snow and Jerome Bruner). The more children are exposed to adult conversation, the more adept they become at holding their own conversations. These ideas are explained in more depth in Jean Peccei's *Child Language: A resource book for students*.

Fig. 5 *Father interacting with baby son*

Politeness too is something that is acquired through interaction, but also through explicit teaching ('say please if you want ice cream'). But politeness is not just about saying please and thank you, it is about shaping your language to avoid imposing on others, and also to make others feel good about themselves. As you will have seen in Section A Language and mode, Brown and Levinson's politeness model puts forward two types of politeness strategies: *positive politeness* and *negative politeness*. Again, these skills are gradually acquired to greater or lesser extents depending on the child, his or her environment and the context in which he or she is using language.

■ Link

For more on Catherine Snow and Jerome Bruner's work on the role of interaction, see Language development theories on pages 118–127.

■ Data response exercise 13

Examine the following interaction. What might the adult change in her utterances to make the language easier to comprehend for the child?

Compare your ideas with the feedback (page 125).

Context: child has just dropped a cup of juice on the floor, breaking the cup and splashing juice everywhere.

Age: 2 years 5 months.

Adult: Oh brilliant. That was really clever, wasn't it?

Child: Cup broken.

Adult: Yeah and the juice is all over the place. Thanks a lot.

Fig. 6 *Language acquisition is more than understanding words and putting them in the right order*

Extension activity

Try to collect/obtain/study child language data from four- to six-year-olds who are starting to use more advanced pragmatic constructions. Look at the ways in which requests and questions are phrased. Is there a gap between a child's comprehension of indirect forms and their own use of them?

Topic revision exercise

Complete the questions on your own, then discuss your ideas with a partner.

1 What is pragmatics and why is it important to communication?

2 What were the seven functions of children's language that Michael Halliday noted?

3 How are idioms, sarcasm and indirectness important to pragmatics?

Children's early reading and writing

■ Moving from speaking to writing

So far, your study of child language development has focused on the language children hear around them and the language that they speak themselves. This topic will move on to consider how children make the transition from speaking to writing.

It should be stressed at this early stage that much of what you have studied on spoken language acquisition will be relevant to your work on early writing. It should play a part in your exam answers.

It is also worth reminding yourself of the work you have done on Language and mode in Section A of this unit, because it is a shift in mode that we are really looking at when considering the move children make from speaking to writing. The ways in which children start to use different blended modes such as e-mail and word-processed texts, and the ways in which different modes are valued in society, are points that we will explore in more detail as the topic continues. To begin with, it is important to remember that for a very long time, the written mode has been considered more culturally 'valuable' than the spoken mode, and it has been afforded more prestige as a result. It is perhaps for this reason that children in the UK are explicitly taught writing from a relatively early age, compared to many other countries.

In this topic we only have space to cover the start of a child's early writing – up to the ages of about seven or eight. You may wish to explore the topic of children's writing in more depth for your own interest, or as part of a more detailed language investigation in your A2 year, so further reading suggestions are given on page 122.

Let's start, though, with a look at some examples of children's early writing across a period of four to five years.

■ Data response exercise 14

Examine the following four examples of children's writing. What do you notice about the ways in which the writing develops as the children get older?

You might find the following questions helpful in organising your ideas:

■ What types or forms of writing are there?

■ Who is the writing aimed at?

■ How does the writing look on the page?

■ How long is each piece of writing?

■ How long are the individual sentences (if sentences are in fact used)?

■ What kinds of spelling are used?

■ What experiences or ideas is each child trying to relate?

■ What kind of discourse structure does the child use?

For some ideas on what you might have found, see the feedback (pages 125–126).

a

b

Invitation

Dear mumiy ano
rooJiy
Please
to my   f o m
assy   (pss)
       embiy
oa
    th urs
    day
from Lidam

Transliteration: mumiy and roudiy please come to my class assembly on thurrsay. Liam.

c

On the wicend I *week*
vent to the
piak and plad on the
swings.

Independent

12/3/07

d

16.1.06   My Weekend news.

Sounds like lots
of fun Mattie

On   Saterday   Mummy

and   Daddy   Built   Our

Bunk   beds.   Then   We

Put   toys   In   My   room.

After   that   We   went to

Grand Mars   and   Granddads

House.   We   stayed   then

for   a   Night   But

Finlay kept   Me   A wake

All   Night.   On   sunday

we fed the Duckes

Transliteration: on the wicend I went to the piak and plad on the
swings.

■ The cultural context

As you are now aware, children generally acquire spoken language in stages, with little or no explicit 'teaching' of what to do. To return to an analogy used in the Introduction, spoken language is 'caught not taught'. This, however, is clearly not the case for reading and writing, which are taught explicitly at home, at nursery and at school. One important aspect of the written mode, though, *is* picked up by children through their environment and *without* explicit teaching: *its importance to adults*. Even before children have established the necessary understanding of the symbolic value of letter shapes and words, they seem to have a good understanding that the written mode has value and meaning in society. This can be seen in children's early scribblings that mimic some features of adult writing, or through the games children play that involve written texts: pretending to take orders for food, drawing treasure maps or pretending to write and then deliver notes to parents and friends.

■ Early reading

For children to read, a grasp of grapheme–phoneme correspondence is required. In other words, they must understand what sounds (phonemes) individual letters or strings of letters (**graphemes**) represent. English has approximately 44 phonemes but only 26 letters, meaning that certain letters have to be combined to create the sounds of the language. This can cause problems for children. Masha Bell, a supporter of spelling reform, points out that the English language 'has different, logically unpredictable graphemes for identical sounds (main/lane; say/grey/weigh; air/care/bear/where/their)'.

In addition, children need to grasp the symbolic system that lies behind written language. Cognitive theorists argue that this symbolic system forms the basis of much of the child's future language development: an understanding that the marks on the page 'stand for' or *represent* the sounds in the real world.

In much the same way as young children segment the stream of sounds around them into meaningful units, such as words or morphemes (see Phonological development on pages 81–85), older children will need to segment the graphemes in a stretch of writing into the corresponding phonemes. In English, this is made much harder by the sometimes tenuous link between the way words are spelled and the way they sound. In fact, the word we know as 'fish' could be spelt as *ghoti* if the following grapheme–phoneme correspondences were applied:

gh as in *rough*
o as in *women*
ti as in *station*

Try saying these words out loud to hear what he meant. Many people have campaigned for the English spelling system to be changed to make it easier for children (and adults) to spell common English words. Bell identifies features such as the *-ee* sound that can be spelled as *ee, ea, ie, ei, eCe, iCe, e, i, ey* and *eo*, and inconsistent consonant doubling in words such as *trolley, hollow, solid* and *holiday* – to name just a few.

Others have argued that the spelling system exists as it does for a reason, and that the contexts in which we use different words, the subtly different spellings between words that sound similar, are there for a purpose. In the June 2007 edition of *NATE English, Drama, Media*, Keith

■ Key terms

grapheme: the smallest functional unit in a writing system

Davidson uses the example of the word *phonics* itself to illustrate why it is spelled like this rather than *fonix*. He argues that the spelling *phon-ic-s* shows that the word consists of three distinct elements (*phon* = the semantic root showing us that this word is based around sound; *-ic* = an adjectival suffix telling us the word is to do with sounds; *-s* a nominal suffix rather like in *physics* or *genetics*), all of which contribute to our understanding of what the word means. He argues that spelling has rules because it is designed to be seen on the page and that this is 'clearly the point of a graphic system rather than a sound system'.

The teaching of reading is a contentious area because of this. The two main positions are:

Phonics

This is a sound-based system that teaches children to break down (segment) words into smaller units and then blend these units together. As part of this, children are taught to recognise digraphs (e.g. *ph* and *ck*) and trigraphs (e.g. *igh* as in *knight* or *eau* as in *beautiful*). They are given reading books that help to emphasise certain sounds that they have recently studied and that help to reinforce the stage they have reached.

Supporters of phonics argue that the systematic approach to breaking words down encourages children to become more active in the reading process, and that it sets out building blocks for children to use in later reading. For example, morphemes like *-ing*, *-ed*, *-er* and *-est* can be recognised as meaningful units and interpreted by the child when they come across them on the ends of words they may never have seen before. (See Grammatical development – morphology on pages 76–80 for more on these morphemes and how children acquire them.)

Critics of phonics argue that the segmenting and blending of sounds is all very well, until the child comes across the irregularities of English spelling. How, for example, would a child brought up on a diet of regular blends cope with the following words: *fight; enough; knight; plough; follow; swallow*?

Whole word

This is a system that is based on the child recognising the whole word rather than the individual units within it. Children are taught to become familiar with the 'shape' of a word and will then recognise it when they encounter it again.

Supporters of the whole-word approach argue that their model lets the child read for meaning and pleasure, and that the books they read are more wide-ranging and not as strictly regimented as those used for phonics: they don't have to focus on certain sounds like the phonics programme does. They argue that if children come across words they do not recognise, they can use their intuition to predict or guess what they will sound like, based on those they have encountered before and the context in which the word occurs. For example, if a child comes across the word *bow* in a story involving knights with swords and arrows, they may read it in one way, whereas if the story involved people visiting the queen they may read it in another way.

Critics argue that this approach has left many children illiterate and that the guesswork applied is not a sound strategy for teaching reading. They argue that the lack of a systematic structure to approaching words and the units that make them up does not equip children for words they come across at later stages in their education and life.

The debate has become fiercer with recent government reports and initiatives, including The National Literacy Strategy in 1998 that embedded literacy teaching in the primary school curriculum, and The Rose Report in 2006 that recommended the teaching of 'systematic phonics' in all primary schools.

As it stands, most primary school teachers probably use a mixture of both methods and try to find a happy medium, but there is a growing pressure from government to move towards a more phonics-based approach. There is heated debate about the benefits of phonics, with many supporters pointing to studies in primary schools that suggest phonics boosts reading, and opponents arguing that none of these studies really proves anything.

Reading and writing

Children's writing relies on their grasp of reading, and many of the patterns you will observe in children's early writing are directly influenced by their perception of how sounds are translated into letters and words. But before children start to produce written 'words' – as an adult might recognise them – they produce letter-like scribbles and shapes in what appears to be a random order. This is called the *precommunicative stage*, as in Data extract 16.

Data extract 16

After this, a child will normally start to write individual letters (graphemes) and combinations of letters in patterns that bear some relationship to how a word sounds. Consonants tend to be more accurately produced than vowels at this stage. This is called the *phonological segmentation stage* and is illustrated in Data extract 17.

AQA Examiner's tip

You will not be assessed on children's reading in the exam, but will need to be able to show an understanding of how children's writing might be influenced by factors in their reading. Being able to discuss issues like grapheme–phoneme correspondence and how particular words might be spelled in different ways, depending on context, will be useful things to revise.

Link

If you wish to explore children's reading in more detail, this is a potentially interesting area for a Language investigation in Unit 4 in the A2 course.

Data extract 17

Transliteration: 'Stanley My dinersor is a vejeetereon and sceree'

Beyond this, children normally reach the *orthographic* or *conventional stage*, in which there is an accurate grasp of how words are spelled and the main patterns of spelling around them. This is illustrated in Data extract 18.

Data extract 18

My weekend News   2nd May 06

Lots of good details

You do make me laugh Mattie!

Finlay had a Twister I a cream.
Mummy had a orange lolly. Then
we went in. We had to put on a
helmet. Finlay's kept falling off. But that
didn't matter because he didn't need one
There was 105 steps When we got to the
bottom we got on boat and a lady with
a big bottom got on and my side of
the boat wobbled. Then we set off. ✓

■ Research point

Clear stages can be identified in the ways that children develop their very early writing skills.

- ■ **Scribbling**: Making marks on paper.
- ■ **Emergent writing**: As above but with some recognisable letter shapes.
- ■ **Copy writing**: Like emergent writing but with an emphasis on copying letter shapes and words.
- ■ **Independent writing**: The child writing on their own, perhaps single words or even whole sentences.

Kroll (1981) develops this and looks at later writing as well, identifying four stages that are summarised here:

- ■ **Preparation**: Learning how to hold pens and pencils correctly, emergent writing and copy writing.
- ■ **Consolidation**: In the first few years of school, most children will start to write independently, but spellings will often be phonetic and punctuation haphazard. The writing will reflect the influence of spoken language.
- ■ **Differentiation**: From about eight or nine years of age, most children will start to use more accurate punctuation and spelling, and more varied and sophisticated syntax. The writing will seem less like a written version of spoken language and more like a conventional written mode.
- ■ **Integration**: The child will be more aware of the difference between modes and might be able to switch between written and spoken mode in a story. They will be writing independently and with some skill.

🔍 The features of children's early writing

As we have already seen, children go through a number of stages in both their spoken and written language acquisition. While it's useful to have a good grasp of these stages, you are not expected to simply recycle these in your exam answers, but to apply your knowledge to questions that look at the transition between spoken and written language. In the exam for this topic you will be presented with extracts of children's writing and asked to comment linguistically on the features of the language, and how the writing exemplifies the transition from spoken to written mode.

With this in mind, the next few pages will present you with some of the main patterns in children's early writing and how these patterns reflect children's progression from spoken to written modes. Again, it will be very useful for you to refresh your memory of Section A Language and mode, particularly the differences between spoken and written language, and to think about how these apply to children's early writing.

Data response exercise 15

Look at Data extract 17 on page 96. Think about how the child has used the following features of language:

■ Graphology: how is the writing laid out on the page?

■ Lexis and semantics: how wide is the child's vocabulary? Are any specific semantic fields used?

■ Grammar: which sentence types are used?

■ Orthography: are there any patterns in the ways words are spelled?

Check your ideas with the feedback (page 126).

Data response exercise 16

Look at Data extract 18 on page 96. Think about how the child has used the following features of language:

■ Graphology: how is the writing laid out on the page?

■ Lexis and semantics: how wide is the child's vocabulary? Are any specific semantic fields used?

■ Grammar: which sentence types are used?

■ Discourse structure: what kind of structure is used to organise the narrative?

■ Orthography: are there any patterns in the ways words are spelled? How is punctuation used?

Check your ideas with the feedback (page 126).

■ **Extension activity**

Research by Read in 1985 suggests that children tend to simplify consonant clusters in their writing much as they do in their production of sounds (as discussed in Phonological development, pages 81–85).

Are there any other patterns in spelling that you notice in the children's writing presented in this topic? How would you go about researching patterns in children's spelling if you were to study this in more depth?

Modes, forms and contexts

Before finishing this topic and moving on to theories related to child language acquisition, it's important to consider some of the wider factors that influence how children write. Writing does not occur in a vacuum, and children are aware from a very early age of the cultural significance of the written word. Even before they are able to hold a pen properly or master the necessary eye–hand coordination to form letter shapes, they attempt to write. Why?

Pam Czerniewska in *Learning English – development and diversity* suggests the answer:

> Characteristically, in a literate community, a set of literacy-related activities would be familiar and well rehearsed within a particular home, some even ritualistic. In this way, it is argued, they become well learned by children from an early age. Many of the interactions with print will happen in combination with different types of talk – oral reading of a family letter, discussion of the day's events, or argument over a cereal packet offer perhaps – and many will combine both reading and writing.

Children exposed to written language in a variety of forms at home and school will soon become aware of the many different purposes to which the written word can be put. In other words, they are soon aware of different forms and genres of writing. But being aware of them is not always the same thing as mastering them.

This attention to the functions of language is part of what is often termed the **developmental** or **societal model** of children's literacy. This **functional approach** places emphasis on the social context to a child's learning. It is usually set against a more **traditional approach** to children's literacy which is based on a **linear** or **cognitive model**. This traditional approach places reading and writing in a sequence from speaking to reading, through to writing then the development of spelling and genre awareness. To simplify, the functional approach tends to highlight the role of interaction, while the traditional approach foregrounds cognitive development. Theories of language development are explored in the next topic.

Key terms

Developmental/societal model (functional approach): an account of children's language development that foregrounds social context.

Linear/cognitive model (traditional approach): an account of children's language development that places literacy skills in a sequence.

Research point

Katharine Perera explains in her book *Children's Writing and Reading: analysing classroom language* that types of children's writing can often be placed on a continuum, characterised by the following features:

Chronologically or non-chronologically organised texts

Chronologically organised texts use many action words (verbs) and connectives like *then*, *next* and *after that*. Non-chronological texts are organised not on sequences of events but on logical relationships between parts of texts: cause and effect; contrasts; connections. Children find chronological texts much easier to write, perhaps mirroring the ease with which children tend to pick up simple and compound sentences, as opposed to complex sentences.

The writer's relationship to the subject matter and audience based on personal/impersonal style

Personal writing often contains a higher density of personal pronouns (e.g. *we, us, I, she, they*) and relates directly to the experiences and world of the child, while impersonal writing contains fewer personal pronouns and often deals with more distant or abstract ideas. As with the continuum theory in Section A Language and mode (page 1), this personal/impersonal style operates on a sliding scale, with plenty of room in the middle. What is clear is that younger children tend to find personal writing easier to produce.

Children are exposed to the written – and increasingly the typed and texted – word through their daily interactions with adults and carers. This can clearly lead to a variety of different types of input depending on the background of the child and the input they receive. Research by Anderson and Stokes in San Diego, USA in 1984 explored the different types of interaction children had with the printed word, and found cultural and ethnic differences played a part in the types of interaction children enjoyed. Meanwhile, research by Shirley Brice Heath in 1982 seemed to show similar differences between the ways different ethnic groups use the printed word with children, but found as many differences between social classes as well.

What emerges from much of this research is the importance of interaction with children, and this is something explored in a bit more detail in the next topic, Language development theories. What is also apparent is that writing as a *mode* is valued in different ways in different cultures. But what does this mean for newer, blended modes such as e-mail, text messages and various forms of web language?

Children's use of computers is increasing both at school and at home, and typing work on a keyboard helps children focus a little more on the content of their work rather than the physical task of forming letter shapes accurately. The conventions of word processing graphology might also become better established but as with any convention, imagination and exploration might be limited as a result. However, there is perhaps a premium placed on more traditional written genres such as thank-you letters, notes to the tooth fairy, and postcards to relatives than their electronic or blended equivalents. Perhaps the day is not too far away, though, when children will be encouraged to create a group e-mail list of relatives and thank them for birthday presents, or to contact their aunts and uncles by poking them on Facebook…

💡 Extension activities

1 Using online resources or your own data, have a close look at the ways in which children make the transition from written and spoken forms of language to blended modes. For example, how does a child use text messaging or e-mail language compared to an adult or older child?

2 Look back to Section A Language and mode to consider the different factors that influence blended mode communication. Could you argue a case for forms like text messaging either damaging or helping speed up children's early written skills?

Topic revision exercise

Complete the questions on your own, then discuss your ideas with a partner.

1 What are the main stages in children's writing?

2 In what ways are children's spoken language and early writing linked?

3 Beyond spelling, grammar and handwriting, what other factors are important to children's early writing?

4 How important are teaching and interaction to children's development of reading and writing?

Language development theories

In this topic you will:

- explore the main theories connected to children's acquisition of spoken language

- consider the arguments for and against these theories

- look at some case studies and research that have been carried out to explore aspects of child language.

Key terms

Behaviourists: theorists who believe that language is acquired through imitation and reinforcement.

Social interactionists: theorists who believe that child language is developed through close interaction with carers.

Nativist theorists: theorists who believe that humans have an inbuilt capacity to acquire language.

Innate: inborn, natural.

Cognitive theorists: theorists who believe that language acquisition is part of a wider development of understanding.

What do we mean by theories of child language acquisition?

As you have seen from the data you have been analysing in this section on language development, there are different possible explanations for why children do what they do when they use language. Various researchers, many of them psychologists and linguists, have tried to offer overarching theoretical explanations of how children acquire language and why they say what they say. Many of the theorists agree on certain main areas of language acquisition; others disagree fundamentally.

The reason we're looking at theories here, towards the end of the section, is because you have gradually been exploring child language data and have probably noted some interesting patterns of your own. It's important to reach your own understanding of some of these patterns rather than trying to shoehorn them into someone else's theory. Of course, when it comes to the exam on language development, you will need to show a solid understanding of the main theories and be able to offer evidence for and against them. More importantly from an examiner's point of view, you will need to display the ability to look at a question and offer your own interpretation of what is going on.

What are the main debates?

Most theorists agree that children gain competence in their mother tongue at a remarkable speed and in a very short space of time. They argue, however, about how this takes place.

Some theorists believe that language is just like any other learned skill – that it can be developed through imitating others' language and gaining positive and negative feedback from adult carers. These theorists are often called **behaviourists**, after the school of psychology that influences them.

Some theorists believe that language is developed through social interaction, and that children's early language can be influenced and improved by adult carers adjusting their own speech patterns. These **social interactionists** believe that, while children cannot learn solely through interaction, many of their language skills are enhanced by it.

Some theorists believe that all humans, whatever language they grow up to speak, share the same language universals. They believe these are imprinted in us, allowing us to acquire language at incredible speed. These **nativist theorists** argue that language is part of our evolutionary inheritance – i.e. it is **innate** – and that we are 'pre-programmed' to acquire it.

Other theorists believe that children's knowledge of language is just another aspect of a child's wider understanding and intelligence. These **cognitive theorists** believe that, as children's ideas about the world develop, their language will grow to match it.

Many child language experts would be happy to mix and match ideas from these different theoretical positions; others are more dogmatic.

Nature: what we are born with; what is inbuilt or innate.

Nurture: what is acquired through experience and environmental influences.

■ Nature versus nurture

The main debate about child language started with Noam Chomsky's response to B. F. Skinner's *Verbal Behavior* in 1959. For many years, children's language acquisition had been viewed as a form of learned behaviour: children were born as 'blank canvases', waiting to be painted on. Chomsky's belief that children are in fact born with some form of inbuilt language machinery, primed as part of their **nature** to acquire language, blew Skinner's widely accepted belief in **nurture** out of the water. We will look at Chomsky's ideas later: first we will examine Skinner's behaviourist ideas.

■ Behaviourism and imitation

Skinner was associated with the behaviourist school of psychology and his research on the behaviour of rats and pigeons led him to believe that language was just another form of learned behaviour. This could be termed a *nurture* argument, in the sense that it foregrounds the influences on the child – the way he or she is brought up or nurtured from birth – rather than the child's genetic inheritance.

In its simplest form, a behaviourist approach to language would argue that children learn through positive and negative reinforcement. In other words, if children say something accurately they are rewarded (with praise or attention), whereas if they get something wrong they are punished (or more likely, corrected).

Imitation is quite an appealing concept and one that seems – on the surface at least – to work. In Data extracts 19–21, you can see a child repeating what an adult has said and appearing to pick up new expressions through imitation.

Data extract 19

Father: Urr, that food's disgusting!

Ruby: Dat's 'gusting!

Data extract 20

Mother: What's that animal?

Ruby: It's a tiger.

Mother: No, that's a lion.

Ruby: Lion?

Mother: Yes, a lion.

Data extract 21

Ruby: When dinner ready?

Father: In about 10 minutes.

Ruby: 10 minutes? Boys! Boys! Dinner ready 10 minutes!

On the surface, the child has imitated pretty much what the parent has said, but does the child actually understand what the words mean? To put it more linguistically, she may have picked up the lexis, but does she grasp the semantics?

If you were to find out that the child in Data extract 19 then used the proto-word 'gusting' every time she saw food (whether it was disgusting or not), or that the same child kept calling lions 'tigers' for another three months, or that '10 minutes' could mean any period of time from a few seconds to a day or two, then you might conclude that imitation does not really account for much of a child's language acquisition.

Of course, it can account for some things. We are probably all aware of how a child picks up words he or she shouldn't, and then uses them in an embarrassingly accurate context among other people (shouting 'bugger!' in their grandparents' kitchen when granny drops a plate), or picks up elements of regional dialect that must have been acquired from the immediate environment. There is even something to be said for how correction and reinforcement can help with learning words. However, imitation cannot account for everything.

Fig. 7 *Children say the funniest things*

The most obvious problem with Skinner's theory is that children are not rats or pigeons. While it might be relatively simple to teach a dog not to use the sitting room as a toilet, children are much more sophisticated and sensitive creatures – and language a more subtle and nuanced form of behaviour than toilet training.

Another problem is that when children speak, they may be speaking the truth, but in a way that appears wrong. Research on interaction between adults and children tends to suggest that parents will correct the truth of their children's statements more readily than their grammar. So, as in Data extract 22, you might expect to see the parent or carer respond to the fact that the child has misnamed the animals, rather than the fact that the child has omitted the copula verb *are* or overgeneralised the plural ending *-s*.

Data extract 22

> *Father*: What are they?
>
> *Child*: They sheeps!
>
> *Father*: No, they're goats.

This could suggest that correction and/or positive or negative reinforcement is only part of the story. As illustrated by Data extract 23 (drawn from data collected by Katherine Nelson), you might expect children's responses to correction to be similar to adults' – responding to the truth or otherwise of what's said.

Data extract 23

> *Child*: I putted the plates on the table.
>
> *Mother*: You mean, I put the plates on the table.
>
> *Child*: No, I putted them on all by myself.

Another factor that seems to disprove a purely behaviourist approach might be the fact that the idea of correction is central to the notion of positive or negative reinforcement. In reality, research has shown that correcting a child's grammatically non-standard utterances might actually impede a child's language development.

With children's written language, it is clear that a certain amount of early writing (especially 'scribbling') is done in imitation of adult writing. But, as with spoken language acquisition, this will only take a child part of the way towards an understanding of what words mean and how the marks on the page relate to sounds and objects around them.

■ Social interaction

Social interactionists built on the behaviourists' ideas, believing that input is vital in helping children acquire language. They suggest that interaction with a child helps them develop a grasp of not only the meanings of words, but also the practical realities of communication: turn-taking, pragmatics and non-verbal communication.

Interaction is said, in the words of Jerome Bruner, to 'scaffold' children's language development in much the same way as builders sometimes support a structure they are erecting with scaffolding. Bruner called his system the **language acquisition support system (LASS)** – as a rejoinder to Chomsky's LAD (see nativist theory on page 106).

According to interactionists like Bruner, Snow and Trevarthen, parents and caregivers engage in collaborative and ritualised exchanges with their children, even before language has fully developed into meaningful words. Data extract 24 is an exchange between a father and his six-month-old daughter as he changes her nappy.

Data extract 24

> *Father*: Have you done a wee wee?
>
> *Daughter*: (smiles and maintains eye contact)
>
> *Father*: Shall we have a look in your nappy?
>
> *Daughter*: (vocalises and smiles)
>
> *Father*: Let's get the baby wipes then, shall we?
>
> *Daughter*: (vocalises and looks after dad as he goes to get wipes)

Even though the daughter is only six months old and cannot realistically be expected to have a meaningful conversation, the adult treats the child as an intelligent conversational participant, giving her cues for her turns in the conversation, and relating what he says to the actions the two are engaged in. It's fairly clear, though, that he is changing his language to encourage the child's responses.

Key terms

Language acquisition support system (LASS): a system that states that interaction helps support a child's language acquisition.

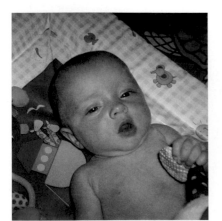

Fig. 8 *An 'intelligent conversational participant' waiting for a nappy change*

For written language and reading, we have already seen how important social interaction is to a child's development, and the work of Lev Vygotsky is relevant here (see Cognitive theories on page 108). He believed that education and interaction with adults equipped children with the 'cultural tools' they needed:

> Using cultural tools, children develop new psychological qualities, which we call abilities. These are the mental habits people need to be successful in particular intellectual or creative fields. The better children's grasp of the appropriate cultural tools, the greater their abilities in any field. The development of abilities leads to a flowering of children's personalities. They begin to plan and organise their own activities, openly express their point of view, provide non-standard solutions for problems, interact freely with other people and, most importantly, believe in themselves and their own abilities.

S. Palmer and G. Dolya, 'Freedom of thought', TES, 30 July 2004

Child-directed speech

According to interactionists, the language used by parents and caregivers to children ('parentese' or **child-directed speech – CDS**) has its own recognised characteristics:

- More pronounced intonation that draws attention to key morphemes or lexemes (see non-verbal aspects of speech in Section A Language and mode, page 17).
- Simplified vocabulary that helps establish keywords ('dog' rather than 'German shepherd').
- Repeated grammatical 'frames' that help draw attention to new elements within those frames (e.g. 'What animal lives in a kennel? What animal lives in a stable? What animal lives in a sty?')
- Simplified grammar – shorter utterances.
- Tag questions used to initiate turn-taking.
- Actions that accompany speech: pointing, smiling, shrugging shoulders, etc. (see non-verbal aspects of speech in Section A Language and mode, page 17).
- More obvious lip and mouth movement to help younger children copy.

Interactionists also point to ritualised scenarios such as dinner times, nappy changes and bath times in which children 'learn their lines'. They also suggest that games such as *Peek-a-boo* or *Walkie round the garden* help children with their turn-taking.

Parents and caregivers often expand, **recast** and develop their children's utterances rather than correct them for grammar or vocabulary. This helps the child develop at a natural pace while providing models for their communication, as in Data extract 25.

Data extract 25

Child: It's a doggie.

Father: Yes, it's a big brown doggie, isn't it?

Child: Brown doggie?

Father: Yes, a brown doggie.

Key terms

Child-directed speech (CDS): the language used by parents and carers towards children, and the features of such language.

Recast: rephrase in a more developed or standard grammatical form.

Critics of the social interaction theory point to cultures around the world such as Samoa and Papua New Guinea, in which interaction with CDS is not believed to take place. They argue that children in these environments do not seem to be impeded by the lack of verbal interaction. Others, such as Hart and Risley (1995), have observed huge differences between social classes in the USA and the verbal interaction children from these different classes receive, with potentially large influences on a child's social and economic development in later life.

■ Nativist theory

As mentioned earlier, Noam Chomsky was the linguist who first challenged the behaviourist model, and his work in many areas of linguistics has been massively influential. Chomsky's own ideas about child language have adapted over the years and been picked up by many other linguists and psychologists. One of his main arguments against Skinner's behaviourist stance was that if children were imitating adult speech, they were being given very poor material to imitate. Chomsky pointed to what he called the 'poverty of stimulus' that children receive. In other words, the quality of the language they hear from parents and carers isn't high enough for them to simply copy it and produce 'correct' grammar. He argued that, as a result, language can't be simply a mimicking or imitating exercise.

Another main plank of Chomsky's attack on behaviourism was that children produce utterances they could never have heard before ('linguistic creativity') and make mistakes ('virtuous errors') that suggest they have an inbuilt grasp of the rules of language. Children commonly produce overgeneralisations, such as 'mouses' for the plural of 'mouse', or 'falled' and 'runned' as past tense forms of irregular verbs that adults would say as 'fell' and 'ran'. They can't have heard these from adults, so something more than imitation must be at work. As discussed in the morphology topic on pages 76–80, these mistakes are often clues that help us to understand the processes at work under the surface of a child's language development.

Nativist theorists suggest that children have an inbuilt **language acquisition device (LAD)** that enables them to extract the rules of their particular language from the words and structures they hear. Chomsky put forward the idea that all human languages, whatever their surface differences, share what he calls **universal grammar**. This is a concept too complicated to do justice to here, but it basically proposes that, deep down, all human languages share similar features. Children are 'pre-programmed' with the underlying rules of universal grammar and simply need to be exposed to their own native language to allow the LAD to extract the particular rules for that language.

A colleague of Chomsky, Eric Lenneberg, has also argued that the LAD needs to be activated with sufficient input before a certain point in the child's development, or the child's language acquisition will be impaired. Cases of 'feral children' – children raised without human interaction and nurture – such as Genie, might give support to this theory.

■ Key terms

Language acquisition device (LAD): a part of the brain that allows humans to develop language through a process of extracting rules from language heard, and then applying those rules to the child's own speech.

Universal grammar: a theory that all languages share a similar grammatical structure under the surface.

■ Extension activity

Find out as much information as you can about feral children and their language development. For a start, try sources such as The Guardian online (www.guardian.co.uk) and Wikipedia http://en.wikipedia.org/wiki/, searching for combinations of keywords such as 'Genie', 'feral' and 'language'.

What do the studies of feral children's language development tell us about the need for interaction and input in child language acquisition?

Another nativist theorist, Steven Pinker, whose book *The Language Instinct* places human language in its evolutionary context, has developed Chomsky's LAD theory and put forward his own principles and parameters theory (PPT).

To simplify a very complex set of ideas, the PPT is essentially a system that allows speakers of a particular language to set the parameters of their own language through listening to the language around them. Some people describe these parameters as being similar to switches that you can turn on or off. In other words, if a speaker of French hears that adjectives follow nouns in the word order of that language (e.g. *le ciel bleu*), the parameter for that feature will be fixed: the switch will be set. Meanwhile, an English speaker will hear the English language word order of adjective + noun (*blue sky*) and their parameter will be set.

This theory is still being debated by many linguists, and Chomsky himself has developed his original ideas in the light of the debate. He seems to have moved closer to what might be seen as a *slightly* more cognitive position, in which the LAD is more like a set of 'puzzle-solving equipment' (as the linguist Jean Aitchison calls it), and less like a unit for just decoding grammatical rules.

Extension activity

Recent research suggests that Chomsky might have overstated the poverty of children's input, with some researchers suggesting that more than 90 per cent of the language children hear consists of standard grammar, rather than the fragmented utterances Chomsky implied.

Record your own data and explore this.

- Do parents and carers tend to simplify anything they say to children?
- Do they use grammatically accurate constructions?
- How is the language adults use to children different from that they use with each other?

Once you have thought about this, make a list of the features of this 'child-directed speech' (CDS).

The innateness theory is supported by a fairly convincing array of evidence. All children around the world, whatever language they learn, pass through very similar stages. Medical research also indicates that there are specific areas of the brain that control language. But even Chomsky's earliest discussions about innateness recognise that *some* input is needed.

Fig. 9 *Programmed for language*

■ Cognitive theories

Followers of the cognitive approach see language acquisition as part of a much wider development of understanding and knowledge in children. They differ from nativists in that many nativists see language acquisition as separate to cognitive development. There is much discussion about the strength of the link between language and thought, but to simplify the debate, you could look at two positions: those of Jean Piaget and Lev Vygotsky.

The Swiss psychologist Jean Piaget's work with children has led to a number of highly influential strands of thinking in children's psychological development. His cognitive approach suggests that language acquisition is part of a child's wider development: language comes with understanding. In other words, a child cannot linguistically articulate concepts he or she does not understand. Meanwhile, the Russian psychologist, Lev Vygotsky (much of whose work was suppressed by Stalin's dictatorship until long after his death) put forward similarly influential views on the connections between language and thought.

Piaget argued that children need to understand a concept before they can use the language terms that refer to that concept. So, a concept like the past would have to be grasped before a child could start to use the past tense, and a concept like **seriation** understood before a child could use comparatives and superlatives.

An idea like **object permanence** plays a part in this too. Once a child has realised that everything has a separate identity and life of its own, even when they can't see it, there seems to be a leap in conceptual understanding that affects language development. The 'naming explosion' that occurs in the third year of a child's life (covered earlier in Lexical and semantic development earlier on pages 73–79) might be linked to this. Pronoun use might also be linked to this conceptual leap forward, perhaps because children start to recognise the symbolic function of words and the power they now have to name all those objects around them.

Vygotsky, on the other hand, viewed language as having two separate roles: one for communication and one for the basis of thought. He saw language in this second role as being a helpful tool for developing understanding, and believed that language and thought become closely related after a relatively short time.

Both approaches might appear to be common sense, but there are exceptions that suggest otherwise. Some children with cognitive problems still manage to use language way beyond their apparent understanding, while others with advanced cognition skills struggle with language. So the two concepts – cognition and language – do not seem to be as inextricably linked as Piaget and Vygotsky might have thought. While there are clearly connections between language development and other aspects of a child's overall development, language is distinct in a sufficient number of ways to make it unique.

■ Research point

Studies conducted in 1996 by Waxman and Balaban seem to show that language labels (e.g. different nouns and adjectival phrases) can help children recognise differences between and within categories more clearly. So in this sense, language does seem to help cognition, as explained in more detail by William O'Grady:

■ Key terms

Seriation: the placing of items in a series, e.g. in descending or ascending order.

Object permanence: the ability to understand that an object still exists even though it is no longer in sight.

In one experiment, a group of nine-month-old infants were shown a series of rabbit pictures as the experimenter said "a rabbit" each time. Another group saw the pictures, but heard a tone instead. Both groups were then shown two pictures, one of a rabbit and one of a pig. The group that had heard the "rabbit" label looked longer at the new animal. The group that had heard the tone made no distinction.

Evidently, hearing a label had helped the first group of infants recognise the category "rabbit", making it easier to see the pig as a new type of animal.

Thinking point

Does research like this tend to offer support to any of the different theoretical positions outlined in this topic?

In terms of children's acquisition of reading and writing, both Piaget's and Vygotsky's ideas have been highly influential. Vygotsky's belief that collaborative play is essential to children's learning has been central to much early years education, where the emphasis has been less on the explicit teaching of new concepts than on the integration of concepts into what the child already knows and does, stretching the child and pushing him or her onwards, even if they are unaware of being taught something new. As Vygotsky himself put it, 'What the child can do in co-operation today, he can do alone tomorrow.'

Extension activity

Put together your own revision chart that offers arguments for and against each theoretical position and examples to support each theory. You may wish to select data from the extracts given in this section.

For more help on essay planning and exam questions, check the final topic in this section, Exam preparation, pages 111–122.

Data response exercise 17

To develop your confidence in analysing child language data, discussing the patterns within it and the possible theories behind it, study the following data. Look for what the children are doing with their language.

1. Can you notice any patterns of 'virtuous error'? Label these with the appropriate terms.

2. Consider whether each child's speech appears to exhibit particular types of competence.

3. Try to link what the children are saying to the different theoretical models we have explored.

Look at the data from as many angles as you can. Check your ideas against the feedback (page 127).

a

Context: twin boys aged 3 years 6 months playing together with toy soldiers, dinosaurs and caveman figures, all loosely grouped into 'goodies' and 'baddies'.

Liam: The goodies are going on their ship cos they've catched a baddie.

Stan: Yeah, they've caught him and throwed him in the dungeons.

Liam: The cavemans are laughing. This one's much more braver than the baddies though… I'm going to build a whole army of goodies.

Stan: Yeah, cos the baddies are coming.

Together: Charge!

b

Context: girl aged 2 years 5 months talking with her father about her brothers who are playing on the computer.

Ruby: What Stan doing?

Father: He's playing on the computer.

Ruby: On the 'puter?

Father: Yeah, he's playing with Liam on the computer.

Ruby: Where Stan going?

Father: I don't know. Probably going to the toilet.

Ruby: To do a wee wee?

Father: Probably.

Ruby: Probly a wee wee?

Father: Yes.

Ruby: Stan back!

Father: Yes, he's back isn't he?

Ruby: Back on 'puter!

Topic revision exercise

Complete the questions on your own, then discuss your ideas with a partner.

1 What is the main difference between 'nature' and 'nurture' theories?

2 What evidence is there that children imitate elements of the language used around them?

3 What evidence is there that children's language development is rule-governed?

Exam preparation

In this topic you will:

- study examples of possible questions on language development and ways to approach them

- look at examples of student responses to previous exam questions and the feedback from experienced examiners on how these students have performed

- gain useful insights from examiners about what makes a good answer at AS Level on this subject

- see how your study of language development can lead to possible areas of study for your A2 English Language investigations.

How this unit is assessed

Unit 1 Seeing through language is assessed externally by examination. Section B Language development is split into two, and you can choose to answer questions on either **initial language acquisition** or **children's writing**.

One question will be set on each of the topics, but this question will be divided into parts. Candidates will be asked to:

- comment linguistically on a small piece of data from children's speech or writing *(10 marks)*

- write discursively in response to an essay cue question based on issues raised by the data *(35 marks)*.

How to prepare for the exam

Everyone has a different approach to preparing for exams, but there are certain key things you need to be aware of to do well. In this exam you are credited for hitting various assessment objectives. The ones that are important for this topic are:

AO1 Select and apply a range of linguistic methods, to communicate relevant knowledge using appropriate terminology and coherent, accurate written expression.

AO2 Demonstrate critical understanding of a range of concepts and issues related to the construction and analysis of meanings in spoken and written language, using knowledge of linguistic approaches.

What do these assessment objectives mean in practice for answering questions on this topic? Examiners want to see a candidate (i.e. you!) focusing on the question set, engaging with the key ideas in the question, showing evidence of knowledge about how children acquire language, and using linguistic terminology to discuss this. Examiners want to see you do well – believe it or not – and they are encouraged to reward your achievements positively rather than penalise your mistakes and misunderstandings. But you need to work to earn the rewards.

Revision is very important, and that doesn't just mean looking back at the whole Language development section after you've finished it. Make sure that you consolidate what you have learned in each lesson by looking back at your notes and the relevant parts of the textbook, preferably topic by topic and framework by framework. Make sure you test yourself using the exercises and activities, so that you can be sure you have covered each part of the section in detail. It's important to see links between the frameworks too, and to be aware of how they all fit together. For example, there are quite close links between how children's understanding of words' meanings links with their development of early grammar.

Examiners will reward candidates who can offer their own interpretations of child language data and who can see connections between what children say and what theorists have said about how children acquire language. They will also reward candidates who include their own examples in their answers. And while we have tried to provide you with a range of data in this textbook, there are other sources of data for you to use: your younger brothers and sisters, nieces and nephews; children whom you may babysit; old copies of your primary school or nursery work that parents might have kept for you; internet sources of data and other books on the topic.

■ Approaching the questions

Since the questions on Language development are split into two parts, it's worth looking at how to approach each one.

Comment linguistically on a small piece of data from children's speech or writing

This is an identification and labelling exercise that will assess your ability to *pick out* significant linguistic features from child language data and to *label* those features accurately. At this stage, you are not expected to offer an interpretation of why these features are there, or different theoretical positions (that comes in the discursive essay part of the question). This is much more about the micro-levels of the text, the little features, rather than the fact that the adult is interacting with the child or that the child may be telling a story.

■ Data response exercise 18

Examine the data below and pick out five features that you think, from your study of language development, are worth commenting on. For example, in line 2, the child uses an overgeneralised plural: '…mouses'.

Context: a father is reading a story (*Tales from Acorn Wood*) to his daughter, at bedtime. (Reading from the text of the book is indicated in italics.)

Age: 2 years 6 months.

1   **Father**: *Bang! Clash! Who's that? Oh no! A band of…*

    Daughter: …mouses!

    Father: *a band of mice*

    Daughter: mice

5   **Father**: *Rabbit's in her…*

    Daughter: …deckdair

    Father: *A doze would be so…*

    Daughter: good

    Father: *Whack! Crack! Who's that? It's…*

10 **Daughter**: Fok he choppin wood

    [later in story]

    Father: *Look! A tent! Is Hen in here? Can you see a long brown ear? What's that?*

    Daughter: mouse!

    Father: No, that's a rabbit

    Daughter: A wabbit

15 **Father**: Yes, a rabbit

Fig. 10 *Bang! Crash! Who's that? Oh no! A band of…*

Data response exercise 19

Examine the early writing in the following data and pick out five features that you think, from your study of language development, are worth commenting on. In **a**, the child has used simple, one-clause sentences.

a

Context: this extract is taken from some independent writing done at home. The first part was a birthday wish and the second a joke at the child's father's expense when the child was told he wouldn't get his birthday wish.

Age: 5 years 5 months.

Transliteration: I want a big g gitar.

My bab daddy wos a wig.

b

Context: this extract is part of independent writing at school.

Age: 5 years 4 months.

Transliteration: On the wicend I went To the piak and plad on the swings.

Write discursively in response to an essay cue question based on issues raised by the data

The second part of each question is worth more marks and takes the form of a more traditional essay answer. In it you will be expected to make more detailed reference to your wider understanding of the processes and patterns of child language acquisition.

An example of such a question might be something like the ones below:

1 How far do children acquire their language skills by imitating adults?

   In your answer you should:

   - refer to particular linguistic features and contexts
   - refer to appropriate linguistic research and theory
   - present a clear line of argument.

2 Examine some of the language issues which arise when children begin to make the transition from spoken to written mode.

   In your answer you should:

   - refer to particular linguistic features and contexts
   - refer to appropriate linguistic research and theory
   - present a clear line of argument.

As you can see, both questions provide you with some guidance as to what should be included to answer the questions effectively. The knowledge of the theory and the research, however, is down to you, as is the way in which you approach the question and the features and contexts you may wish to explore.

Remember, examiners are not looking to catch you out, and there is no one correct way of answering questions like this. You should be able to achieve high marks – perhaps even full marks – in a number of different ways. Again, there are key things to include, and a good understanding of what is actually assessed in this part of the question will really help you to do well.

On the mark scheme for this question, you will find that the top band (13–15 marks) requires that a candidate:

Shows good knowledge about linguistic concepts, theories and research.

Identifies and comments on different views and interpretations.

Candidates are likely to explore:

- a range of well selected examples
- syntax, semantic relations, negation, systematic phonological variation
- acquisition as an active & deductive process
- theories of acquisition critically, using evidence to evaluate
- links between cognitive theory and linguistic development
- the role of imitation, input and correction.

The top two sentences remain on the mark scheme from year to year, while the bulleted descriptors are changed each year to suit the actual question set. So, the basic demands of the question remain the same each year, but you might be expected to cover different areas of the topic to answer the question well in different years.

As you should be able to see from the bulleted descriptors, examiners are looking to reward a candidate who can:

■ draw on his or her knowledge to use linguistic frameworks
■ explore patterns and processes
■ choose examples of child language data that suit the question
■ express knowledge of existing child language theories and to approach those theories critically and with an open mind
■ see connections between different elements of the topic
■ engage with the actual question and the topic itself.

For the remaining five marks on the paper, you are expected to write clearly and accurately, using the correct linguistic terminology, and to organise your answer.

■ Candidate responses

With these points in mind, let's look at some examples of candidate responses to exam questions and what examiners have said about them.

Examination-style questions

2 (a)   Read **Data Set 1** below. Comment linguistically on **five** features of language use which you find of interest.

Data set 1

(The child is two years old.)

1   *Child*: The daddy doll's more big than this one.
       Mother: Yes, it's much bigger isn't it?
       Child: It's more bigger.

2   *Child*: My want to hold your hand.

3   *Child*: Mummy's got a poorly ankle. She hurt it when she felled over.

4   The child uses the following terms:
       Helicuck = helicopter.
       Little helicuck = seagull
       Big helicuck = aeroplane.   *(10 marks)*

2 (b)   Discuss competing theories about children's language acquisition by exploring the data in Data set 1 and examples of your own. In your answer you should:
   ■ refer to particular linguistic features and contexts
   ■ refer to appropriate linguistic research and theory
   ■ present a clear line of argument.   *(35 marks)*

Question from AQA specimen paper, data set from AQA 2005

Student response

Question 2(a)

- The child has said 'more bigger' instead of 'bigger'.
- The child has overextended the word 'helicuck' to include all sorts of flying objects.
- The child has said 'my want' instead of 'I want'.
- The child has made a virtuous error by saying 'felled' instead of 'fell'.
- The child says 'helicuck' instead of 'helicopter', which is a phonological error.

Question 2(b)

Child language acquisition is a wildly debated area, in which there are many theories suggesting how it happens.

The first theory suggested was that of imitation and reinforcement by Skinner. He believed it was operant conditioning that taught a child language, and through a system of rewards for being correct and punishment for being wrong, the child would acquire language. It assumed two functions of language; getting attention and getting what is wanted. It did not take into account the other functions of language: heuristic; representational; imaginative; regulatory; personal; performative; instrumental; and interactional.

These functions are as valid as Skinners two and do not revolve around his suggested functions. Children want to gain information, show creativity, express themselves and quite often control what is around them. Skinner's theory also does not take into account children's logical mistakes, 'The daddy doll's more big than this one', that they have never heard before and therefore could not be imitating. It also ignores their resistance to correction:

'Mum: Yes, it's much bigger isn't it?

Child: It's more bigger.'

For the theory to work, children would have to be corrected all the time and Nelson discovered that mothers who are generally more accepting have more quickly developing children than those always corrected.

It also ignores the critical age aspect (that children who learn late may never learn) and exceptions. Children who cannot hear or speak still understand language though they cannot imitate. It is thought that perhaps language is partly imitation and reinforcement, taken through interaction. The interaction theory suggests that caretaker speech, which is often changed to involve children, is a major factor of children learning language. They learn through tag questions adults ask of them to keep their interest and topics that directly involve them. Speech is slower, the pitch is higher and commands are frequent. It is not certain how much of what a child learns through interaction is used but it is clearly beneficial and provides a good basis for future relationships. Vygotsky suggested that interaction is important in helping them know the difference between written and spoken speech, drawings being an early attempt to write. Interaction teaches children turn-taking in conversation.

The cognitive theory is one that believes that as intelligence increases and concepts are understood, so is language. A child must understand the differences between the colours before they can name them. This is shown by overextension and the semantic development of language.

'Helicuck' for helicopter and 'Big helicuck' for aeroplane. It does not account for children over 18 months as it is difficult to measure intellectual and physical development. Though phonologically the child does take longer to develop. At the age of one the child can understand 50 words but speak only three consonants and a vowel sound. It is a gradual process. The nativist theory, proposed by Chomsky, suggests that learning language is innate. There is a language acquisition device (LAD) in the brain that puzzles words and structures that are heard and causes the child to speak language. This theory largely ignores other input from caretakers and the child's ability to imitate. It does not acknowledge why mistakes never before heard are made 'she felled over' (Example 3). Grammar does not always come out right 'My want to hold your hand' (Example 2). It cannot all be innate, though to an extent it is.

All these theories singularly do not stand out as being perfectly correct but it can be suggested that together they are. Not one theory can account for everything but it is possible that bits of all of them are correct and together could explain children's language acquisition.

Examiner's comment

Question 2 (a)

The response to this question is fairly reasonable and shows some knowledge of language development, but is a little lacking in detail and precise use of terminology. A short, focused answer is desirable here, and the candidate's use of bullet points and short answers is perfectly acceptable, but each answer needs a bit more content.

Positive points

■ The identification of features such as overextension and virtuous error.

■ The identification of relevant features such as picking out 'my' for 'I' and 'felled' for 'fell'.

Points to improve

■ Once features such as those above have been noted, they should be labelled more accurately. For example, the use of a first-person possessive pronoun 'my' instead of a first-person subject pronoun 'I', or inconsistent use of alternatives to the comparative adjective 'bigger'. There are, also spelling errors ('hevistic' instead of *heuristic*) and punctuation mistakes ('Skinners two' should read *Skinner's two*), which could have been checked more carefully.

■ 'Virtuous error' is still quite a general term. Why not label it fully as an 'overgeneralisation'?

■ Similarly, 'phonological error' is partly right, but it could be developed to explain exactly what has happened: deletion of an unstressed syllable and assimilation of consonant sounds.

■ The language of the carer towards the child could also have been considered, with the recasting of 'more big' into 'bigger' being worth a look. The child's resistance to correction by saying 'more bigger' is also a valid point.

Marks

This candidate would probably score 5 out of 10 on an answer like this, and would have to be more precise and detailed to achieve a higher mark.

Question 2 (b)

This is a response that shows some good knowledge of different theories of language development. It would benefit from closer attention to written expression and more development of the examples quoted.

Positive points

■ Good knowledge of different theories and how they interrelate.

■ Willingness to explain evidence for and against each theory.

■ Some awareness of case studies and research.

■ Some examples of child language data.

Points to improve

■ Clearer written expression: many points are left undeveloped and some sentences are left hanging without being properly finished.

■ Better use and explanation of examples: the examples are largely limited to those in the data set and more examples from elsewhere – with fuller linguistic explanations – would help a great deal.

■ Some areas of the theories need to be explained more precisely: innateness is left rather sketchily outlined, while imitation and interaction are better handled.

■ The rather formulaic structure can lead to a rather average response: answers that are more data-driven, or which take an approach that makes more explicit use of linguistic frameworks will often secure better marks and make for an examiner having a more interesting read!

Marks

This is a fairly solid and focused answer with some good moments of discussion, but these are offset by some rather imprecise expression and undeveloped areas. The candidate would score around 20 out of 30 for AO2 and 3 out of 5 for AO1, giving a total of 23 out of 35.

Examination-style questions

3 (a)   Read **Data Set 2** below. Comment linguistically on **five** features of language use which you find of interest.

(10 marks)

3 (b)   Examine some of the language issues which arise when children begin to make the transition from spoken to written mode.

In your answer you should:

■ refer to particular linguistic features and contexts

■ refer to appropriate linguistic research and theory

■ present a clear line of argument.

(35 marks)
AQA specimen paper

Data set 2

(The writer is aged 5 years and 10 months.)

Key
e – letters reversed in the original

I made a tim**e** macine. I tuc me to London **b**ac in time.

it was darc and silent. I decided **t**o camp. I had a tent w**it**h me.

it was cold out side. und**e**r me tent **t**er wos a funy noie it whent

woowoo. I cep wcking up and the woo cept **g**oing on.

I wowc up in **t**he moning I whent to buy som br**e**cfest and when I

got out of the I Sor a Gost I wheintto the timemachine.

I got home and when to be**d**

Student response

Question 3 (a)

1) The child uses the proper noun London to illustrate the place that s/he went to and uses a capital letter to represent this.

2) The child begins by using a simple sentence that is formed of the subject 'I', the verb 'made' and the adverb 'time machine'.

3) Some of the data is written in the past perfect tense, for example, 'I made a time machine', which shows the child's completed action.

4) 'Sor' and 'wos' are both spelt incorrectly and are written like how the child would pronounce the word instead.

5) The progressive verb 'wcking' is used to show the ongoing fact that s/he couldn't sleep.

Question 3 (b)

Spoken language is something that is not taught; imitation theorists believe that children start off with a blank slate and imitate the language they hear around them, whereas linguists such as Chomsky believe that children have an inbuilt 'learning acquisition device' from which they can extract the rules of language. Written language on the other hand is taught and it has been said that children have the ability to recognise that written language serves some importance to adults and this may be one reason why we tend to teach children written form at an early age compared to other countries and so it is seen to be quite prestigious.

Childhood games such as writing a shopping list or even playing 'schools' with one another can be seen to reflect the fact that children understand that the written mode does serve some value and meaning in society. They also are aware of the different genres of writing; however they can not always successfully apply them. This shows that in child language acquisition they understand more than they can comprehend.

The stage before a child can produce 'written' words is called the precommunicative stage. This is then followed by the phonological segmentation stage where the child will normally start to write graphemes and a combination of letters in patterns that show some similarities to how a word sounds. This is an example of how a child puts what they have learnt phonologically and translates this into written form, which shows that their learning process is active. The final stage is the orthographic stage where words are spelt accurately and in the right context.

As children become older their written language tends to improve and become more complex. The older a child normally gets the more focused their writing becomes, for example, whether or not they have written for an intended target audience and this generally reflects the child's age and ability.

Another issue that arises when children make the transition from spoken to written mode is the way that they develop their handwriting and how they form letters together to try and make a word. Sometimes this does not work as children often use the letter 'd' in places where 'b' should appear and vice versa for example 'bog' for 'dog' and perhaps when a child first starts to write it may not look like 'proper' letters and instead may look like a shape. It is inevitable that this transition from spoken to written mode is something that will not take place overnight and will take time and so children are bound to make 'virtuous errors'.

Some linguists have recognised the fact that the English spelling system can be seen as a barrier for child acquisition and think that it should become somewhat easier for them to be able to comprehend. George Bernard Shaw for example said that 'fish' could be spelt as 'ghoti' if certain grapheme-phoneme correspondence is applied. Language acquisition can be difficult for children to understand especially as some letters are combined to create one sound such as -*ch*.

Bell identified features such as the –*ee* sound that could be spelt as *ee, ea, ie, ei eCe, iCe, I, ey* and *eo*. This may confuse children and even some adults when they attempt at spelling words in their written communication.

Children's writing may be influenced by factors in their reading. For example, a child who recognises that particular words such as night/knight and see/sea can be spelt differently depending on their context is likely to be more accurate with their written language. Also, children who read more and have experienced the use of phonics and whole-word systems may find it helpful to apply this to their written language.

Just like spoken language, when a child will go through the stages of babbling, the holographic stage, and the telegraphic stage and then the post telegraphic stage, written language is also very similar. They begin with scribbling, emergent writing, copy writing and then finally independent writing. Kroll (1981) identified four stages in how children develop their very early writing skills. These were: preparation (a mixture of emergent writing and copy writing); consolidation (spellings are often phonetic); differentiation (more accurate punctuation and more varied syntax); and integration (writing is more independent and creative). This again shows that there is a process involved in written language.

Perera's research shows that children find chronological texts easier to write that use connectives like then, next and so on and personal writing that contains personal pronouns such as 'we', 'us' and 'I'. Both of these ideas could be used to show how children enjoy speaking and writing about their own experiences and things that are personal to them.

It is important to recognise the fact that all children do not learn language in the same way and some are quicker at learning the 'correct' language skills than others. However, evidence does show that children are aware of the different forms of language and their previous knowledge of spoken language is used to help them through acquisition.

Examiner's comment

Question 3 (a)

The response to this question is definitely along the right lines, even if all the technical terms are not fully applied. A short, focused answer is desirable here, and the candidate's use of bullet points and short answers is perfectly acceptable.

Positive points

- The identification of elements such as a simple sentence.
- The capitalisation of a proper noun.
- The identification of tense and aspect.
- Awareness of spelling irregularities.

Points to improve

- The simple sentence in fact consists of a subject, verb and object.
- 'I made a time machine' is past tense but not past perfect.
- There could be more accuracy in the discussion of how 'sor' and 'wos' are spelled – they could be termed **phonetic renditions** of vowel sounds.
- The point about the simple sentence could be developed to include wider reference to other sentences in the data.

Key terms

phonetic rendition: when words are spelled as they sound

Marks

This candidate would probably score 6–7 out of 10 on an answer like this, and would just have to be slightly more precise to secure a top mark. An answer that offers a bit more of an overview of some of the main features of the data would also help, i.e. an answer that includes something on each of: sentence length and type, orthography, phonetic rendition, discourse structure.

Question 3 (b)

This is a generally well-organised response to the question that makes good use of links to spoken language acquisition and to theories of reading and writing.

Positive points

- The straightforward and focused response to the question.
- The references to different stages of reading and writing and how these relate to spoken language acquisition.
- Theoretical knowledge (Chomsky, Perera and Kroll).
- Some examples when referring to spelling and reading issues.
- A good awareness of how context influences individual children's written language.
- Awareness of how written language varies depending on genre and purpose.
- Awareness of the prestige of written language and its influence on children.

Points to improve

- More examples are needed for discussion of how children develop their grammar and writing for different genres and audiences.
- A greater focus on the transition issues referred to in the question: perhaps reference to the problems children face with grapheme–phoneme correspondence.
- A better contextualisation of writing within the whole framework of children's language development would help, i.e. a sense of when a child might start to write as compared to their spoken development.
- Some more developed links to some of the overarching patterns in children's writing and theoretical explanations for them. For example, some kind of link to Vygotsky's or Piaget's ideas about cognitive development and the use of the past tense in narratives.

Marks

The candidate covers quite a lot of material here and has some good knowledge, so she would score around 22 out of 30 for AO2. The answer is well organised and clear, so gains 4 out 5 for AO1 – giving a total of 26 out of 35.

■ Further reading

Bell, M. *Understanding English Spelling*, Pegasus Elliot Mackenzie Publishers, 2004

Crystal, D. *Listen To Your Child*, Penguin, 1982

Mercer, N. and Swann, J. (eds.) *Learning English: development and diversity*, Open University Press, 1996

Myszor, F. *Language Acquisition*, Hodder Education, 1999

O'Grady, W. *How Children Learn Language*, Cambridge University Press, 2005

Peccei, J. S. *Child Language: a resource book for students*, Routledge, 2005

Perera, K. *Children's Writing and Reading*, Blackwell, 1984

Pinker, S. *The Language Instinct*, Penguin, 2000

Pinker, S, *Words and Rules*, Basic Books, Perseus, 1999

■ Developing your work into A2

Once you've taken your Unit 1 exam on Language development, you may never have to look at child language again – at least until you perhaps have children of your own! Then again, if you find the topic interesting, there are opportunities for you to take it further in A2 in your Language investigation coursework (Unit 4).

As the focus of your investigation will be spoken language, some areas you may want to look at in more detail are suggested below:

■ A longitudinal study of a child's developing phonological competence over a 12-month period.

■ A study of how different children develop their skills of reading.

■ An investigation into the language of carers and parents towards children.

■ An apparent time study of children's application of grammatical rules in spoken language.

■ A study of how teachers and classroom assistants use spoken language during the literacy hour in years 1–3.

The possibilities are varied and interesting, and we hope you have found your introduction to children's language development a stimulating start to this subject. Many different linguists and experts have written extensively on this area and a further reading list is provided here should you wish to go into more detail.

Feedback

This part of the book provides all the feedback for the Data response exercises in Unit 1, Section B. For the answers to the Topic revision exercises, please go to pages 202–205.

Introduction

Data response exercise 1

There are many things you could have said about the utterances here. They might include some of the following:

- Some of the 'words' aren't 'proper words' at all.
- The utterances seem to get longer – there are more words – as you read from a to k.
- Some of the utterances seem to be incomplete – words are missing.
- Some of the utterances make sense but sound 'wrong'.
- Some of the utterances seem to use 'rules', but in cases where you wouldn't expect them to be applied.
- The utterances become more sophisticated and convey more complex information as they run from a to k.
- Many of the words seem to be linked to the world immediately around the child.
- Some of the words seem to be linked to imaginary worlds and play.
- The utterances seem to have a range of functions: from demands, questions and statements through to more advanced comments about what might happen in the future.

You might also have considered how little you know about the context to each utterance:

- Were they all from the same child?
- At what ages did the children say these things?
- What were they doing or referring to?
- Who were they talking to, if anyone?
- What were they trying to say?
- Where were they?
- What sort of background do(es) the child(ren) come from?

Lexical and semantic development

Data response exercise 2

Naming words		Action words	Social words	Modifying words
Jasper	woof	more	bye bye	more
socks	bot-bot	poo	hello	my
Daddy	Marmite	book	hiya	hot
shoes	jam	quack quack	no	nice
juice	ball	woof	yes	two
Nana	cup	bang	yeah	
Grandad	spoon	cuddle	ta	
poo	bowl	jump	please	
book	Mummy		wassat?	
duck	bang			
quack quack	cuddle			
biscuits	cat			
bubbles	laa Loa			
eyes	weeble			

While many of these words are fairly easy to place into the right categories, others are less clear. You may have noticed that some of the words appear in two categories and this is because particular words might be used in different ways depending on the context. Examples are 'woof' and 'quack quack', which could be used as action words (verbs) to describe the noises animals make, but some children also use these terms as naming words (nouns) – a duck might be referred to as a 'quack quack', for example. 'Cuddle' is another example, which could be both a verb and a noun.

Data response exercise 3

Tiger: categorical overextension. Tiger appears to be the term used to refer to all the similar animals within this category.

Socks: analogical or categorical overextension. There are two alternatives here. One is that the child is making an analogical overextension and likening some property of the glove to that of the 'concept of sock' they already have (perhaps because it is placed on a part of the body or is made from a similar material). The other could be a categorical overextension in which the word 'socks' is being used as a hyponym for all types of clothing.

Duck: categorical overextension or mismatch. Again, there are two possibilities here. The child may be using the term 'duck' to refer to all birds, or might be using the holophrase 'duck' to refer to the whole process of feeding birds in the park, or even to the whole activity of walking to the park and then feeding the birds.

Cat: a mismatch. The cat is often there, so the word is conveying some abstract information about its absence.

Shoes: underextension. The child is using the word 'shoes' in a very narrow sense, relating its meaning only to her own shoes and not to those belonging to others.

■ Grammatical development – syntax

■ Data response exercise 4

	Utterance	MLU and explanation
a	'What you doing?'	4 *What* and *you* *do + ing* = 2
b	'Not eat that daddy.'	4 1 for each morpheme
c	'Where's man going?'	5 *Where + 's* (contracted form of 'is') = 2 *man* = 1 *go + ing* = 2
d	'The cavemans are laughing.'	6 *caveman + s* = 2 *The* and *are* = 2 *laugh + ing* = 2
e	'The soldiers falled over when they got hitted.'	11 *The, over, when, they* and *got* = 5 *soldier + s* = 2 *fall + ed* = 2 *hit + ed* = 2
d	'Doctor made my ear better.'	Telegraphic stage. The absence of the determiner *the* from the possible adult target *the doctor* suggests that while this is a fairly sophisticated utterance, it is still telegraphic. Nearly a post-telegraphic utterance, but not quite.
e	'How long is it till my birthday?'	Post-telegraphic stage. This is probably the same as the adult target. The utterance is a question and formulated in the correct syntax.

■ Data response exercise 5

a	Doer + action.
b	Possessor + thing.
c	Nonexistence.
d	Action + undergoer.
e	Thing + location.
f	Thing + property.

■ Data response exercise 6

a	'I sit Daddy lap.'	Telegraphic stage. The adult target might be something like 'I am sitting on Daddy's lap' or 'I want to sit on Daddy's lap', which would suggest that the preposition *on* has been omitted and some form of auxiliary verb (**am** *sitting or* **want** *to sit*) is missing. The absence of a possessive -'s suffix on Daddy is a morphological feature.
b	'Cat gone.'	The adult target might be 'The cat has gone', in which case the absence of a determiner *the* and auxiliary verb *has* mark this as being the two-word stage.
c	'I done it.'	This could be the telegraphic stage or post-telegraphic, depending on the context. Some regional varieties use *done* instead of *did* as a past tense. In this case, the child has used a full adult target correctly. If, however, the child is used to hearing 'I have done it', then this would be a telegraphic utterance because of the omission of the auxiliary verb *have*.

■ Grammatical development – morphology

■ Data response exercise 7

As you will already have seen from the section on syntax, words like 'walked' and 'steamer' consist of two morphemes (*walk + -ed* and *steam + -er*). The first morpheme is called the free morpheme because it can stand independently and act as a meaningful unit on its own, while the second morpheme in each example is called a bound morpheme. The bound morphemes can only have meaning when attached to free morphemes, and in these cases they act to show past tense (-*ed*), plurals (-*s*), progressive aspect (-*ing*), comparatives (-*er*), objects performing certain verbs (-*er*) and possession (-*'s*).

■ Data response exercise 8

The following comments are suggestions for what the child might have been trying to say. When you analyse your own child language data, be open-minded in your approach and offer a range of possible interpretations.

a 'I runned.'

The child has used an overgeneralised past tense -*ed* ending on an irregular verb.

b 'There was three mans.'

The child has used an overgeneralised plural -*s* ending on an irregular noun and formed a version of the past tense without creating grammatical agreement between the verb and the nouns (i.e. the verb is a singular form and the noun plural).

c 'I eating.'

The child has successfully used a progressive -*ing* ending on the main verb, but has omitted the auxiliary verb (*am* or *was*).

d 'This goody is braver than that one.'

The child has successfully used a comparative -*er* ending on the adjective brave.

e 'That baddy got a shooter.'

The child has omitted the verb *has* and created a noun *shooter* from the verb *to shoot* plus an -*er* ending that turns it into 'a thing that shoots'.

f 'They shotted their arrows at the baddies.'

The child has used an overgeneralised past tense -*ed* ending on an irregular verb, but has applied the ending to the correct past tense form (*shotted* rather than *shooted*).

g 'Daddy go work.'

The child may have omitted two words and a morpheme: the auxiliary *is*, the *-ing* morpheme and the preposition *to work*.

Data response exercise 9

nighty: affixation. Noun *night* with adjective *-y* ending added.

plant-man: compounding.

sharped: conversion. Adjective *sharp* converted into a verb.

cycler: affixation. Clipped noun (*bicycle*) with *-er* ending added to describe someone who cycles.

Phonological development

Data response exercise 10

a **Deletion** of final consonant sound (*s*).

b **Deletion** of unstressed syllable (*com*).

c **Substitution** of *w* for *r*.

d **Deletion** of first consonant and addition of final consonant sound.

e **Consonant cluster reduction** of *bl* to *b*.

f **Substitution** of final consonant sound (*t* for *k*).

g **Substitution** of *b* for *r* and **assimilation** (*b–b*).

Pragmatic development

Data response exercise 11

Utterance	*Possible* Halliday function
'Put me down!'	*Regulatory* – telling father what to do
'Biscuit!'	*Instrumental* – expressing a need or *Representational* – showing knowledge of what's in the tin
'Why, daddy?'	*Heuristic* – asking questions to find out more about her environment
'I walking.'	*Personal* – expressing identity and pride in achievement or *Representational* – stating a fact
'Look at me, I'm a fairy.'	*Imaginative* – showing role-playing and imaginative abilities and/or *Regulatory* – seeking to control others' behaviour

Data response exercise 12

a uses instrumental functions of language along with a deictic (context-dependent) expression, which relies heavily on non-verbal communication (the pointing) and the parent's understanding of context (that it's the biscuit within the tin that is required, not the tin itself, or that the child is just naming the object she sees).

b is very similar to **a** but with use of the noun *biscuit* itself.

c is a direct statement of personal need that relies on the parent responding to the child's need. The modality employed in question form in **d** and **e** (through the modal auxiliary verb *can*), along with the politeness marker *please* in e), shows that the children are starting to use less direct, perhaps more tentative and polite approaches.

f and **g** rely on inference to make their point and thus demonstrate a greater pragmatic awareness. In **f**, Liam makes a simple statement using a *subject – verb – complement* structure (as opposed to the less subtle *subject – verb – object* structure of **c**, which leaves his father to supply the next logical step ('Do you want a biscuit, then?'). Meanwhile in **g** he alludes to what his brother has received without any obvious reference to his own needs.

Data response exercise 13

While it's an understandable reaction to the incident, the adult probably hasn't adopted the most helpful linguistic strategy for dealing with it. Then again, this is probably a more helpful reaction than screaming or sobbing quietly in a darkened room.

A child of 2 years 5 months is unlikely to understand the pragmatics of the sarcasm in such seemingly positive terms as 'brilliant', 'clever' and 'thanks' when they are used in such a strange context. A more direct and semantically straightforward response might be more clearly understood by the child, but it's probably worth pointing out that not all parental utterances to children are for the child's sake, and this reaction may be better suited to serving the parent's needs at this time.

Children's early reading and writing

Data response exercise 14

What you might have noticed is that the writing here takes several different forms: some texts are clearly written in school and marked by teachers, while others are less obviously context bound. The narrative forms of Data extracts 3 and 4 are consistent with the kinds of task set for early writers at primary school.

The target audiences for these pieces of writing seem to differ too: a) may not have any intended audience at all, and might have been written as a form of 'scribble play' – the child mimicking writing conventions but not necessarily communicating anything in particular through the letters and shapes themselves.

The handwriting and letter formation appear to become clearer as the examples progress. The uncertain shapes of a) are recognisably letters in b), while in c) and d) the letter forms themselves are much more elaborate, capital letters are occasionally – if somewhat inconsistently – used, and punctuation has started to appear. The conventions of writing are more strictly adhered to in d), with horizontal rather than sloping lines and a much more consistent and individual style of handwriting.

Example d) is a much longer piece of writing than the others, perhaps reflecting the child's age and ability.

The syntax becomes progressively more complex as the examples progress. In b), the single sentence is simple, with added greeting and sign-off. In c) the sentence is compound, featuring two independent clauses, but perhaps imitating speech style in its use of ellipsis. Example d) makes use of compound and simple sentences, with some more varied syntactical patterns, including fronted adverbials of time such as 'On Saturday', 'Then', 'After that' and 'On Sunday'. The discourse structure of d) is organised chronologically using these adverbials.

The spellings become more accurate as the examples progress, with greater precision over vowels in d).

These are just some initial observations, and there are probably many more things you could say about what each child has done.

■ Data response exercise 15

Graphology

The writing accompanies a picture of a dinosaur. It is laid out across the page in two recognisable lines, following the conventions of adult writing. There are recognisable gaps between most individual words.

Lexis and semantics

The writing is themed around what the child has been studying at school, and the lexis used reflects the fields covered in class – different dinosaurs and their diets. But the word 'vegetarian' is used instead of *herbivore* as the child himself is a vegetarian and uses this word to describe himself.

Grammar

The sentence is grammatically simple (one clause) but seems to be constructed in a way that resembles the spoken mode: the structure up to the noun phrase 'a vegetarian' is a fairly standard S–V–C structure (subject – verb – complement), but a conjunction and further modifier are then employed ('and scary'), which might be seen as an elliptical construction (i.e. a short version of 'and he is scary'). This suggests that the 'and scary' part has been added as an afterthought, which is much more like spoken language.

Orthography

Out of the seven words used, four are accurately spelled ('my', 'is', 'a', 'and') and three reflect phonetic rendition of vowels: 'din**ersor**', 'vej**eetereo**n', 'sc**eree**'. One of the consonant sounds shows a virtuous error in the way in which grapheme–phoneme correspondence has been applied: **j** for **g** in *vegetarian*. The letter shapes are clearly formed and it's apparent that the work has been redrafted with the rewriting of 'and' to correct a possible earlier misspelling.

Overview

This extract would appear to illustrate a child well into the phonological segmentation stage of his writing. His consonants are generally sound, while his vowels are still developing. The work is imaginative and the child responds to the topic being studied at school with his own perspective.

■ Data response exercise 16

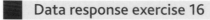

Graphology

The writing is laid out in conventional lines, and the heading 'My weekend news' sets it in its context. The child is used to the form she is being asked to write in and lays out her page in the conventional way. There is no picture this time, which might suggest that the written mode has achieved more importance.

Lexis and semantics

A degree of detail has been added through the use of proper nouns ('Finlay' and 'mummy') and a specific brand name ('twister ice cream') while extra details are added in the form of descriptive modifiers ('*orange* lolly', '*105* steps', '*big* bottom').

The semantics revolve around the family and family events, but this is to be expected when the purpose of the writing exercise is to recount weekend experiences.

Grammar

The whole narrative is written in the simple past tense and this seems confidently done. At one point, a progressive verb 'kept *falling*' is used and this adds an extra element of detail to the story.

The sentence structures are a mixture of simple ('Finlay had a twister ice cream'), and some longer and more grammatically sophisticated compound–complex sentences that feature coordinate and subordinate clauses ('When we got to the bottom we got on boat and a lady with a big bottom got on and my side of the boat wobbled'), including an adverbial clause ('When we got to the bottom').

Discourse structure

The structure is organised through adverbials such as 'then', and takes a straightforward chronological structure to events. The use of the adverbial clause ('When we got to the bottom') suggests a growing maturity in sequencing events.

Orthography

The handwriting is very clear and the child has used joined-up writing throughout.

The use of punctuation marks and capitals is quite secure, with some occasional lapses ('Ice cream' is capitalised rather than 'twister'). The use of apostrophes of the contraction *didn't* is accurate, and full stops are accurately used to mark out sentence boundaries.

The spellings are very accurate and seem to reflect a growing understanding of different vowel sounds and consonant doubling ('ma**tt**er', 'wo**bb**led', 'bo**tt**om'), with only one phonetic rendition ('bo**tt**em').

Overview

For a six-year-old child, this is confidently written and largely accurate. The conventions of narrative-based school writing tasks seem well understood. There appears to be a little too much assumption that the reader understands the full context of the story (*Where* were they going, for example?), but this is fairly typical of children at this stage.

Language development theories

Data response exercise 17

a The conversation between the boys here is very much based on what they are doing and is very context-dependent. They share an understanding of the 'rules' of the game they are playing ('goodies' v. 'baddies'), which could link to pragmatics and the influence of interaction with others who have used these 'rules': family; TV programmes and films they have followed; computer games they might have seen or played.

Their interaction seems natural, which is probably partly down to the fact that they are twins; but it is just as likely related to the fact that they happen to be boys of the same age engaged in a shared activity. The smooth interaction is evident in the regular turn-taking and shared topics, while the amount of agreement between them is another sign that they are on the same wavelength. Much of this would tend to support elements of social interactionist theory, as these forms of conversational behaviour would probably have been picked up through interacting with others.

On a syntactical level, the boys are clearly beyond the telegraphic stage and producing utterances made up of a mixture of sentence types: simple ('The cavemans are laughing') and complex ('The goodies are going on their ship cos they've catched a baddie'). Morphologically, the overgeneralised *-ed* endings on 'catched' and 'throwed' would seem to be virtuous errors supporting nativist theories of language acquisition: the *-ed* endings have been actively applied to irregular verbs. Likewise, the overgeneralised *-s* ending of 'cavemans' would support the same nativist theories, as the boys' environment does not contain 'cavemans', 'catched' and 'throwed' as models to imitate.

The cognitive approach might be linked to Liam's utterance 'This one's much more braver than the baddies though'. This is because he seems to be aware not only of the abstract quality of bravery but also of the fact bravery is a relative term. He is comparing the qualities of his toys with others, using the comparative adjective 'braver', but 'doubling up' the comparative element by adding 'more' in front of it.

b The interaction between parent and child in this extract lends itself to an interpretation using the social interactionist model, but there are other elements to consider. First, the clear turn-taking is again an example of interaction that has been picked up through regular conversations that have created an awareness of conversational 'rules'. The father is using several features of child-directed speech (CDS), such as tag questions ('isn't he?') to elicit a response, and recasting in a more standard grammatical form ('Yes, he's back isn't he?'), using the copula verb 'is' that Ruby had omitted. But he also uses ellipsis ('Probably going to the toilet') when a fuller grammatical form may have been more helpful as a model ('*He is* probably going to the toilet').

Looking at possible examples of imitation gives us some food for thought. While Ruby clearly echoes her father's utterances ('On the 'puter?' and 'Probly'), there is evidence to suggest that these are not just parroted, but that she has a conceptual grasp of the words' meanings. For example, when Ruby's father replies that Stan is going to the toilet, Ruby has an understanding of what that word means and what it is related to ('To do a wee wee?'). This suggests this is not an example of a child simply copying what a parent has said, but a more intuitive process of labelling, packaging and network building (along the lines of what Jean Aitchison has proposed).

There is much more to explore in each extract – for example, phonology, functions of utterances and lexical variety. This is just a start to show how the everyday examples of child language can be examined with a theoretical eye, and maybe to lead you into asking questions about why these things happen.

Exam preparation

Data response exercise 18

The kind of features you would be expected to find in a text like this are included below:

- Overgeneralised plural ending: 'mouses' instead of mice in line 2.
- Correction and recasting from father in line 3.
- Substitution and assimilation of *ch* for *d* sound in line 6.
- Consonant cluster reduction of *ks* in 'fox' to *k* in line 10.
- Omission of auxiliary verb *is* in line 10.
- Deletion of final consonant sound *g* in 'choppin' in line 10.
- Overextension of 'mouse' for *rabbit* in line 12.
- Substitution of *w* for *r* sound in 'wabbit' line 14.

In the exam you would be awarded two marks for each feature correctly identified: one mark for identifying it in the first place and another for correctly labelling it. As you should be able to see from this example, you are expected to find single words and phrases rather than talk about the text as a whole. So the key to this part of the question is knowing what kinds of feature to look for and having the terminology at your fingertips to label them correctly.

Data response exercise 19

The kinds of feature you might be expected to find in written texts like these are listed below:

- The use of simple sentences in **a**.
- Phonetic rendition of vowels (*wos/wears* and *wicend/weekend*).
- Irregular capitalisation in **b** ('To').
- Use of adverbial phrase to start writing in **b**.
- Use of past tense in **b** ('I went').
- Use of compound sentence in **b** ('I went to the park and played on the swings').
- Orthographical irregularities (*b=d*) in **a**.

Representation and language

- AO1 Select and apply a range of linguistic methods, to communicate relevant knowledge using appropriate terminology and coherent, accurate written expression.

- AO3 Analyse and evaluate the influence of contextual factors on the production and reception of spoken and written language, showing knowledge of the key constituents of language.

- AO4 Demonstrate expertise and creativity in the use of English in a range of different contexts, informed by linguistic study.

Unit 2 focuses on building on the skills and frameworks you were introduced to in Unit 1. This second part of the book requires analytical and creative skills: you need not only to explore texts written by others, but also to produce a text yourself. The focus of the unit is on representation, so both sections will help you explore what this term means and how it is important to language study. This time you are assessed through coursework, so this part of the book introduces you to the two distinct tasks required for the coursework, and offers you advice, guidance and ideas.

Section A Investigating representations

This part of the unit relates to your first piece of AS coursework – investigation. It helps you develop an analytical framework for use when exploring how different individuals, groups of people, events, issues and institutions are represented through language. Some of the wider linguistic concepts relating to how language can shape meanings and how audiences can be influenced by language are considered. You are then given guidance on how to collect texts for analysis, how to approach an investigation of these texts, and the kinds of questions to ask about them.

Section B Producing representations

Section B relates to your second piece of AS coursework – production. It guides you through some of the different types of writing you might consider when creating your own text, and helps you plan both your creative piece and a commentary. The emphasis in this section is on treating writing as a process, so you will be encouraged to research, plan and redraft your ideas until they are exactly how you want them to be. The frameworks you have used to analyse texts in Section A will feed into this second section and help you to see links between the representation of issues and the creative process behind the representation.

A Investigating representations

Introduction

The first part of the coursework consists of a written investigation of 1,000–1,500 words into how language is used to represent one or more of the following: individuals; social groups; events; issues; or institutions. You will be expected to analyse between three and five texts or extracts of texts in order to explore how language is used to represent your chosen focus. Your texts must be linked temporally (by time): all from the same time; each from different time periods; or tracking an unfolding story. They can be written texts, or spoken texts that have been transcribed.

Further guidance on how to choose a focus for your investigation, collect data and plan an investigation are given at the end of this section on page 164.

What do we mean by 'representation'?

The word *representation* has a number of different meanings, many of which are relevant to your work on this topic. *Representation* is made up of two elements: *re + presentation*. This suggests that all forms of representation present something to us *again*, or in a different way. So in this sense, a written account of an event or a written 'picture' of a person *re-presents* them to an audience through language.

Another meaning of *representation* is *to stand for*. As you will have seen from the work on Language development in Unit 1, Section B, language is a symbolic system: sounds (phonemes), letters and words (graphemes) *stand for* ideas and objects in the real world. And because this symbolic system is largely arbitrary – decided on and agreed by people rather than set in stone – meanings are not always fixed. Even a dictionary, which most people would refer to if they were unsure of a word's meaning, is just one set of agreed meanings. As you will see in Unit 3 of the A2 course, meanings change over time: sometimes very quickly, and at other times drifting gradually over centuries. Meanings are often contested, too, which can lead to fierce debates about what particular words and phrases mean to different people.

Any text produces within it an idea of the author and the ideal target audience. A charity advertisement may be created to represent the 'writer' as a concerned, sympathetic and determined crusader for social justice – and address the 'ideal reader' as a responsive, caring and preferably wealthy supporter. A newspaper editorial may be designed to represent the 'writer' as the voice of the paper and the nation – thoughtful, educated and socially conscious – and address the 'ideal reader' as people who share the worldview of the editor. But these are idealised models: there is no real ideal reader and we all interpret texts in different ways, depending on our own backgrounds and experiences, our own understanding of the associations different words have.

Additionally, the perspective from which events are related to us is important. One event can be viewed from a number of different

Key terms

Subject position: the perspective from which events or issues are perceived.

subject positions, and a writer can choose to foreground certain positions to create different effects.

Language is crucial to representation as it gives us a means of relating events, ideas and emotions to others. But most people would probably agree that language is not neutral or, if it is, it can still be put to various uses and for various ends that are not neutral. As you will see in Why representation matters, on pages 163–167, language can be crafted carefully to create a particular picture that reflects the views of the writer. It can also shape our views as readers and perhaps even alter our behaviour towards different groups of people or individuals.

Language does not exist in a vacuum. It is very much a product of the society it is used within: language is a loaded weapon.

For example, what seems on the surface to be a 'common sense' representation of a straightforward event may not be as clearcut as it first appears. Indeed, the whole concept of 'common sense' is itself problematic.

■ Data response exercise 1

Study the sentences or phrases below. Look at what might make these simple expressions problematic. Why would linguists take issue with the representations created in these examples?

Check your ideas against the feedback (page 171).

a The discovery of America by Christopher Columbus.

b Each student should bring his own pen and paper to class.

c The disabled deserve our sympathy.

d The nation mourned when Princess Diana died.

e Sixty protesters were injured at the demonstration.

f 'If you kill the dragon, you can have the princess,' cried the King.

Looking closely at language enables us to see what it reveals and what it conceals – which in turn helps us to analyse how particular groups, individuals or events are represented. What perhaps emerges from the sentences and phrases above are patterns to do with pronouns, semantics, grammatical constructions and broader lexical choices. You have met these terms in Unit 1, and used them with the support of The linguistic frameworks toolkit, but we need to look at them again here in relation to representation in language. Try building a framework specifically for this unit. It will assist you in teasing out the meanings and structures of texts, and you can add to it as you select texts and issues to explore.

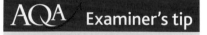
Examiner's tip

Remember that The linguistic frameworks toolkit on page 206 can give you clear definitions of some of the more tricky areas of grammar you encounter.

■ A suggested framework for investigating representations

■ **Pronoun and determiner use** – which pronouns and possessive determiners are used and how is the reader addressed? Are pronouns used to include and/or exclude?

■ **Active/passive constructions** – which voice is used within the text and how is agency handled?

- **Modification** – are adjectives used to modify nouns and create specific effects? How are adverbs used to present ideas?

- **Metaphor** – are metaphors used in the text to present one idea in another's terms?

- **Nominalisation** – are processes and actions turned into nouns? Does this obscure agency?

- **Register and lexical choice** – does technical, specialist or academic language create an impression of an educated and knowledgeable writer? Does a colloquial register seem to 'bridge the gap' between reader and writer, creating a more believable tone?

- **Graphology** – does the text present information in a graphical or pictorial form that might anchor particular meanings? Does the use of bullet points or headings 'close down' other possibilities for discussion?

- **Rhetorical devices** – does the author structure an argument and use language in such a way as to create a persuasive and convincing effect?

- **Sentence and clause linking** – does the use of particular grammatical structures signal dependent relationships between elements in a sentence?

- **Tense and aspect** – how does the use of past or present tense affect the meanings of the text? Does the use of aspect – progressive or perfective – affect meanings?

- **Subject positioning** – from which perspective are events or issues perceived and recounted? Is one position given particular prominence and credibility?

Pronouns and determiners

Are these inclusive or exclusive? Is the audience included through plural pronouns such as *we, us* or possessive determiners such as *our* and *your*? Are 'them and us' divisions created through pronoun use? Pronouns are very important in establishing solidarity and closeness between participants, or excluding and separating them as outsiders. Some pronouns have been used in a generic fashion in the past: *he* is an example of this that now causes some debate. Is it right to assume that *he* includes *she*, or should separate pronouns, or a gender neutral pronoun like *they*, be used instead?

Data response exercise 2

Read the extract on the next page from a charity advertisement. How are pronouns used to present a narrative, include or exclude the reader, and what might be the intended effects of this use?

Check your ideas against the feedback.

Banished by her father, Katy arrived on our doorstep, distraught and disbelieving

Christmas Eve 2005. The year's most magical night had become a nightmare for this poor young girl. Katy had spent the past month arguing with her parents. That evening, a row had erupted and Katy had broken a family heirloom.

Her furious father had decided **she had to go**. He drove her to The Children's Society's Check Point Project, with Katy weeping in the back seat.

That year Katy spent Christmas with strangers

Katy's father was still enraged when they arrived and insisted that she be placed in **emergency accommodation**. After he left, Kay was shown to a room. It meant on that cold winter's night, she wouldn't be sleeping on the streets.

She couldn't believe she would be spending Christmas – and, so she thought, the rest of her life – away from her family. That night **she cried herself to sleep**, traumatised.

How our counsellor helped Katy

Angela, our counsellor arrived on Christmas Day, **she persuaded Katy to open up** and tell her side of the story. Kay had recently been dumped by her boyfriend for her best friend. She felt humiliated but felt she couldn't confide in her parents or her best friend. Christmas made her feel even more lonely, depressed and angry.

Angela explained to Katy how to talk to her parents about her personal life. She also encouraged her to see things from her parents' perspective, not just her own.

Getting the family back together

With Angela's help, Katy was welcomed back home. She and her parents are now much happier and talk to each other in times of trouble.

Katy says: *"If it hadn't been for The Children's Society, I could have been out on the streets that Christmas. Thanks to Angela, me and my mum and dad are all getting on better and know how to deal with problems together and stop them getting out of hand."*

- **Each year in the UK, 100,000 children run away from home and many are so desparate that they resort to begging, stealing or prostitution to survive**

- **1 in 6 say they were forced to sleep rough or with strangers**

- **1 in 12 say they were hurt or harmed while away from home**

Key terms

Active voice: a name given to grammatical constructions that relate to the roles of subject and object in a clause.

Passive voice: a name given to grammatical constructions that relate to the roles of subject and object in a clause.

Active and passive constructions

Choosing an **active** or **passive voice** can be an important decision. As noted above, the passive voice can hide agency: there is no grammatical need to include the agent of the verb. A sentence like 'Mistakes were made' (made famous first by American President Ronald Reagan and then George Bush) hides agency quite neatly, allowing the President or his administration to distance themselves from the mistakes. Who made these mistakes?

This point is acutely noted by Charles Baxter, author of *Burning Down the House*, when he compares the language of Reagan with that of General Lee after the battle of Gettysburg in 1863: 'All this has been my fault,' Lee said. 'I asked more of men than should have been asked of them.' Who sounds more honest here?

Data response exercise 3

What do you notice about the use of active and passive voice in the examples shown in the data below? How straightforward is it to tell who is doing what to whom?

Check your ideas against the feedback (page 171).

a Over 60 demonstrators were injured in the disturbances.

b Police retaliated to missiles being thrown from the demonstrators and charged the crowd, leading to over 60 demonstrators sustaining minor injuries.

Modification

The ways in which nouns and noun phrases are modified by adjectives is another area to explore. We often expect to see evaluative adjectives attached to nouns – pre-modifying them – to express opinions: 'an *excellent idea*'; 'a *brilliant book*'; 'a *terrible song*'. But certain adjectives do their work more subtly, evoking an attitude and covertly constructing a perspective. Noun phrases such as *suspected terrorist, discredited education policies, stifling red-tape* often signal an ideological position through the pre-modifying adjective.

Adverbs can also be **modifiers**. Particular interpretations can be foregrounded with the use of adverbs such as *obviously, clearly, evidently* and *of course*. These often work by making it appear that any other interpretation of the evidence runs contrary to popular opinion or common sense. These adverbs of comment, or disjuncts, act differently from many adverbs in that, instead of telling us how, why, where or when something happened, they give a writer's particular stance or opinion on it.

Metaphor

The English language is full of metaphor. In fact, the previous sentence itself includes a metaphor that presents the language as a container to be filled. Many metaphors are used without us even noticing, but some are crucially important to the issue of representation.

Key terms

Modifier: a word, usually an adjective or a noun used attributively, that qualifies the sense of a noun. Adverbs of comment also act as modifiers, e.g. obviously.

Data response exercise 4

Read the phrases and sentences. They are taken from a *Daily Mirror* editorial on the day after D-Day, when British and American Allied troops started their mainland offensive against Hitler's armies. (You can get an idea of the complete article from the illustration in the margin.)

How is war represented through the metaphors used?

Check your ideas against the feedback (page 171).

...bloody game of war...

The curtain rises on the closing scene of the greatest human conflict the world has ever known.

Other metaphors or similes that might be worth considering are those of illness and infection when related to social problems (drugs spreading like a virus, or antisocial behaviour infecting communities), and metaphors of war being used in sports reports ('Blitzed' was the headline of the *Daily Mirror* on the morning after the England football team beat Germany 5–1). Other metaphors from business and finance have found their way into the everyday language of education and health care.

Nominalisation

The linguist David Hyatt describes nominalisation as the process of 'presenting as a noun or noun phrase something that could be presented with other parts of speech'. Another linguist, Norman Fairclough, points out that as there is no verb, no agency need be ascribed. In simple terms, once something has been nominalised, no one need be responsible for having done it. Take the following examples:

- *Policeman's murder* horrifies colleagues.
- *Foot and mouth outbreak* stuns farmers.
- *Race attack* leads to protests.
- *Violent clashes* mar Chelsea game.

In each of the noun phrases italicised above, a process or action has been *nominalised*, i.e. somebody has murdered the policeman, someone has caused an outbreak of foot and mouth, someone has attacked someone else, people have been clashing. The nominalisation of these processes obscures agency (i.e. *who did what*) and might potentially be used to hide responsibility. On the other hand, not every example of nominalisation is part of a big conspiracy; as the linguist Geoffrey Hughes puts it in *Words in Time*, 'the conflict between syntax (with its requirements of clarity, causation and sequence) and fact (elusive, complex and often incoherent) is very evident'. So, the conventions of journalism could be seen to be part of the reason why grammar becomes compressed and agency hidden, rather than a deliberate attempt to obscure agency.

Register and lexical choices

Lexical choices can also influence the reader. Sophisticated, technical lexis can create the impression that the writer is well educated and knowledgeable, and may lead the audience to take his or her words more seriously. On the other hand, a casual, colloquial register can create the impression that the writer is addressing the audience as equals, bridging the gap between the two. Another factor here is that complex ideas can be **naturalised** when **colloquial language** is used. If an idea is presented in colloquial language, it can achieve a degree of resonance with its target audience that it might not achieve if it were written in a higher, more distant register. The potential here is to perhaps present 'common sense' views in the language of the people. But the notion of 'common sense' is very problematic, and linguists like Fairclough and Hyatt argue that common-sense ideas are in fact ideologies or ways of thinking about the world, which themselves have been naturalised. In other words, a 'common sense' idea such as 'making money is good' is only common sense because the ideology that has given rise to it – capitalism – is in the ascendant in the western world. As a political system, there are probably much better ways of protecting the planet's future, treating each other fairly and existing peacefully!

■ Key terms

Naturalisation: a process in which certain ideas can gradually appear to become normal or natural.

Colloquial language: everyday, spoken-style language.

Data response exercise 5

Read the football team extract below that is adapted from an article by Tony Parsons in *Arena* in 1991. How does the writer's choice of register and style help position the writer's views as 'common sense'? What kind of audience positioning is at work in this text?

Check your ideas against the feedback (page 171).

Punk beggars, drunk beggars, beggars with babies. Beggars in shell suits and beggars in rags. Beggars stinking of cheap lager with snot on their chin and a mangy mutt on the end of a piece of string. Lots of them.

And gypsy beggars who try to stuff a ratty flower into your buttonhole with some sentimental line – 'For the children,' coos some obese hag. Old beggars too shagged out to beg, young beggars who look like they could run a four-minute mile if they ever made it up off their backsides. Beggars in King's Cross, beggars in Covent Garden, beggars on the street where you live. All kinds of beggars everywhere in this city, and they will be with us forever now. They have no shame. Because begging is no longer taboo.

I think that my father would rather have seen us go hungry than have to go out there and ponce for our supper. I think that the old man, may he rest peacefully, would have preferred to rob, cheat or watch us wither with malnutrition before standing on a street corner with a Uriah Heep look in his eye asking for a hand-out. He would have been happier seeing us sleeping in a shoebox full of shit than he would have been *begging*.

The fact is that my father's generation was incapable of begging. The children they raised were also incapable of begging. There were standards that were not negotiable. There were certain lines you never crossed; there were taboos. Respect the elderly. Don't rat on your friends. Never hit a woman. Never stand on a street corner with snot on your chin and a dog on the end of a piece of string asking passers-by if they have any change. Of all the taboos, *don't beg* was the greatest of all.

Extension activity

Look at the student production piece 'A Letter from a Ghost' on page 196 of Section D in this unit. How do the writers create opposing ideas of beggars/homeless people through positioning?

Graphology

The layout of a text and its use of images can have an impact on its representation of an issue, group or person. Images help anchor particular viewpoints and ideas. In the *Daily Mirror* editorial on page 158, the image of a grim-faced British soldier kicking down a swastika-emblazoned door reinforces the idea of heroic, patriotic and single-minded battle against the Nazis. Bullet points can be used to give the appearance of simplicity and a limited range of choices, when the truth might be more complex.

Sentence and clause linking

The ways in which clauses and sentences are linked can affect the ways representations are created and understood. Some sentence structures signal interesting grammatical relationships between clauses and are common in charity advertisements or political campaigning. For example, in the complex sentence, 'If you donate £5 a month, we can save the sight of up to one hundred children', the first clause – a subordinate clause of condition – sets up a grammatically dependent relationship between the two clauses. In this way, the grammar works to mirror the charity's dependent relationship on the target audience.

Tense and aspect

The structure of a text can often be organised using tense and aspect. These grammatical terms are applied to the use of past and present tense, and perfective or progressive aspect. For a simple introduction to these terms, have a look at the Grammatical toolkit on page 206. In terms of their effect on representation, tense and aspect can be very significant. For example, the simple present tense can be used to suggest a habitual and recurring process.

■ Data response exercise 6

Read this extract from John Gaunt's column in *The Sun* newspaper (9 January 2007). How are tense and aspect used to create a particular impression of the state of the country?

Check your ideas against the feedback (page 172).

> Whole estates the length and breadth of this country have been turned into no-go areas where thugs with no intention of working and every intention of fiddling the dole hold sway and decent people live in fear.
>
> The liberal elite who run this country don't live in these areas and have turned a blind eye to the development of these urban wastelands and only seem to worry about them when another kid gets mauled by one of these morons' illegal dogs.

Subject positioning

As outlined at the beginning of this topic, subject positions are perhaps best seen as different perspectives that might be taken when describing events and issues. For example, an event such as a fight between two boys at a bus stop might be viewed from a number of subject positions:

■ Each participant in the fight.
■ Friends of each boy standing nearby.
■ People walking by on the way back from work.
■ A shopkeeper next to the bus stop.
■ People in passing cars.
■ The police officers who pull up in a car to deal with the fight.

Each participant might have a different subject position in relation to the event taking place, and their account of events could use very different language devices to construct a representation of the event taking place. And that's before we even consider the possible prejudices and ideological mindsets of the observers, or the ways in which language might affect their recall of the events. The shopkeeper may see two boys fighting and simply fit this into her wider worldview that young people are out of control and in need of more discipline in school. A passer-by pushing his daughter in a buggy may be more concerned about the welfare of his child in this situation. The police officers may consider the incident in the context of recent violent incidents in the area and view the participants accordingly.

Fig. 1 *Different subject positions reveal different version and experience of events*

So while the fight itself may well be the centre of attention for many participants, each subject position is, in the words of Rob Pope, author of *Textual Intervention*, 'its own centre … each subject position offers not just a slightly different version of the *same event* but substantially *different events*'.

When applied to more complex events, such as wars between nations or experiences of perceived racist or sexist behaviour, subject positioning can become a very important and contentious issue.

Extension activity

Look back at the different subject positions suggested above. Think about how you might write each version of events from three very different subject positions. How might your language choices help encode your representation of events?

Data response exercise 7

Have a look back at the extract on page 132 from the charity advertisement. What are the possible subject positions represented in this text? How are certain subject positions highlighted or foregrounded in this text?

Check your ideas against the feedback (page 172).

Topic revision summary

■ Your coursework requires you to produce an investigation of 1,000–1,500 words based on an analysis of between three and five linked texts.

■ Your texts must be linked temporally (by time): all from the same time; each from different time periods; or tracking an unfolding story.

■ You can choose a focus for your investigation from the following broad categories: social groups; individuals; institutions; events or issues.

■ Representation can be interpreted in different ways: be clear about how you intend to define it.

■ You will need to build up your own linguistic framework to enable you to explore and analyse your chosen texts.

■ Language is a powerful tool!

Why representation matters

Link

Check the next topic, Social groups and representation, for more ideas on some of these 'offensive' terms.

Key terms

Reflectionism: the theory that language reflects our thoughts.

Determinism: the theory that language determines or shapes our thoughts.

The debate about representation and language is more than just about politeness and causing offence, although that is a part of it. Language is a powerful force: every time we use language we can shape other people's attitudes, either towards us or towards the ideas we choose to represent. Language can be at once a reflection of our attitudes and a means to shape attitudes, and this is at the heart of the debate about why representation matters.

Extension activity

Think about some of the words in the English language that people view as offensive: words used to label different ethnic groups, sexualities, age groups, genders. Where do the words come from and how might they be used offensively? What are the objections to using such words?

Reflectionism and determinism

The terms of the debate about the connection between language and thought can be reduced to a very simple **reflectionism** versus **determinism** opposition, but the true picture is more complicated.

Language is created by humans and used as a tool, so to some extent it's clear that what we say is at least partly a reflection of our thoughts, opinions and attitudes. The great dictionary compiler, Samuel Johnson, described language as 'the dress of thought'. But all of us carry within us different interpretations of word meanings that relate to our background, culture, experiences and individual identity, and we inhabit a world in which language is constantly manipulated and reshaped by other individuals and, perhaps more significantly, institutions such as the media and government. The meanings of words, and the shades of meaning associated with words, shift over time and can undergo quite significant changes in the space of just a few years. Take *gay*, *sick* and *wicked*, for example, words whose meanings have shifted significantly.

So, are we truly in control of language, or does it exert an influence over us? Some would argue that language is a force that can alter the way we perceive the world and recall events, and that to some extent we are not masters of language but servants of it.

Extension activity

Explore the concepts of linguistic determinism and linguistic reflectionism by searching for them as keywords on the internet. Many different linguists, anthropologists and psychologists, such as Benjamin Sapir, Edward Lee Whorf, Elizabeth Loftus, Steven Pinker and Jerry Fodor, have come up with ideas about the extent to which language can shape our thoughts.

■ Dominant and muted groups

Another model that looks at how language and thought are linked, and which has an impact on representation, is the theory of dominant and muted groups. On one level, this works as an economic or sociological model: those who have most economic and social influence within a society have the most chance to make their voices heard. On another level, it links directly to language: those in power dominate language itself, creating a form of language that privileges themselves and excludes others. Shirley and Edwin Ardener, whose ideas form the basis of muted group theory, argued that there are 'dominant modes of expression in any society which have been generated by the dominant structure within it'.

Feminists in particular have argued that language has been constructed by men, dominated by men and used by men to deny women's voices the space and power they deserve. In her introduction to *Man Made Language*, Dale Spender sets out such a feminist position:

> Language helps form the limits of our reality. It is our means of ordering, classifying and manipulating the world. It is through language that we become members of a human community, that the world becomes comprehensible and meaningful, that we bring into existence the world in which we live.
>
> Yet it is ironic that this faculty which helps to create our world also has the capacity to restrict our world … Having learnt the language of a patriarchal society we have also learnt to classify and manage the world in accordance with patriarchal order and to preclude many possibilities for alternative ways of making sense of the world.'

D. Spender, Man Made Language, *1980*

Spender goes on to argue that as language is a 'human product', we can 'unlearn' the patterns of thinking that have been created by patriarchal language and challenge the status quo, creating new, fairer alternatives to the language of the past.

Fig. 2 *Does vocabulary sometimes exclude women?*

■ Extension activity

1 Think about the linguistic frameworks you have studied so far and how they might be applied to the language used to describe gender.

■ Does semantics play a part in the different connotations of words used to describe men and women's behaviour? Look, for example, at the words used to describe men and women who have more than one sexual partner. (See Social groups and representation, pages 168–176.)

■ Is syntax important when looking at how women and men are represented in romantic novels? Consider, for example, who are the agents of verbs when men and women interact, and who are the objects.

■ Is pragmatics relevant to how discussions about men and women in everyday discourse rely on shared understanding of 'common sense' ideas about how men and women behave? What might a speaker be getting at, for example, when he says 'Women drivers!'

■ Is morphology relevant to the ways in which women's job titles differ from men's? (For example, titles such as 'usherette' and 'waitress' use bound morphemes to mark the female job title as different from the male 'usher' and 'waiter'.

■ Extension activity

■ To what extent do you agree with Spender's view that the English language reflects the patriarchal nature of our society?

■ What linguistic evidence is there that men are treated more favourably in language than women?

■ How would you go about finding out more about the origins of particular words used to describe the genders?

The same arguments about gender could be applied to any 'disempowered group' within society: ethnic minorities; sexual minorities; the working class and people with disabilities. Largely as a result of feminists campaigning for equal rights for women, but also because of simultaneous struggles in the black and gay communities, language has become a battleground in the fight for equal rights.

■ The political correctness debate

Political correctness (PC) is a term guaranteed to provoke strong arguments among many people. The aim of this topic is not to preach a particular line in favour of PC or against it, but to clarify what PC means in terms of language and to offer ideas about it.

The origins of PC, according to the linguist Deborah Cameron, are rooted in the left-wing and liberal political movements of the USA in the 1970s. The phrase may have originally had an ironic twist to it – the campaigners perhaps self-consciously poking fun at their own radical zeal – but it has undergone a form of **pejoration** in recent years (which itself might make the basis of an interesting study for AS Level coursework!). We can rarely open the newspaper these days without a report claiming that 'PC has gone mad' or that 'PC has gone too far', and the phrase now seems to come weighed down with negative associations.

Broadly speaking, the intentions behind the early PC movement were to draw attention to laws, behaviour and language that might discriminate against ethnic minorities, women, people with disabilities and sexual minorities. Moves were made to deal with words and expressions such as 'chairman' and 'mankind', and generic pronoun use.

■ Link

For more on the links between language and gender, see Social groups and representation on pages 144–152.

■ Key terms

Political correctness (PC): the name given to the movement that began in the 1970s, campaigning for the removal of offensive language from everyday vocabulary.

Pejoration: a process whereby words 'slide down' the scale of acceptability and pick up negative connotations over time.

■ Link

You will look again at political correctness at A2, in Unit 3, but with more of a focus on its context within the wider scheme of language change over time, and attitudes towards it.

AQA Examiner's tip

Be careful when dealing with stories about 'Political correctness gone mad'. Reports in the media about the nursery rhyme 'Baa baa black sheep' being changed to 'Baa baa green/rainbow/multi-coloured sheep', 'black coffee' to 'coffee without milk', 'Christmas' to 'winterval' to avoid offending minority groups often fail to have any genuine basis in fact. We can term these 'PC myths'.

Data response exercise 8

Look at Table 1, which lists politically incorrect words and their politically correct alternatives. What are the potential problems with the politically incorrect words and why might the politically correct alternatives be less problematic? Consider the key term offered on this page and check your ideas against the feedback (page 172).

Table 1

Politically incorrect terms	Politically correct terms
Manageress	Manager
Postman	Postal worker
Male nurse	Nurse
Each person must provide his own lunch	Each person must provide their own lunch
Mankind	Humanity/humankind

It was believed by many campaigners that if the words could be changed then perceptions might also be changed. This view of the power of language links to the Sapir-Whorf hypothesis that language shapes or influences the way we think. It could be argued that by removing a word like 'policeman' from the popular lexicon and replacing it with the gender-neutral 'police officer', women may feel more welcome to join the police, and the popular stereotype that police are male might also be dispelled. Even if the PC alternatives did not have a huge effect on perceptions, the debate itself and the media interest in the discussion around the language might have an impact on challenging certain attitudes.

As the linguist Deborah Cameron puts it in *Verbal Hygiene*:

> Linguistic conventions help to naturalise and reproduce certain beliefs and assumptions, but these are not necessarily dependent on language or 'caused' by it … then again, drawing attention to someone's use of language is one way of making previously unremarked assumptions manifest to them; and this can on occasion be the first stage in changing their attitudes.

D. Cameron, Verbal Hygiene, 1995

AQA Examiner's tip

Supporters of PC argue that the backlash against non-sexist and non-racist language is part of a wider attempt by the right-wing media to discredit fundamental principles of equality by rubbishing language reform. Opponents of PC see the PC movement as a linguistic straitjacket, making us feel uncomfortable and overly sensitive about our language use, and therefore fair game for ridicule. The whole debate is one you should approach with caution and some discrimination.

The idea that language can 'naturalise' certain beliefs is very significant when considering representation and language. The linguist Norman Fairclough explores this in more detail in his influential book *Language and Power*. He argues that once particular discourses, ideas and word meanings have become accepted as 'common sense' they no longer appear open to scrutiny.

> Such assumptions and expectations are implicit, backgrounded, taken for granted, not things that people are consciously aware of, rarely explicitly formulated or examined or questioned.

N. Fairclough, Language and Power, 1989

Part of your role as a student of English language is to develop the tools to analyse and challenge 'common sense' assumptions, and see what lies behind them. The work you have already done on ideal readers, actual readers and subject positions in the Introduction (What do we mean by 'representation'?) has been part of this process.

One example of how a word has become naturalised in some contexts is 'bitch'. The origins of this word are noted by the Online Etymology Dictionary as:

> **bitch**
> O.E. bicce, probably from O.N. bikkjuna 'female of the dog' (also fox, wolf, and occasionally other beasts), of unknown origin. Grimm derives the O.N. word from Lapp pittja, but OED notes that 'the converse is equally possible.' As a term of contempt applied to women, it dates from c.1400; of a man, c.1500, playfully, in the sense of 'dog.' In modern (1990s, originally black English) slang, its use with ref. to a man is sexually contemptuous, from the 'woman' insult.
> 'BITCH. A she dog, or doggess; the most offensive appellation that can be given to an English woman, even more provoking than that of whore.' ['Dictionary of the Vulgar Tongue,' 1811]

www.etymonline.com

Fig. 3 *'Where my bitches at?'*

The derogatory usage of bitch towards women is not really in doubt, but the naturalisation of the term to refer to women in general is a more recent process. Some would lay the blame for this process at the door of rappers such as Snoop Dogg and Jay-Z. Snoop Dogg's 'Can U Control Yo Hoe?', which makes lurid reference to controlling his 'bitches', and Jay-Z's '99 Problems' ('I got 99 problems but a bitch ain't one') could be cited as examples.

It could be argued that Snoop Dogg's performance as a pimp-style character in this song and many others is just playing a role – few people would accuse an actor of really *being* a hobbit just for acting as one in a film – but the casual use of 'bitch' and 'hoe' to describe women suggests that the terms are unproblematic for the rapper and that they have become naturalised. And part of the process of naturalisation could then be the adoption of such language use by the performer's audience.

Topic revision summary

- Language and attitudes are closely linked: words can reflect social attitudes but also shape them.
- 'Common sense' representations about how people behave or how society operates should be challenged through focusing on language: there may be more to these representations than meets the eye!
- Language can be seen as a product of society as much as it is a product of individuals.
- Efforts have been made by campaigners to remove offensive words from the vocabulary and replace them with more 'neutral' terms.

Social groups and representation

What do we mean by 'social groups'?

On a simple level, the term social groups is used to refer to groupings of people within society. The individuals within these groupings may be related by factors such as their *gender* (male or female), their *social class* (upper, middle, working), their *ethnicity* (black, white, Asian, mixed race, etc.), their *age, sexuality, dis/ability*, adherence to a particular musical *subculture* or *special interest*, among any number of other factors.

On a more complex level, you might want to ask:

■ why anybody would want to label a group of people

■ why a particular feature is used to group particular people together

■ who's doing the labelling

■ whether or not the labels are used to stereotype, generalise or demean those labelled

■ whether or not these labels have a particular history to them

■ whether or not the meanings of these labels are contested or accepted by those they are applied to.

In this topic, we hope to be able to explore these issues, look at existing debates around some of the terms used to label particular groups, and start looking at ways in which you might wish to explore the representation of different social groups in your own investigation.

Gender

Data response exercise 9

Read this extract below that is adapted from an article by Eve Kay in *The Guardian* (29 June 2007), and think about the questions which follow it.

Call me Ms

When Eve Kay entered her title as Ms on a government form she found herself embroiled in a row about the word's definition. For heaven's sake, she says, surely it's time to ditch Miss and Mrs for good.

The title Ms was first invented by accident back in 1961 by the American civil rights activist Sheila Michaels. A typing error on a radical newsletter her flatmate received in the post gave her the idea. Michaels' parents weren't married, so she had always been considered 'illegitimate', and notes now that she 'was looking for a title for a woman who did not 'belong' to a man. There was no place for me. No one wanted to claim me and I didn't want to be owned. I didn't belong to my father and I didn't want to belong to a husband – someone who could tell me what to do. I had not seen very many marriages I'd want to emulate. The whole idea came to me in a couple of hours. Tops.'

In those days many women were married off at 18 – you couldn't even get a loan from a bank as a single woman. Michaels was 22 and being a

'Miss' implied she had been left on the shelf. 'All employment for women, then, was regarded as being an anteroom to marriage. The first thing anyone wanted to know about you was whether you were married yet. I'd be damned if I'd bow to them.'

Michaels' Ms brainwave did not take root as quickly as she hoped – 'It was terribly frustrating, because no one wanted to hear about it. There was no feminist movement in 1961, and so no one to listen. I couldn't just go ahead and call myself Ms without spending every hour of every day explaining myself and being laughed at, to boot. I had to learn to be brave.'

It took 10 years for Ms to get a wider hearing. In 1971 a friend of the American feminist Gloria Steinem heard Michaels use the term in a radio interview and suggested she use the name as a title for a new national feminist magazine. In the same year, New York congresswoman Bella Abzug introduced legislation into Congress that said that women did not have to disclose their marital status on federal forms. In 1971 the first issue of *Ms* appeared on newsstands and by July 1972 *Ms* magazine began life as a monthly, taking the concept of Ms into the mainstream.

Mary Thom, one of its early editors, recalls that both the magazine and the word had a huge impact. 'I adopted Ms from the first time I heard it. And since the title was designed for bureaucracy it was accepted immediately by bureaucracy.'

Thom also offers an explanation for the immediate appeal of Ms to American women. The title 'had a real practical value. When I applied for a department store credit card, they wanted my father's name because I wasn't married – even though he lived 500 miles away, even though I was in my 20s and living away from home.' Ms was needed to help end such breathtaking discrimination.

But the title also has an earlier antecedent. In the 17th century the term Mistress had two meanings. One of these was its current meaning – a woman kept by a man who is already married. But it was also the title of a woman in charge of a household and, surprisingly, no marital status was attached. With the development of capitalism and the modern family, Mistress fell out of use as a form of address as women entered a more refined era of oppression.

Miss and Mrs are marks of the old world, reminders of women's second-class status as wives-to-be (Miss) or simply wives (Mrs). If you are a woman who doesn't use Ms – particularly a woman under 30 who has never even thought of it – then ponder this: how do you want to present yourself to the world? Are you an appendage or an appendage-in-waiting? Don't be branded and marked by old-world convention. Let's kick against those fools at companies such as Atlantic Data. Let's put two fingers up to employers and bureaucrats who want to define us by our marital status. Choose Miss and you are condemned to childish immaturity. Choose Mrs and be condemned as some guy's chattel. Choose Ms and you become an adult woman in charge of your whole life.

Questions on 'Call me Ms'

- What disadvantages of the titles Miss and Mrs are highlighted in this article?
- How did the existing titles for men and women in 1971 (Mr, Miss and Mrs) reflect patriarchal values?
- What kinds of problem have there been with establishing alternatives to Miss and Mrs?
- Why is Ms seen to be a better option by this writer?
- Why is language important in this debate?
- As you can probably see from the issues raised by Eve Kay in this article, language is central to the debate about how women and men are perceived in society.

Language and its relationship to gender has probably been a battlefield for about as long as language has existed. This is hardly surprising given the different roles and positions in society occupied by men and women. And the different status afforded to the genders has been one of the most long-running **dialectics** throughout human history.

Language and gender has been a particular focus of formal language studies for the best part of 50 years, and many different linguists have put forward their own theories, pieces of research and opinions on how language and gender are interlinked. Much of the early work on language and gender is based on Dale Spender's highly influential 1980 book, *Man Made Language*. Some might argue that her arguments are rooted in the culture of the 1960s and 1970s, but how much has really changed?

Some of the key concepts surveyed by Spender and others are explained in Table 2, along with examples.

Table 2 *Linguistic concepts*

Linguistic concept	Explanation	Examples/comments
Lexical asymmetry	A form of imbalance between the meanings of two ostensibly matching words. Where you might expect to see some equivalence in these pairs of words, the reality is that the female terms carry much less positive connotations than the male terms.	*bachelor/spinster* *master/mistress* *lord/lady* *wizard/witch* *king/queen*
Pejoration	A process whereby words 'slide down' the scale of acceptability and pick up negative connotations over time	*Hussy*: originally a shortened version of housewife, this word has become much more negative *Wench*: once meant a small child of either sex, but became a young girl and then pejorated to mean a 'woman of easy virtue'
The semantic rule	The idea first coined by Muriel Schulz that words associated with women tend to undergo pejoration	See the examples above or find your own by exploring word etymologies
Semantic over-representation	The idea that there are many more words used to describe sexually active females than males	*slut, slag, tart, whore, hoe, sket, slapper*
Lexical gaps	In effect, the flipside of overrepresentation, when we find there are no equivalents for certain terms	Are there male equivalents for the examples above? You may find that the nearest equivalents have much more positive connotations: *stud, playa, Casanova, Romeo.*
Metonymy/ synecdoche	*Synecdoche* is a concept in which a part of an object or idea functions as symbolising the whole. *Metonymy* – rather like metaphor – substitutes one usually related idea for the thing it is representing, e.g. Whitehall represents the British government, or Washington the US administration. Feminist linguists argue that many of the terms exemplified here dehumanise women (treating them as objects rather than people) or associate women with a particular body part or sexual function, rather than treat them as complete people.	*She was a nice bit of skirt.* *Piece of ass.*
Marked terms	Terms in which the gender of a person is (often unnecessarily) foregrounded through a gendered pre-modifier or suffix	*Lady doctor, male nurse, usherette, actress*

Default assumptions	Stereotypical ideas about the gender, age, ethnicity, etc. of a person in a particular occupation	The assumption that a nurse would be female; a doctor male; a professor white, male and old
	In an attempt to redress these stereotypes, more harm than good can be done by adding unnecessary marking of gender, etc.	When these terms are marked – male nurse, lady doctor, female professor – the marking actually draws attention to the 'strangeness' of it.
False generics and generic pronouns	The use of gendered nouns and pronouns to encompass both genders. Many linguists argue that these false generics exclude or marginalise women, as most people don't see them as being truly generic (i.e. representing both sexes).	*Mankind* used instead of *humankind* or *humanity*. *He* used instead of *he or she*
Objectification	The use of language to represent people as objects, to be admired or derided. It's argued that many of these usages demean, belittle, trivialise or infantilise women (make them appear as children).	*Tart, sweetie, cupcake, baby, shortie, bit of fluff*

Some have argued that these are not just gender issues. For example, words associated with any relatively powerless or oppressed group in society often pejorate: *chav* was once believed to have meant a young child in Romany Gipsy slang ('chavvy'), *villain* a rural worker ('villayne') and *faggot* a heavy bunch of sticks, or burden. Likewise, it could be argued that lexical asymmetry might be applied to ethnicity too: *black* and *white* for example, have very different connotations. Not all of these etymologies (word origins) are accepted as fact and there is much discussion about the roots and development of a number of contentious terms, along with discussions about whether or not some of the concepts above are still relevant in the 21st century.

Extension activity

In the early 1970s, Julia Stanley claimed that the English language had over 200 derogatory terms for women and only about 20 for men. More recently, linguists and teachers have tried to test this and have carried out their own research that suggests that while there may be slightly more negative terms for women now, there are many for men as well. How would you go about investigating this further?

Ethnicity

The language used to label different ethnic groups has been another contentious area for many years, but has perhaps reached a peak in the last decade or two. As you will have seen already in Why representation matters on pages 139–143, the PC movement in language has led to an increased sensitivity towards the terms used to label people from different ethnic groups and has led to many new alternatives being introduced.

Historically, in Britain at least, the words used to label black and Asian people have been at the forefront of this debate, largely because immigrants from the Caribbean, Africa, India, Pakistan and Bangladesh have been the most visible non-white ethnic groups in Britain, but also because of a longstanding colonial history between Britain and these areas.

🔍 **Data response exercise 10**

Take a look at the list of words below.

1 What are your views on the meanings of the words listed here?

2 What do these words mean to you?

3 Do you think that any of these words carry any particular connotations?

4 Do any of these words seem particularly positive or negative to you?

5 Are there any words that you haven't come across before?

Check your ideas against the feedback (page 172).

■ **Key terms**

Semantic reclamation: a process whereby the victims of a particular word's offensive usage adopt the word themselves.

a   Nigger.

b   Paki.

c   Half-caste.

d   Cracker.

e   Yid.

f   Mongrel.

g   Chink.

h   Raghead.

One theme that probably stands out is the strength of the negative connotations connected to the words used to label non-white groups, and the weakness of those used to label whites. Many words here have tortuous histories to them or are used to generalise groups of people. Another is the way in which some words appear to have no derogatory denotation, but exist as offensive or taboo terms because of the connotations they have developed over time.

Fig. 4 *Shock tactics*

■ Sexuality

Labels are often used to mark out those who differ from the norm, and sexuality is an area in which language is often used to describe and derogate those who are not attracted to the opposite sex. Even a statement such as 'those who are not attracted to the opposite sex' carries with it assumptions that the norm should be opposite-sex attraction.

The words used to label men and women who prefer same-sex relationships, who are not exclusively attracted to the opposite sex, or even those who do not wish to engage in any form of sexual activity, are also a hugely contested area.

■ Data response exercise 11

Look at the list of words below.

1 What are your views on the meanings of the words listed here?

2 What do these words mean to you?

3 Do you think that any of these words carry any particular connotations?

4 Do any of these words seem particularly positive or negative to you?

5 Are there any words that you haven't come across before?

Check your ideas against the feedback (page 173).

a Gay.

b Faggot.

c Lesbian.

d Homosexual.

e Straight/bent.

f Battyman.

g Person of same-sex orientation.

h Queer.

■ Extension activity

Look for recent articles in newspapers or websites and consider the different views about the changing use of the word gay. You may wish to start with sites like the BBC News website, *The Guardian* or this blog: http://englishlangsfx.blogspot.com that links to and comments upon English language stories for A level students.

■ Dis/ability

As with many other labels, words related to people's ability or impairment through illness or accident of birth are a subject of some debate. In fact, the difficulty involved with choosing a heading for this part of the topic highlights the problematic nature of this issue: the lexical gap in English for a word that neutrally represents 'disability'. Overarching terms such as *disabled people* or *handicapped people* have become unpopular for a number of reasons. They are thought to have a generalising effect, linking together people with no use of any limb and those who have a minor hearing impairment, those with cerebral palsy and those with epilepsy into one homogeneous mass. Critics argue that by generalising people in this way, the individual needs of particular people fail to be addressed.

Another criticism is based on the way in which each of the quoted examples seems to put the condition in front of the person. Looking at each example syntactically, it's clear that the adjectives *handicapped* and *disabled* pre-modify the noun *people*. This word order might be interpreted as placing more emphasis on the condition than the person, highlighting the difference rather than the individual. One proposed alternative to such terms changes the word order: *people with disabilities*. These are sometimes referred to as people-first alternatives.

Others take issue with the words themselves. Disability is made up of the bound morpheme *dis* (meaning *not* or *without*) and the free morpheme *ability* (see the Grammatical and morphological framework on pages 207–212) suggesting that the person who is disabled has no ability. This is another example of a **marked term**. Clearly, this is not the case. *Handicapped* (defined in many dictionaries as meaning suffering from an *impairment* or *restriction*) has proved equally contentious and has given rise to one particular **folk etymology** related to begging (cap-in-hand).

Other terms are much less subtle and are often used unthinkingly as playground insults. Words like *spastic* and *mong* have in the past been used as medical terms: *spastic* was used to refer to people with cerebral palsy, a condition that among its symptoms includes uncontrollable spasms or movements, while *mongoloid* was a word used from the late 19th century up to the 1970s to refer to people with Down's syndrome, because the doctor who later gave his name to the condition (John Langdon Down) believed that the facial characteristics of the patients he examined were similar to those of people from Mongolia in the Far East.

■ Age, social class and subcultures

While these three areas are grouped together for the sake of space in this textbook, each could prove a fruitful area of investigation as part of your work on this unit. Consider some of the following terms used to label people in certain social groups. How do they represent different age groups, classes and subcultures?

> *Age: youth, yob, pensioner, hoodie, wrinkly.*
> *Social class: chav, posh, trailer trash.*
> *Subcultures: emo, goth, grunger, townie, hippy, urban.*

■ Key terms

Marked term: term in which the gender of a person is (often unnecessarily) foregrounded through a gendered pre-modifier or suffix.

Folk etymology: a fairly widely accepted, but generally mistaken, belief about a word's origins.

■ Extension activity

Read the following extract and consider how social class is being represented through the language choices made by this writer. Use The linguistic frameworks toolkit on page 206 to guide you.

Ahh – York. Arrive at the wonderful Victorian train station, walk up towards the Minster through the beautiful streets and many snug little pubs, and you feel as though you're in heaven … but wait! The place is teaming with evil gangs of rat-faced charvers! You wonder if it's only you who can see them, spitting and snarling and destroying everything that they cannot steal, lurking in the back alleys and parks to pounce on or torment the tourists and students, tease old and disabled people, and when they feel brave, rob them in broad daylight. They are all Burberry-clad with tracksuits and prison white trainers, and a large cross-bred fighting dog is de rigueur.

York is surrounded by a ring of shite – huge post-war council estates which are true no-go areas for the buses and the police, and real shit-ridden ghettos. Small, sunken-eyed undernourished feral little charver boys with cracked-cornered mouths hunch over spliffs and drink lager in every green space. With often less than 50 words in their vocabulary, they speak out of one nostril and have permanently knitted brows. Heroin and crack cocaine are rife. Car crime, burglary, drug dealing and mindless violence are the norm. A feeling of menace pervades these chav estates, and like in many other English towns, that menace has moved into the city where hooded rat boys move in gangs robbing, destroying and committing acts of random violence against ordinary people going about their business.

Adapted from www.chavtowns.co.uk

Rather like the semantic rule discussed in relation to gender, words that are linked to the working class often undergo a form of pejoration. As Geoffrey Hughes points out in his book *Words In Time*, many words linked to social status have undergone what he terms a process of 'moralisation' in which words associated with the ruling class have gained positive connotations (*noble* and *gentle*, for example), while those associated with the poor have picked up negative connotations (*churl*, *villain*, *wretch*, *knave* and *slave*).

Concerns about the behaviour of young people and the subcultural groups they align themselves with can be traced through language too. Hughes notes that words like *hooligan* (1898), *teddy boys* (1954), *mods* and *rockers* (1960s), *skinheads* (1969), *punks* (1974) all tended to carry connotations of threat or violence in their day, much as terms like *rudeboy*, *gangsta*, *ASBO* and *chav* do these days. Hughes points out that even a relatively neutral word like *youth* now has quite negative connotations. But this cuts both ways: terms used to label older people have undergone pejoration too (*senile* used to be linked closely to *senior* and had no negative associations), while many exist solely to insult (*wrinkly* and *coffin dodger*).

Meanwhile, terms like *emo*, *goth*, *grunger*, *raver* and *hippy* have been used (and still are in various ways) to describe youth groups who associate around particular genres or subgenres of music. The labels – while not necessarily pejorative in their own right – are often used to label and generalise whole groups of individuals, stereotyping their behaviour, lifestyle and attitudes in certain ways.

ⓘ Ⓠ Extension activity

How would you go about investigating the ways in which different age groups are represented?

One idea might be to look at the different birthday cards aimed at particular age groups and to explore the assumptions about the target audience that are expressed through the language used in them. Is there any tendency to assume older people live quieter, less active lives and don't have as much fun as their younger counterparts?

Extension activity

How are young people represented in the mass media?

One interesting representation occurred in a TV programme when the former Conservative Party minister Ann Widdecombe interviewed young people on a council estate in Islington, North London. The young people she interviewed and passed opinions on were so incensed at their portrayal that they produced their own video called *Beyond the Hoodie*. Widdecombe has since produced her own follow-up to the teenager's response. This could run and run!

Fig. 5 *Hoodies, thugs and yobs?*

Topic revision summary

■ Different social groups are represented in different ways through language – often unequally.

■ These social groups are often broken down into categories of people linked by features such as: gender; ethnicity; sexuality; age; dis/ability; social class; and subcultural allegiance.

■ Some have argued that words can be 'reclaimed' from negative connotations.

Individuals and representation

In this topic you will:

◼ look at the ways in which particular individuals in British society are represented through language

◼ examine how individuals represent themselves in print and online.

As you will have explored already in the last topic, Social groups and representation, language can be used to create particular representations of whole groups of people in ways that are often linked to their ethnicity, age, social class, sexuality and gender. Individuals can be represented in a similar way and also represent themselves through language. This topic takes a look at how some of these representations are constructed, pointing you towards some potential subjects for investigation in the coursework for this unit.

Political animals

The representation of prominent local or national politicians can offer you plenty of material to explore. The ideological stances of various newspapers and columnists within those newspapers can often be revealed through a detailed textual analysis of articles on a given day or across a wider time range.

An example might be the reporting of different party leaders' speeches to their political conferences, or even an analysis of the speeches themselves for how issues such as crime, education and health are represented to the party faithful and the wider public. Most newspapers now offer a very detailed breakdown of the political leaders' conference addresses, including in some newspapers a mini **corpus analysis** of keywords that crop up. So in *The Guardian's* coverage of Gordon Brown's first address as Prime Minister to the Labour Party conference, they noted that while words like *education* and *health* turned up over 30 times, the word *Iraq* was only mentioned twice.

The drug-addled serial swordsman versus the tearful blonde beauty

Celebrity culture is a fruitful area of research for representation issues. Each year, a string of new celebrities emerges either through the various reality TV shows, talent shows such as *The X Factor* and *Fame Academy*, or success in sports or popular music, and more established celebrities undergo the trials and tribulations that now seem associated with a life in the public eye: rehab; custody battles; prison terms ... and more rehab.

Taking a quick look at recent years, the celebrities who seem to have featured most heavily in the tabloid press have been Amy Winehouse, Jade Goody, Pete Doherty, Paris Hilton, Lindsay Lohan, Calum Best and Britney Spears. There are probably many more too, but by looking at samples of what has been written about some of these celebrities we can examine how particular representations are created through language and how these might link to wider issues such as gender, ethnicity, age and sexuality. This kind of textual analysis lends itself to corpus analysis, an approach outlined in more detail on page 164 (What sort of investigative method should I use?)

The linguisic framework you have been using throughout this unit (see page 130–131) can be applied to how celebrities are represented, and an analysis of a range of articles about a particular celebrity could form the basis of a good representation investigation. On a small scale, a textual analysis of a particular newspaper article might give you a snapshot

Key terms

Corpus analysis: a systematic investigation of the language of a collection of texts.

Fig. 6 *Amy Winehouse and husband*

■ Link

More guidance on the use of language corpora is given in Coursework preparation on pages 164–170.

of patterns of labelling that can then be explored in more depth using frameworks such as semantics and syntax. So, for example, in the *News of the World* (19 August 2007), the celebrities Calum Best and Gail Porter were referred to in different articles as follows:

> ***Calum Best***: 'drug-addled serial swordsman', 'blond, bed-'em-all bad boy'

> ***Gail Porter***: 'brave Gail Porter', 'tearful', 'the blonde beauty'

While these are just a few quotations, they do suggest that the representation of gender may be something worth looking at in more detail. For example, the noun phrases 'bed-'em-all bad boy' and 'serial swordsman' tend to suggest an almost approving tone to Best's sexual achievements. On the other hand, Gail Porter is described adjectivally in altogether more sympathetic or patronising terms as 'brave' and 'tearful'. Interestingly, both are described as 'blonde', which might offer you a different angle of interpretation, perhaps prompting you to look for similarities in representation rather than differences across genders.

By using a corpus analysis of how particular celebrities' names are pre- or post-modified, you can often observe patterns of labelling at work on a much larger scale. Try searching for two or three words either side of a celebrity's name across 15–20 different newspaper or magazine articles and you will probably find some more telling patterns.

■ Representing the victim

The language used to represent individuals who have died or been subjected to crime can be a fascinating if sensitive area to explore. Obituaries and tributes on websites to people who have died can be crafted by writers to position subject, writer and reader in many different ways. The rise in sites such as gonetoosoon.com and muchloved.com provides you with the chance to look at how language is used to convey responses to people's untimely deaths, and often tells us as much about the person writing the tribute as it does about the person who has passed away.

For example, the use of the phrase 'fallen soldier' to describe a young person who has been killed in a street stabbing or shooting is a case in point. By using language drawn from the semantic field of war, the deceased is represented – perhaps glorified – as a combatant in a large-scale national or international conflict, when in fact they may well have been killed in a petty brawl over postcodes and territory between rival groups.

Equally, the analysis of the use of language drawn from the semantics of religion can offer different perspectives on how death is viewed by different cultures, while the language of death is itself full of euphemism and attempts to ascribe sense to often senseless and incomprehensible acts of violence.

Tributes to well-known people who have died can offer a broader perspective and perhaps reveal a sense of how wider society mourns its dead. Sites devoted to the rapper Tupac Shakur, Ian Curtis (singer of Joy Division), Princess Diana, Elvis Presley, John Peel or Kurt Cobain (singer of Nirvana) all provide material for deeper investigation, including how language is used to construct a sense of the deceased's achievements, failures, struggles and place in the wider scheme of things.

Media reports about crime can not only reflect society's concerns about the issue, but also become part of the issue itself, as you will see in Events, issues and representation, pages 185–189. The representation of individuals who are suspected of crimes, have committed crimes, or have been the victims of crime can give you the chance to carry out in-depth case studies.

When looking at how victims of crime are represented, issues of agency and nominalisation could be key framework areas to explore: for example, is the individual represented using active or passive voice, and does this have a potential impact on how they might be perceived and positioned in relation to events?

Self-representation

Language is used not just to represent others but to represent ourselves. In effect, every time we open our mouths we represent ourselves, but it is written self-representations of individuals we will look at here.

Fig. 7 *Kurt Cobain*

Extension activity

How would you use language to represent yourself if you were to write some of the following?

- an extract from your autobiography
- a blog entry about your day so far
- a profile on Facebook, MySpace or similar social networking site
- a letter to a problem page, agony aunt or advice column
- a diary entry from the last week
- a personal ad in a newspaper seeking a partner
- a curriculum vitae (CV)

You might want to try sketching out an outline of how you would craft your vocabulary and grammar to write in each of these forms. Notice how the conventions of each form dictate how you shape your language.

Investigation ideas

- Analyse a selection of personal ads from different publications or websites on the same day. Look at how the conventions, style and content of the ads compare.

- Analyse a range of personal ads in the same publication over a period of 30 years, looking for changing patterns of language or shifting representations.

- Compare a set of heterosexual personal ads of men seeking women, with some homosexual, men seeking men, ads, looking for patterns of representation.

- Compare a range of Facebook or other social networking profiles using one of the following as a variable: age; gender; nationality.

- Investigate the differing representations of three dead pop stars on internet tribute sites.

- The evolving representation of a sportsperson like Paul Robinson, Wayne Rooney, Johnny Wilkinson or Maria Sharapova during a major tournament.

- The evolving representation of a celebrity such as Amy Winehouse or Pete Doherty over a six-month period.

- Analyse a set of obituaries drawn from national newspapers.

Topic revision summary

- Individuals are represented and can represent themselves in different ways through language.
- Individuals in the public eye, such as celebrities and politicians, are often good focal points for investigation.

Institutions and representation

In this topic you will:

◾ look at the ways in which different institutions in British society are represented in different ways through language

◾ examine how audiences can be positioned in relation to debates about these institutions.

◼ Church, state ... and football team

Along with social groups, individuals, issues and events, the major institutions of society provide us with areas to investigate when we consider how language can shape and create representation. 'Institutions' can be a little hard to define, so the definition we'll work with here is a custom, a practice or an established organisation, such as the institutions of marriage, religion and the nation state.

Using this definition of institutions, we will look at how language is used to represent Christianity and the police as two examples, and then suggest some other areas to investigate at the end of the topic. Institutions such as the monarchy, state education and the NHS can provide plenty of material to explore, while the national football team could also qualify for this category, even if they can't qualify for anything else.

◼ Christianity

The role of religion and its influence on wider social attitudes have been discussed for centuries, and recent world events – 11 September, the 7 July suicide bombings in London, arguments about creationism and 'intelligent design' in the USA, debates around faith schools and social integration in the UK – have pushed it to the front of the news agenda in this century. The ideologically opposed viewpoints of secularists and fundamentalists are often very interesting to explore from a linguistic perspective, while the representation of different faith groups in the media has become a sensitive topic, with accusations of prejudice and 'Islamophobia' in some quarters.

◼ Data response exercise 12

Read extracts a and b which are taken from *The God Delusion* by Richard Dawkins. How does the writer use language to represent the Bible and those who follow it?

Check your ideas against the feedback (page 173).

Fig. 8 *"Nice use of pre-modifiers, Mr Dawkins, but pity about the subject positon..."*

a To be fair, much of the Bible is not systematically evil but just plain weird, as you would expect of a chaotically cobbled-together anthology of disjointed documents, composed, revised, translated, distorted and 'improved' by hundreds of anonymous authors, copyists, unknown to us and mostly unknown to each other, spanning nine centuries. This may explain some of the sheer strangeness of the Bible. But unfortunately it is this same weird volume that religious zealots hold up to us as the inerrant source of our morals and rules for living.

b The God of the Old Testament is arguably the most unpleasant character in all fiction: jealous and proud of it; a petty, unjust, unforgiving control-freak; a vindictive, bloodthirsty ethnic cleanser; a misogynistic, homophobic, racist, infanticidal, genocidal, filicidal, pestilential, megalomaniacal, sadomasochistic, capriciously malevolent bully. Those of us schooled from infancy in his ways can become desensitized to their horror. A naïf blessed with the perspective of innocence has a clearer perception.

The police

The police service, the police force, the cops, the old bill, the Feds, the boy dem ... the words that abound for the police are as varied as the attitudes that exist towards them. In Data extract 1, the Commissioner of the Metropolitan Police, Ian Blair, considers the role of the police service in modern Britain. In Data extract 2, former journalist turned-screenwriter, David Simon, takes a more cynical view of the day-to-day life of a police officer in the USA.

Data extract 1

The citizens of Britain now have to articulate what kind of police service they want.

For this reason: after atrocities in New York, Madrid and London, after Bali, Casablanca, Istanbul, Delhi and Jordan, fears for personal and communal safety are inextricably part of contemporary life.

Moreover, these events coincide with another development, the increasing sense that anti-social behaviour, as the opposite face of a civil society, is also threatening our ability to lead free lives.

Three trends have coincided. First, the agencies of community cohesion, the churches, the trade unions, the housing associations, the voluntary clubs have declined in influence.

Secondly, the agents of social enforcement, such as park keepers, caretakers and bus conductors, have disappeared.

The third was the laudable but under-funded and imperfectly implemented decision to close so many long-stay psychiatric institutions.

This has left many people looking – in the absence of anyone else – to the police service for answers to the degradation of communal life – for answers to the neighbours from hell, the smashed bus stop, the lift shaft littered with needles and condoms, the open drugs market, the angry, the aggressive and the obviously disturbed.

And it is clear that how the police deal with these often very local issues will determine whether we are considered to be successful in everything we do, local or not.

An extract from Metropolitan Police Commissioner Sir Ian Blair's Dimbleby Lecture, November 2005

Data extract 2

This is the job:

You sit behind a government-issue metal desk on the sixth of ten floors in a gleaming, steel-frame death trap with poor ventilation, dysfunctional air conditioning, and enough free-floating asbestos to pad the devil's own jumpsuit ... You answer the phone on the second or third bleat because Baltimore abandoned its AT&T equipment on a cost-saving measure and the new phone system doesn't ring so much as it emits metallic, sheeplike sounds. If a police dispatcher is on the other end of the call, you write down an address, the time,

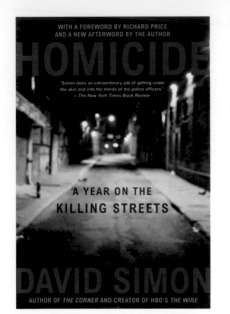

Fig. 9 *Homicide: A Year on the Killing Streets by David Simon*

and the dispatcher's unit number on a piece of scratch paper or the back of a used three-by-five pawn shop submission card.

Then you beg or barter the keys to one of a half-dozen unmarked Chevrolet Cavaliers, grab your gun, a notepad, a flashlight and a pair of white rubber gloves and drive to the correct address where, in all probability, a uniformed police officer will be standing over a cooling human body.

You look at that body. You look at that body as if it were some abstract work of art, stare at it from every conceivable point of view in search of deeper meanings and textures. Why, you ask yourself, is this body here? What did the artist leave out? What did he put in? What was the artist thinking of? What the hell is wrong with the picture? ...

You walk around the edges of the scene looking for spent bullets, casings, blood droplets. You get a uniform to canvass the houses or businesses nearby, or if you want it done right, you go door-to-door yourself, asking questions that the uniforms might never think to ask.

D. Simon, Homicide: a year on the killing streets, *1991*

Data response exercise 13

Read Data extracts 1 and 2. Examine how each speaker/writer conveys his attitudes to the role of the police and how different lexical registers are used to create a sense of expertise, inside knowledge and social conscience. How is language used to represent the police and how does the context and form of each extract influence its message?

Check your ideas against the feedback (page 173).

■ Investigation ideas

- How different religious groups (e.g. Muslims or Mormons) have been represented over time in national media.
- How opponents of religion (secularists, communists and/or anarchists) have represented religion in their campaigning literature.
- The language of different versions of the Bible aimed at different age groups.
- The representation of the police in lyrics by rappers such as KRS-one, NWA and Dead Prez, or in the lyrics of punk/rock musicians such as The Clash, Rage Against The Machine and Dead Kennedys.
- The representation of the police on websites such as those of the Police Federation and ACPO (Association of Chief Police Officers), and blogs by serving police officers such as 'copper's blog' and 'pc bloggs'.
- How language is used to represent the monarchy in politically opposed publications.
- How the national football, rugby, cricket or athletics teams are represented around key sporting events.

Topic revision summary

- Institutions such as the Church, police service, military, monarchy or national football team can provide fruitful areas for investigation.
- It's important to define exactly what you mean by an 'institution'.

Events, issues and representation

War, famine, pestilence, death

The ways in which natural and human-made disasters are represented through language is another area to investigate. Alongside these subjects, there are issues that recur in society and are debated perennially – crime, death, poverty, inequality.

To explore how language is used to represent some of these ideas, we will look at some examples of texts. Applying the linguistic framework you were introduced to on page 155, you will be able to examine how language can often shape our perceptions of events, how language can position us in relation to events and how audiences respond to these representations. What is covered here is just a brief snapshot of two main areas – war and crime. Ideas on other areas to investigate are suggested at the end of the topic.

War

The language of war is fertile territory for investigation. News reports on armed conflicts, website articles offering different opinions about such conflicts, and the ways in which soldiers themselves discuss their experiences are just a few examples of ways in which language is used in different ways to represent war. The language of war has also worked its way into many other aspects of our lives, with metaphors of conflict appearing in sport (*attack, defend, strike*), politics (*ambush, rearguard action, sound the retreat*) and many other areas.

The extracts in this topic have been chosen to illustrate some of the ways in which you might use a linguistic analysis to explore issues of representation

Data response exercise 14

The following extract is taken from an interview with a British soldier fighting in Iraq, reflecting on the recent troop withdrawal from central Basra. Using your representation framework, analyse this text, looking particularly at how the soldier conveys his own experience of the conflict.

Check your ideas against the feedback (page 174).

Corporal Lucas Farrell

Age 23, Liverpool

[One night] we had left Basra Palace on a supply convoy to the PJCC in Bulldogs, Warriors and military trucks. As we were unloading the supplies in the base, we came under attack from mortars and rockets. It was pretty fierce. An officer who had been briefing us one minute was then killed. We were stunned, like, shocked.

But then there was no more time to think about that. We were told that they [the militias] would know when we went out and that they would be waiting for us. And that's what happened. As we left, there

Fig. 10 *Group of British soldiers in Iraq in 2007*

was firing from all sides. We were getting repeatedly ambushed, they were hitting the vehicles [with] small arms, RPGs [rocket-propelled grenades]. What they were trying to do was hit the ones in the rear and separate the convoy and trap some of us. There was a lot, a lot of shooting. I don't know how much was fired in total, I was using a GPMG (General Purpose Machine Gun) and I myself fired around 600 rounds.

We drove straight back to Basra Palace with the officer's body – then you thought about what had happened, and it was very sad.

Extension activity

Which other texts might you use alongside this one to look at how war is represented through soldiers' voices?

■ Perhaps you could explore soldiers' voices in different wars or conflicts: this might allow you to look at wars over time (First and Second World Wars, wars in Vietnam, Korea, the Falklands, the former Yugoslavia or Iraq).

■ You could also look at the ways in which First World War poets (Wilfred Owen, Siegfried Sassoon, Isaac Rosenberg, *et al.*) write about the conflict, perhaps comparing their versions of events with those of newspapers of the time, or prose accounts by serving soldiers.

■ The voices of the families of soldiers are also an interesting area to explore.

■ You could expand your focus by exploring how war is represented by those not directly involved – politicians and journalists. An example of an editorial about war is given on page 134.

AQA Examiner's tip

Don't assume that you have to look at texts on paper! There are some fantastic online resources, including databases of newspapers, facsimiles of older documents and archives of texts. Looking at texts over time is one approach you may want to use in your investigation, and these resources allow you to do just that. A list of suggested websites and resources is provided in Coursework preparation, pages 190–196.

The language used to justify wars and to persuade the public of the need for armed conflict is interesting for a number of reasons. Opinions are often polarised and language is used at full stretch to argue passionately for or against. A comparison of an anti-Iraq War editorial in a newspaper like the *Daily Mirror*, with one in *The Sun* which supported it, might prove a fruitful way of comparing how war is represented from different positions.

Likewise, the reporting of war in different media outlets can provide some interesting angles to explore. The foregrounding of military objectives or the fate of enemy combatants can offer an insight into the positioning of the writer, while the reports' use of language from the military lexicon can be revealing. In his book *The Language of War*, Steve Thorne looks at a number of military terms that have now moved into mainstream usage.

Blue on blue	the accidental death of allied soldiers.
Collateral damage	the accidental death of civilians.
Demographic targeting	the premeditated killing of civilians.
Export the risk	to shoot first and ask questions later.
Mop up	to finish off the last remnants of enemy resistance within a specified area.
Smart bomb	a computer-guided or electronically controlled missile.
Surgical strike	an attack aimed at destroying an individual target.
Transfer tube	a casket containing the dead body of a soldier.

As Thorne explains:

not only do these terms give a false sense of accuracy and sophistication, but they are also deliberately cryptic, abstruse, vague and highly evasive ... the term "Blue on blue" is derived from war games where allies are usually blue and enemies, in a hangover from the cold war, are red. Used in this context it appears to imply that war is just a game ... the term "mop up" makes war sound like a domestic chore ... smart bomb and surgical strike make military operations and items of military hardware sound more precise than they actually are.

S. Thorne, The Language of War, 2006

■ Crime

It would be naive to think that newspapers simply represent political and social issues such as crime, famine and immigration in a neutral way. As we have already seen, representation is not a neutral, value-free process. It might be argued that each time an issue or event is represented an **intervention** is made in the debate. So in 1998, when the editor of the *Dover Express* newspaper described asylum seekers and bootleggers (people importing cheap cigarettes and drink from Europe to sell on at a profit) as 'human sewage', his was clearly not an unbiased take on the issue.

The reporting of crime is another case in point. On one hand, the media are responsible for reporting on events that take place – that's their job after all – but on the other hand, the prominence they give to particular stories, the emphasis they place on the relative importance of certain

■ Key terms

Intervention: an attempt to take part or engage in a debate.

incidents and the ways in which language is used to construct a particular version of events, can all shape the reader's response and become part of the issue itself. The reporting of crime can often lead to an exaggerated perception of crime and an increased fear of crime, which in themselves can make people feel that crime is rising and society is becoming more dangerous.

Data response exercise 15

Read the following extract from *The Sun* feature on crime figures (17 July 2003) and examine how language is used to represent crime and the government's response to crime, and to address the reader. Use your representation framework to pick out language features which help to create a particular impression.

Check your ideas against the feedback (page 174).

> **BRITAIN is living in fear as crime soars across the nation, two damning reports revealed last night.**
>
> Official figures showed that rapes and street violence were rocketing – despite attempts by Home Secretary David Blunkett to twist the statistics and play down the crisis.
>
> And a survey proved that many *Sun* readers were terrified of falling victim to thugs, muggers, aggressive drunks and junkies.
>
> Police numbers disclosed that violent crime leapt 22 per cent last year, with female rape increasing by 27 per cent – from 8,990 to 11,441.
>
> *Overall, police recorded 5,899,450 crimes compared with 5,525,316 the previous year.*
>
> That represented a **RISE** of 7 per cent. But the Home Office claimed instead there had been a 3 per cent **FALL** because the figures were inflated by changes to the classification of crimes and the way they were recorded.
>
> *The disturbing statistics showed:*
>
> ■ Murder, manslaughter and killing of infants *JUMPED* by 18 per cent, from 891 to 1,048. Violence against individuals *ROSE* 28 per cent from 650,474 cases to 835,101.
>
> ■ Wounding and violence involving weapons was up 11 per cent from 28,796 cases to 32,104. Offences under the Firearms Act *LEAPED* from 3,247 to 3,572. Assaults on police officers were *UP* 12 per cent to 33,742.

Non-fiction reports of crime are not the only sources of language for an investigation into this theme, and a range of other texts are worthy of exploration (see Investigation ideas opposite). Each of these ideas needs consideration before being turned into an AS investigation, but they all have the potential to provide fresh perspectives and insights into the topic as a whole.

Find examples of media reports from different sources or different times that are focused on immigration, and compare the ways in which language is used to represent the issue. You might want to look at the investigation ideas that follow.

Investigation ideas

- The language of the Victim Support website.
- An analysis of the lyrics of 'Sirens' by Dizzee Rascal (*Maths & English* album, 2007) or 'Chinese New Year' by Clipse (*Hell Hath No Fury* album, 2006), both of which appear to celebrate or glorify elements of crime and the lifestyle associated with it.
- The language of political parties in election literature addressing crime as a political issue.
- First-hand testimonies from death row convicts in America.
- The language of crime reporting in local newspapers.
- The language of TV cop shows such as *The Wire* and *The Shield*.
- The language of first-hand victims of crime in books such as *The Surprise Party* by Stanley N. Alpert and *Steve and Me* by Duwayne Brooks.
- The language used in novels about crime, such as *Homicide: a life on the streets* by David Simon or *The Black Dahlia* by James Ellroy.
- A range of stories about immigration in the same week as covered by different newspapers (e.g. *The Sun, Daily Mail, The Guardian, Daily Mirror, Socialist Worker*) or three to five stories from the same newspaper over a period of 50/100/150 years.
- A sample of stories about immigration on the same day from different news and current affairs websites (e.g. BBC news, Sky news, Newsround).
- A range of feature articles exploring the lives of refugees from three different broadsheet newspapers from the same year.
- Extracts from party political manifestos on immigration (Labour, Conservative, Liberal Democrat, Respect, Independent Working Class Association, UK Independence Party).
- Campaigning literature from opposing sides of the argument: *No Borders* v. *Migration Watch*, for example.
- Explore the evolving coverage of the 2007 floods in the UK across local and national newspapers during a two- to three-week period.
- Investigate the representation of British victims of natural disasters in foreign countries compared to indigenous victims.
- Examine the representation of different social groups in the coverage of Hurricane Katrina's devastating aftermath (perhaps looking at how working-class African Americans have been represented in relation to working-class whites).
- Study the changing representation of war veterans through the Imperial War Museum's website.

Topic revision summary

- Any significant event or issue could prove interesting territory for an investigation.
- Topics such as war, crime, poverty, racism and immigration are among many that could make suitable subjects to explore.

Coursework preparation

☑

■ What is an investigation?

An investigation is not an analysis: it might consist of a selection of different analyses of a variety of texts, but it has to be more than this. An investigation should have clear aims and some sense of direction. You should be able to plan in advance what kind of focus you want, which topic area you are going to explore, which methodology/ies suit/s you best and which examples of language you will be looking at.

The AQA A specification explains the investigation as follows:

Candidates should analyse between three and five texts (which may be extracts from longer texts).

There should be a temporal relationship between the texts. An investigation may focus on a number of texts:

■ produced at the same time (e.g. surveying newspaper articles published on the same day)

■ evolving over time (e.g. a news story spanning a period of time)

■ produced at different times (e.g. texts produced in the 1950s, 1970s and the 21st century).

The analysis should be 1,000–1,500 words long. Copies of the analysed text should be presented with it.

■ What does an investigation involve?

The key focus of this investigation has to be 'representation'. You should be looking at how language creates and shapes representations of individuals, events, issues, institutions or social groups.

■ What is meant by 'investigating representation'?

The AQA A specification puts it like this:

Work should focus on how lexis, grammar, semantics and discourse structure in individual texts produce representations. Candidates will need to use the linguistic frameworks developed in Unit 1 to carry out a critical discourse analysis.

Candidates should explore the texts':

■ purposes

■ construction of an author identity

■ construction and positioning of an ideal reader and the shaping of response

■ representation

■ possible actual audience and interpretations

■ genre.

As you will have seen from the earlier topics in this section, a 'critical discourse analysis' is an approach that looks at how language features such as word choices, grammatical structures, and choices of reader and writer positioning create particular effects and shape a reader's understanding. You should be applying your own linguistic framework to explore how a topic or subject of your choice is represented through language, and to explore the implications of this.

How do I choose my topic?

The key areas for investigation are individuals, social groups, institutions, events or issues. You can choose whatever focus you want within these areas – for example, how a particular social group such as women, or a particular issue such as poverty, is represented in your choice of texts – in discussion with your teacher/s. Ultimately, they will have to mark it, so you should take their advice if they feel that you will not be able to perform a good job on a particular task.

Choosing a suitable topic is part of your planning stage, and more ideas are given later to help you think through your options.

How do I find texts to investigate?

The texts you choose and the language data you investigate will depend on your choice of topic, but you can use spoken, written or blended mode texts for this unit, so a huge range is open to you.

If you choose written texts, you may decide that one way of approaching the task is to keep a scrapbook – physical or virtual – of newspaper cuttings about a particular issue or person. You could, for example, track the coverage of a politician or celebrity in a particular newspaper over a period of some months, or collect a range of newspapers on a given day and choose to examine these. Older newspapers are kept online on databases such as Infotrac, and most newspapers have searchable archives on their websites.

You are not limited to newspapers of course: you could look at how language is used in comic books such as *2000AD*, *Preacher*, *Hellblazer*, *SpiderMan* or *X Men* to explore the representation of superpowers or justice; you could examine the language of political parties' or charities' websites; you could examine literary texts for younger children by authors such as Philip Pullman, J. K. Rowling or Enid Blyton to explore issues of representation of religion or gender; or literary texts for an adult audience such as Toni Morrison's *Beloved*, Roddy Doyle's *The Deportees*, Jeanette Winterson's *Oranges Are Not The Only Fruit*, George Orwell's *Homage to Catalonia*, or many more. The possibilities are endless …

If you choose spoken texts, you need to have access to either recording equipment or transcripts. This can be very time consuming and takes a bit of organisation, but may offer you valuable material to investigate. The fact that you transcribe the material yourself often gives you greater understanding of the details of a spoken text too.

What sort of investigative method should I use?

The way you approach your data (the spoken, written or blended language that you're exploring) depends on a number of factors. In the end it's up to you how you go about this, but here are some possible methodologies.

Corpus analysis

A *corpus* is a body of language (*corpora* is the plural). This could be a collection of texts of one particular form, such as newspaper or magazine articles, extracts from short stories, examples of rap lyrics, transcripts of political speeches. A corpus analysis is a systematic investigation of the language of this body of texts. So you will probably use a linguistic framework such as that outlined on page 155 to investigate your chosen focus in a range of texts from your corpus. As explained above, your investigation has to be more than just an analysis, so you must explore three to five texts and they must be linked *temporally* (i.e. either three to five texts from across different periods of time, or three to five texts from the same day). As well as corpora that you assemble yourself by selecting texts, electronic and online corpora are available, which allow you to search using a range of different criteria. A very simple way of searching for particular words and how they are used is through the search engine Google, but more sophisticated corpora such as those below allow greater precision:

- The Oxford English Corpus www.askoxford.com/oec contains about 2 billion words from literary novels, websites and newspapers from all over the world.
- The British National Corpus www.natcorp.ox.ac.uk contains 100 million words (90 per cent from written sources, 10 per cent from spoken) from the late 20th century.
- The Collins Cobuild corpus www.collins.co.uk/corpus/CorpusSearch. aspx contains around 56 million words (46 million from British sources, 10 million from the USA).

One such criterion – *collocates* – allows you to search for words either side of the keywords you choose. So, for example, if you were looking for ways in which the name of a celebrity had been pre-modified, you might want to look for two to three words preceding the celebrity's name. Alternatively, you could explore patterns of post-modification by looking for five to six words after the keywords. Corpora also allow you to trawl huge banks of texts for patterns of usage, so you could look for appearances of words such as *immigration*, *war*, *crime* and be directed to texts where such themes are dealt with. This approach can also assist you with a quantitative approach to data – helping you see the frequency of words in particular texts (e.g. the appearance of the words *half-caste*, *housewife* or *gay*), which can then allow you to explore the implications of such words in more detail.

These online corpora can appear a bit baffling at first glance, so you might want to ask your teacher for help should you wish to use this methodology. Or for a relatively straightforward explanation, visit the Oxford English Corpus site and click on the links that explain how it works and what it's for.

Case studies and participant analysis

These are in-depth investigations with a particular focus that allow you to find out more about how a particular issue, event, institution, social group or individual is dealt with. A case study might take the form of tracking a particular focus through time (e.g. how crime is represented in the same newspaper across five decades or how an event is represented as evolving over a period of time, e.g. how the 2007 floods were represented across two weeks, or how an outbreak of foot and mouth disease was reported over a five-day period), or across different texts (e.g. how a politician is represented in five different newspapers on the same day). Participant analysis is a technique that allows you to track the ways in which a particular participant in a text is described, i.e. you may wish to track the ways in which a particular character in a novel is given certain verbs to purpose or how the word *immigration* is premodified in a newspaper story.

💡 Planning your investigation

1 Decide on a focus and aim.
2 Choose your texts and methodology.
3 Develop an analytical framework.
4 Analyse and investigate.
5 Overview.
6 Conclusions.

The first step is to decide on a focus for your investigation. Which areas do you find interesting? Which areas would you like to find out more about? Do you have a particular reason for choosing an area to focus on? The best investigations are driven by a genuine interest in the subject matter, so give this some thought and look back through this section of the textbook for areas that might have sparked an interest. You can also use resources such as language blogs and the websites of national newspapers to sift through language issues in the media and pick up on areas that might appeal.

Often you will have an idea about where you want to look and which texts you'd like to explore, based on the subject you're investigating. For example, you may wish to examine how the England women's football team is represented and a logical place to look would be the sports pages of the national newspapers. However, it's worth thinking laterally about this and investigating less mainstream sources of news too: internet discussion sites; blogs; regional and local newspapers; women's interest and sports magazines.

Once you've selected and collected your texts – be they written, spoken or blended modes – develop a methodology for analysing them and a linguistic framework that will help you explore them in more depth.

The key part of your investigation is the analysis of the texts or extracts you've chosen and the investigation of the focus you've set yourself. This is what you should plan and redraft as much as possible to achieve the best end results.

Planning your analysis

There's no one perfect way to do this, but thinking through different approaches, as in Table 3, will probably help.

Table 3 *Different approaches to planning your analysis*

Question	Positives	Negatives
Will you analyse your texts framework by framework e.g. lexis – semantics – grammar – graphology?	Helps you to cover a range of areas Gives you more chance of seeing connections between texts Allows you to make a point of prioritising the top band features of grammar	Can be rather formulaic Can prevent you from exploring one text in detail if you're not careful
Will you analyse one text at a time?	Allows some in-depth coverage of each text Helps you engage with the ideas in each text	Might prevent you from exploring patterns of language use if you remain focused on one text without comparing

Reaching an overview

The overview of your analysis is the chance to look at the wider representation issues your investigation might have uncovered. This is your chance to consider:

■ the possible implications of the representations you have explored

■ how your findings link to the contexts in which the texts were produced

■ how the representations you've explored link to established theories or concepts

■ how the representations you've explored challenge such theories and concepts.

It's also your opportunity to pull together the different strands of your analysis and see what kinds of patterns might emerge.

Concluding your investigation

With such a small-scale study you need to be careful not to make grandiose claims about 'proving' one theory true or another untrue. It's best to err on the side of caution and show some awareness in your conclusion that what you have done is just a brief snapshot of how language works in the particular context that you have investigated. Given your relatively small word count for this coursework task (1,000–1,500 words), you should probably write about a paragraph for this part.

🔆 Sample investigation work

Here we'll look at two short extracts of analysis from longer investigations, and offer some examiner commentary on what makes these successful or otherwise. Extract A is taken from an investigation into the language used to represent the England rugby team on the day after their defeat in the 2007 World Cup Final, while Extract B is taken from an investigation into the language used to represent different age groups in birthday cards.

Extract A

> In my investigation I have looked at the *News of the World* and *Observer* newspapers, and the BBC news website from 21 October 2007.
>
> In the *News of the World* article it states 'England's brave heroes were beaten 15–6 by the Springboks after winger Mark Cueto was denied a crucial second-half try by Aussie video ref Stuart Dickinson' this is very bias and takes the side of the England team by making them look like heroes. The writer of the article says they are 'brave' and this word is very powerful when it goes with 'heroes'. There is also lots of field specific lexis which makes this difficult to understand for the target audience.

Examiner's comment

While this is just a very short extract, it is clearly quite a long way short of what's expected at AS Level and needs to be developed substantially to give the candidate any realistic chance of a decent grade.

On one level, the candidate is picking out some relevant material but, on another, there's very little analysis of the language used or its effects on creating a representation of the team. It's also rather carelessly written with some fairly basic grammatical and spelling errors (e.g. the lack of a sentence break after the quotation from the article, and the spelling of the adjective *biased* as *bias*).

To improve the analysis the candidate would be advised to look at word classes, the passive voice and the use of audience positioning. The noun phrase *England's brave heroes* could be analysed as using a pre-modifying adjective *brave* to accentuate the qualities of the team already established by the use of the noun *heroes*, while the use of the proper noun (and possessive apostrophe) *England's* casts the team as a national institution who belong to us all … if we're English. Meanwhile, the use of the passive voice in the clause 'winger Mark Cueto was denied a crucial second-half try by Aussie video ref Stuart Dickinson' is interesting because the agency is made absolutely clear to the reader: the England player 'was denied' – making him the object of this verb, while the agent of the verb 'to deny' is none other than an 'Aussie' (a colloquial term for an Australian), perhaps hinting at some kind of bias from the rugby rivals? The audience is positioned as England rugby supporters and the use of field-specific lexis referred to in the candidate's answer is relevant in helping identify this audience as people who know something about the game and understand its terminology.

Extract B

Pre-modifiers used in an informal way are only found in the cards for the younger people; when they are used they make the noun phrase more casual and friendly e.g. 'groovy birthday'. This gives young age a positive tone and emphasises the need to be young and since there is a lack of these pre-modifiers for older people it gives a more negative attitude towards aging and places a stress on being young. This seems to feed the stereotype of old people and therefore represent them negatively. This stereotyped image of an old person may be the reason why the majority of words used to describe an old person were negative. Since we have this set image of old people in our minds then these views may be reflected in the way we talk and write about old people thus supporting the reflectionism theory. Younger adults were mostly described with neutral words; this is because there is no set stereotyped image of what an adult should look and behave like so neutral words were used.

Examiner's comment

Again, this is an extract from a longer piece so it's quite difficult to see the wider context to which the candidate is referring, but it should be clear that this is heading in the right direction when compared to Extract A. The more assured use of technical terminology ('pre-modifier' and 'noun phrase') suggests that the candidate is better equipped to identify significant linguistic features, while the ability to start linking ideas to issues such as stereotyping and concepts such as linguistic reflectionism are steps in the right direction.

There is a noticeable lack of examples here, which doesn't help, and the conclusions are a little broad for such a limited investigation. However, with a bit of work this could be turned into a detailed, original and analytical investigation of the representation of age. One of the most positive features of this extract is the candidate's willingness to link the details of language to wider issues, and this is an approach that should be encouraged.

Further reading

If you want to know more about what the linguists and other authors mentioned in this section have said about representation and language, look at some of the titles listed below.

Cameron, D. *Verbal Hygiene*, Routledge, 1995

Fairclough, N. *Language and Power*, Longman, 1989

Pinker, S. *The Stuff of Thought*, Allen Lane, 2007

Pope, R. *Textual Intervention*, Routledge, 1995

Spender, D. *Man Made Language*, Rivers Oram Press/Pandora List, 1980

Thomas, L., Wareing, S., Singh, I., Peccei, J. S., Thornborrow, J. and Jones, J. *Language, Society and Power*, Routledge, 2003

Thorne, S. *The Language of War*, Routledge, 2006

In the end, the success or failure of your investigation will depend on you and what you find interesting about language. There is a wealth of material available to explore in written, spoken and blended mode forms; it's a question of finding an angle, asking interesting questions and applying linguistic frameworks to the texts you choose. The more inquisitive you are about *how* and *why* language is used, the better your investigation will be. Now it's over to you, so good luck with this part of your coursework.

Topic revision summary

■ Careful planning and considered selection of texts to analyse is vital to doing well.

■ Thinking about a methodology – a way of approaching your texts and what you want to find – is really important.

■ Applying a detailed linguistic framework to the texts is crucial: you don't get many marks for talking about layout and pictures, but you do for looking at word classes and grammatical structures.

■ Making sense of the language features and the effects they create is very important.

■ Spotting connections and patterns between texts will be helpful to achieving a good mark.

Feedback

This part of the book provides all the feedback for the Data response exercises in Unit 2, Section A.

Introduction

Data response exercise 1

Some of the ideas that you might have come up with, and maybe a few others are included here for discussion.

a Christopher Columbus may well have been the first westerner to land on north American shores (although many would debate this, the Vikings included), but did he really 'discover' the country? There were already people living there, whose existence is ignored or sidelined by the semantic construction of this phrase. The language seems to encode within it a particularly western mindset: that if there were people there, their opinions don't really count. The subject positioning seems to foreground one experience over another.

b This sentence seems to assume that students are uniformly male, because of the use of the pronoun 'he'. Does this exclude female students? Does *his* really mean *his and her*?

c The noun phrase 'the disabled' is problematic because it represents people with disabilities as a homogeneous group. Would expressions like 'the blacks' or 'the Asians' be acceptable? The determiner 'the' establishes a group identity. It could also be argued that the whole sentence is patronising: what people with disabilities deserve is up to them to decide, and sympathy is probably not the first thing that would spring to mind. The perspective from which this is delivered is also interesting: the first-person plural pronoun or possessive determiner *our* is employed, suggesting that the audience is perceived as being able-bodied and that disabled people are not included as part of the audience. The effect is to exclude and to separate.

d The abstract noun 'nation' is used here to suggest a shared and unified group identity. This assumes – or strives to assert – that everyone within the nation shared the same perspective as the writer. The 'ideal audience' would share the writer's viewpoint, but others may not have particularly cared, or in some situations would have seen the pressure to conform as an infringement on their freedom of thought.

e The grammatical structure here is perhaps more interesting than the words. The use of the passive voice, in which the subject of the sentence 'the protesters' has the verb *to injure* done to it, allows the writer to hide agency. In other words the agent of the injuries – the ones who did the injuring – are not mentioned. Someone must have done the verb, but they are left out of this sentence.

f The issue with this example is perhaps best seen in terms of what's not included, or rather *who* is not here: the princess. The use of the verb *have* carries connotations of dominance and ownership, suggesting that the brave knight in this story (to whom this example is directed) will be rewarded for his act of violence by being given the princess, as if she were an object to be passed from one man to another. Perhaps this example, taken from a children's book, might be seen to reflect a patriarchal (male-dominated) society.

Data response exercise 2

The pronoun use here seems designed to place the reader in the shoes of the homeless young person, using second person synthetic personalisation (the technique where a writer/speaker uses the second-person pronoun to synthesise or fake a personal relation to the audience) with the possessive determiner '**your** home' and pronoun with contracted verb 'Now imagine **you're** 12 years old'. The charity creates an ideal reader as someone who can empathise with the victim's situation and then join the campaign to help. Moving into third person ('**her father**') on the second page before using a first person plural possessive determiner ('**our** doorstep'), Katy's plight is revealed in narrative form. Later in the advert, there is a shift to first person as Katy tells her own story ('**I** could have been out on the streets…'), perhaps suggesting that she has survived to tell her tale herself.

Data response exercise 3

a A passive sentence: the subject 'Over 60 demonstrators' receives the action of the verb *to injure*, but no agent is required – grammatically speaking – so there is no explicit acknowledgement of who did the injuring.

b An active sentence is used here, with the subject *the police* acting as agent to the verb *charged* whose object is *the crowd*.

Data response exercise 4

'…bloody game of war…'

War as a sport or competition between two sides and with a clear victor.

'The curtain rises on the closing scene of the greatest human conflict the world has ever known.'

War as a performance, a crafted, stage-managed and ultimately fictional event presented to an admiring audience.

Data response exercise 5

Some observations you might have made are as follows:

1 The use of a colloquial register ('snot on their chin', 'mangy mutts', 'ponce for our supper') and taboo language ('shoebox full of shit') helps to position the writer as a 'normal bloke', speaking the common-sense language of the streets.

2 The references to family and traditional values ('my old man', 'my father's generation', 'never hit a woman', 'don't rat on your friends') stop just short of some kind of Dick Van Dyke parody of working-class life, but present to us a set of values that appear honest and simple.

3 The rhetorical momentum, created largely through repetition of keywords and phrases, helps the writer to develop his argument in a straightforward, no-nonsense style.

4 The reader is positioned as a resident of 'this city' and the use of proper nouns such as 'King's Cross' and 'Covent Garden' help to map out a familiar terrain to Londoners, perhaps making us feel more at one with the writer who trots out these place names so casually.

Data response exercise 6

Gaunt has used a present perfect construction in the first line 'have been turned' that is also in the passive voice. The present perfect allows him to talk about an event that has already taken place but which is relevant to the moment at which he is writing. The simple present tense of 'thugs … hold sway' and 'decent people live in fear' is used to create a sense of habitual action. The simple present creates an impression that this occurs day in day out.

In the second paragraph, the simple present reappears ('who run this country', 'don't live', 'seem to worry', 'kid gets mauled'), and a present perfect, but this time in the active voice ('have turned a blind eye'), is used again to create the impression that the damage has been done and to indicate who is responsible.

There are other areas of the framework that might be applied to this text, for example its use of pre-modification ('**liberal** elite') and colloquial register ('morons'), but the writer uses tense and aspect to help reinforce his view that this is how things are.

Data response exercise 7

The different subject positions in the Children's Society advertisement allow a range of angles on this issue. We come across Katy's story as the most prominent position and are granted access to some of her inner thoughts through first-person quotations. Her father's position is also important, but he remains nameless, with adjectives such as 'furious' and 'enraged' being used to describe his mood. The active voice used to describe the father's decisions and actions creates a sense of his power, and perhaps Katy's lack of control of the situation. The charity's counsellor, Angela, is named, giving her a more recognisable identity; and her helpful role is emphasised through the description of her as 'our counsellor', a noun phrase using a first-person plural possessive determiner, which casts her as an ally of the charity and its aims. There are other subject positions hinted at: the mother, the ex-boyfriend and the friend he has dumped Katy for.

Why representation matters

Data response exercise 8

1 *Manageress/manager*: the politically incorrect term uses a suffix (-*ess*) to mark gender unnecessarily. If a woman happens to be a manager, why should her title be any different to a man's doing the same job? Some people argue that the term *manageress* confers a lower status on women, suggesting that they are not as powerful as managers.

2 *Postman* is a marked term that potentially excludes female workers from the job. *Postal worker* is a more inclusive and gender-neutral alternative.

3 *Male nurse* marks the job title for gender and problematises the word *nurse*. If the male modifier was added to counter a default assumption that all nurses are women, then it only really draws more attention to the strangeness of a man being a nurse. This operates in much the same way as *doctor* and *lady doctor*, where the marking of gender is completely unnecessary.

4 *His* is a male pronoun and potentially excludes females. *Their* is gender neutral and avoids this problem. Some purists might argue that *their* is a plural pronoun and should therefore not be used with each, but most linguists see this as a minor problem.

5 *Mankind* is a male noun: some would say it is being used generically and thereby excluding women or denying their equal status. *Humankind* is more inclusive.

Social groups and representation

Data response exercise 9

There is no feedback for this exercise.

Data response exercise 10

A brief explanation for these terms is given below, but these are by no means the full story for each word.

a Nigger — A term for a black person (usually of African origin) that derives from the Latin for the colour black (*niger*) and which has passed through Spanish, Italian and possibly French before becoming a recognised term of abuse in English.

The respelling (*nigga*) and, some would say, **semantic reclamation** of the word, are still hotly debated.

b Paki — A shortened version of the word *Pakistani*, referring to a person from Pakistan, but often used to refer to anyone from Asia or the Middle East. Many people view the word as having a racist function.

c Half-caste — A term used to label people of mixed race. The word derives from the Latin *castus* meaning pure, so literally comes to mean half-pure. No prizes for guessing which half was seen as 'pure'.

d Cracker — A term with contested etymology that is used to label poor white people in the USA. Some have argued it comes from the diet of cracked corn eaten by poor white labourers, or that the crack refers to the whip used by slave-owners to discipline their slaves.

e Yid — A term to label a Jewish person that derives from the word *Yiddish*, meaning Jewish.

f	Mongrel	Originally used to refer to mixed-breed dogs, this term developed pejorative connotations and was applied to mixed-race people from the 16th century onwards.
g	Chink	A term used to label people from China. One suggested etymology is that it relates to the physical appearance of the eyes and to an older meaning of *chink* as *slit*.
h	Raghead	According to the *Etymology Online* website this word has been around from 1921 to describe a person of South Asian or Middle Eastern appearance, presumably in reference to headgear.

Data response exercise 11

A brief summary of possible definitions for these words is given here, but it is important to explore word origins and definitions in more depth yourself. Suggestions for further study and tips for research methodology are given in Coursework preparation, pages 190–196.

a	Gay	This is a word that has undergone some significant semantic shifts over time. Once meaning bright and happy, it's been applied to sexually active men (hetero- and homosexual) 3–4 centuries, but has more recently been applied to homosexual men, first as a pejorative label, then as a self-labelling badge and now as a broader term in slang use for *useless*, *rubbish* or *pathetic*.
b	Faggot	Now used as a term of abuse for gay men, this term is believed to have originated from a word for a bundle of sticks, semantically drifted to mean a burden and then drifted again to relate to a useless person who followed an army around.
c	Lesbian	A term that derives from the Greek island Lesbos, home to the poet Sappho whose work included celebrations of homosexual love between women.
d	Homosexual	A 19th-century coinage derived from Greek and Latin (same + sex). Many gay men object to it because it was first used as a medical term to describe what was perceived as a sexual abnormality.
e	Straight/bent	A metaphorical pair that connotes deviance from the norm, or some kind of twisting out of shape.
f	Battyman	Originally from Jamaican patois (batty = bottom), this has spread into wider usage as a term of abuse for gay men. The synecdoche of the body part standing for the whole person's identity is widely considered offensive.
g	Person of same-sex orientation	A politically correct alternative to some of the above terms. This example perhaps illustrates the concern that some examples

of PC language are complex and wordy phrases that are prone to criticism and mockery themselves.

h	Queer	Originally an adjective meaning *strange*, this has now shifted to relate to sexual orientation, with some gay activists reclaiming the word to celebrate their difference from the norm.

Institutions and representation

Data response exercise 12

Dawkins' position is clearly stated, to say the least! His antipathy towards religion is well documented and these two Data extracts offer a rhetorical demolition of some of Christianity's most fundamental beliefs.

Register and lexical choices: Dawkins uses a mixture of sophisticated and quite colloquial registers to achieve different results. By using a list of quite sophisticated, Latinate adjectives in the second extract, he appears well educated but also humorously self-aware. There seems to be a clear relish to the hyperbole used in his list, which is undercut a little by his more casual use of terms such as 'control-freak' and 'bully', nouns that perhaps draw a reader's attention to the mix of registers he uses and the playfulness behind that. He uses a similar approach in the first extract, mixing 'inerrant' with 'weird'.

Modification: Dawkins' use of 'jealous and proud' post-modifies the proper noun *God*, while his rhetorical listing of adjectives ('misogynistic, homophobic …') pre-modifies the noun *bully*. Elsewhere he modifies his adjectives with adverbs ('*chaotically* cobbled-together anthology' and 'much of the Bible is not *systematically* evil but *just plain weird*'). Dawkins' use of adverbials is interesting in other ways: his apparent even-handedness in the adverbial phrase 'To be fair' at the start of the first extract, and the adverb 'arguably' in the second extract is deceptive, as he is only being 'fair' by not claiming the Bible is 'systematically evil'. Damning by faint praise indeed!

Data response exercise 13

The Ian Blair extract is characterised by its spoken mode and is organised around a clear discourse structure and rhetorical techniques. The use of several abstract nouns and noun phrases ('community cohesion', 'anti-social behaviour', 'civil society') is a result of the focus on the police service and its role in wider society, while nominalisation ('the degradation of communal life') is used as a form of shorthand to describe a set of conditions that are presented to the reader as a form of unquestionable truth. Elsewhere, a more colloquial and accessible register, full of concrete nouns, is employed to strike a chord of recognition: 'the neighbours from hell, the smashed bus stop, the lift shaft littered with needles and condoms.' A reader might question some of these assumptions – that society is going to the dogs, that the police can fill the vacuum created by social decay, that these 'three trends' are the only factors in the bigger picture – but Blair's language is designed to position himself, the police and us as readers in a particular way.

In the other extract, David Simon's style is very different, and probably related to the non-fictional written form adopted, as well as his own outsider's view of police life. His register is much more colloquial, his grammar more self-consciously casual (actually rather less formal than Blair's spoken mode and his use of technical lexis ('AT&T equipment', 'police dispatcher') more hard-bitten. This perhaps creates a sense of him as a jaded, cynical surveyor of the reality of police life and its mundane grimness, rather than the visionary and socially engaged position Blair attempts to project.

And while Ian Blair's language strives to elevate the police to the position of an essential social institution, Simon's language evokes the day-to-day rituals of a serving police officer and the concrete nouns ('spent bullets, casings, blood droplets') reflect the investigative procedures and the attention to detail that are required to solve cases.

■ Events, issues and representation

■ Data response exercise 14

Some of the features that you might have noticed are suggested here.

1 **Pronoun use**: The predominant use of the first-person plural *we* in a subject position ('We drove straight back') and *us* in an object position ('They were trying to … trap some of us') is linked to the soldier's perception of himself as part of a wider team. The use of *they*, the third-person plural refers to the militias and establishes a clear distinction between 'we' the British soldiers and 'they' the enemy.

2 **Lexical choices and register:** The text is apparently from an interview with British soldiers and appears quite colloquial in its register at times. Phrases such as 'a lot of shooting' and the sentence 'It was pretty fierce' sound rather mundane, but perhaps hint at the way in which this soldier treats armed conflict as a day-to-day occurrence in his life. In a sense, the language he uses naturalises his experience: his spoken, casual register making the conflict seem less out of the ordinary to a reader. Elsewhere, a quite specialist lexis is used, with initialisms like 'GPMG', 'RPG' and 'PJCC' used, perhaps suggesting technical expertise and experience of conflict to the reader, while less specialist terms such as 'rounds' and 'mortars and rockets' are all drawn from the semantic field of warfare, but are less technical to most readers.

3 **Active and passive voice**: The use of the passive voice is quite noticeable in this extract, with two examples showing that the British troops ('we'), while functioning as grammatical subjects, are the receiver of different verbs' actions. For example, 'we were getting repeatedly ambushed' and 'We were told'. Looking at the use of the active voice in some constructions, when the 'enemy' ('they') are subjects in some examples, the British troops and their vehicles are the objects of the verbs ('they would

be waiting for us', 'they were hitting the vehicles' and 'they were trying to … hit the ones in the rear and separate the convey and trap some of us'). The combined effect of these passive and active constructions might be to show the control that the enemy had in this situation and the lack of control the soldier felt he and his colleagues had. Rarely do we see an active construction in which the British troops seem to have the enemy in their sights. Even when the soldier talks about firing his weapon, he isn't specific about who he is aiming at, only about how many rounds he fires.

4 **Tense and aspect**: The tenses used to organise this account are quite interesting. The opening use of past perfect ('we had left Basra') sets up a distant time frame against which other actions in the past can be sequenced. This is then followed by the past progressive 'as we were unloading …', which helps establish a sense of ongoing action that is about to be interrupted by a simple past tense clause 'we came under attack'. The use of the past progressive crops up in 'We were getting repeatedly ambushed', 'they were hitting the vehicles' and 'What they were trying to do …', all creating a sense of continuing action, adding to the effects discussed above with **voice** to create an impression that, for a while, the British troops seemed to be constantly under attack.

■ Data response exercise 15

1 **Tense and aspect**: The text opens with a present progressive followed by a simple present tense ('BRITAIN *is living* in fear as crime *soars*'). These help create the impression that the situation is ongoing and affecting us even as we read the text.

2 **Register and lexical choices**: The lexical style of the article is quite typical of the tabloid press in many respects. Verbs like 'rocketing', 'leapt' and 'jumped', which are used to describe the crime statistics, are semantically powerful choices that accentuate the newspaper's viewpoint. Meanwhile, the choice of verbs and verb phrases such as '*twist* the statistics and *play down* the crisis' help position the paper as disbelieving observers of the government. Other verb choices are interesting too, setting up a neat distinction between the factive verbs 'revealed', 'proved' and 'disclosed' (in paragraphs 1, 3 and 4 respectively) and the less certain 'claimed' that is used in paragraph 6 to characterise the government's position.

Elsewhere, colloquial terms such as 'thugs', 'muggers' and 'junkies' adopt the register of the target audience, perhaps naturalising the use of such terms and the 'common sense' notion that society is falling prey to such people.

1 **Sentence and clause linking**: Simple sentences are used repeatedly at the end of the extract to draw attention to particular statistics. While quite lengthy noun phrases are used to begin these sentences ('Wounding and violence involving weapons' and 'Murder, manslaughter and killing of infants'), the basic grammatical structure still follows a subject – verb – adverbial form. This simplicity of structure helps to emphasise each statistic.

Introduction

The second part of the coursework folder is a text you've produced that consciously contributes to the representation of someone or something. This topic briefly looks at what's involved and how this section of the book can help you.

Decisions, decisions...

The specification demands that you create a text that 'produces or challenges' a representation, and that you submit a commentary with that text showing how you've created it. There are three key initial decisions to be made:

1 Are you going to produce or challenge a representation?
2 What or whom are you representing?
3 What kind of text are you creating?

This section of the book shows some possibilities to make these decisions easier. You will examine texts, as in the previous section, but from a different perspective, using them as genre examples to see how texts can be crafted to challenge representation, rather than how texts can unintentionally create representations.

The actual submission

This part of the coursework will consist of a text of about 600 words, and a commentary of about 400 words. The specification states:

The text should have a clear genre other than an academic one such as an essay. The intended audience, purpose and place of publication should be specified as much as is appropriate to the genre. Genres may be literary or non-literary.

The commentary will defend the representation and explain linguistically how you have created it. Basically, a commentary is a kind of analysis of your own writing using linguistic frameworks to explain how the desired effects have been produced. You can give a brief indication of graphological features of the text, but this is not a key aspect and need not take up much time.

There are examples and exercises in this section of the book, and it's a good idea to try out different kinds of writing before you decide. You may feel that it's wasted work, but view it as valuable practice that will improve your writing overall and ensure that you submit the best piece possible. There are probably forms here that you haven't tried writing before, and if you don't try a few, you'll probably choose something you're familiar with. Maybe you're a born satirist and you don't know it yet ...

AQA Examiner's tip

Although there will be a range of possibilities presented in this book, it should **not** be viewed as a list to choose from. Any text is suitable as long as it centres on a representation issue and is recognisable as an example of its intended genre. Don't be limited by the suggestions, use them as a starting point!

Your text can therefore:

- be **about** representation, for example:
  - a newspaper article about the media treatment of someone in the news
  - a blog piece about rappers and their use of 'the N word'

- **create** a different representation of something, for example:
  - a fairy tale in which a princess wants a career and doesn't want to be married off
  - a comedy sketch describing Christians in the alarmist way other religions are sometimes treated.

Making those decisions

You'll probably find that one (or even two) of the three choices is far easier than the others. You may know that, no matter what else, you'll be writing about gender representation, or defending a celebrity who's getting a bashing in the tabloids, or showing how football fans aren't automatically hooligans. Alternatively, you may love the idea of writing for children, or doing a polemical piece for a newspaper, or creating a character introduction to slot into a novel. The production of a representation may appeal, or you may feel that challenging existing ideas is the way for you. Having studied Unit 2, Section A Investigating representations, you'll have a good idea of the range of people, groups and institutions that could be covered. You've also encountered some of the types of possible text, both here in Unit 2 and in the Language and mode section of Unit 1. You may want to link your production piece to your investigation, to challenge the representations that you've been examining. You may feel that the opportunity to work with the representation of two completely different things is more exciting. It is your coursework, and the moderators like to see a range of things, so don't make an instant, rushed decision about what and how to write. You've more chance of producing something good that way.

Topic revision summary

- Your coursework requires you to produce a text of 600 words with a commentary of 400 words.
- You have three decisions to make: what to write; whether to produce or challenge a representation; and who or what to represent.

Writing skills

In this topic you will:

- understand the planning and drafting process

- learn to avoid some common errors in writing

- develop checking and editing skills

- consider how writing can be used to challenge representations in a deliberate way.

Writing is a valuable skill

Writing is a process; it is not all accomplished in one go. Part of the pleasure of studying English Language at an advanced level is to improve and develop writing skills. Also, writing is probably the key skill that many employers will assume you've gained from the study of English Language at A Level. Moreover, it is a marketable skill.

In this topic, you'll start thinking about the process and craft of writing, practise checking and editing, and examine a list of errors commonly made. If you have developed some bad writing habits, such as a tendency to misspell certain words, now's the time to sort them out. You'll also start to think more carefully about how a writer may plan to challenge or confront stereotyped and problematic representations.

■ Checklist: stages of production work

1 Gather ideas.

2 Consider a few ideas in detail and narrow down to one.

3 Write a plan. Include:
   - ■ detail about the content
   - ■ detail on possible linguistic features to use (this will help enormously at stage 8).

4 Draft the piece.

5 Re-read it for a basic check, noting changes on the draft:
   - ■ Is it accurate? (Check spelling, punctuation, register.)
   - ■ Does it make sense?

6 Re-read it for effect, noting changes on the draft:
   - ■ Have you used the right features?
   - ■ Have you overdone it?

7 Make the necessary changes to the piece.

8 Draft the commentary.

9 Check and edit the commentary for accuracy and for meaning.

10 Read both pieces through again and make any final amendments.

■ Ideas – getting and keeping them

You should be prepared to consider a few ideas for your production coursework, rather than picking something early in the process and rejecting everything else. Writing is above all a *creative* process, even if the kind of writing you're doing is not 'creative writing'. It's worth having a place to record any ideas you have about this coursework, so that when you really need to decide, you have some options to consider. Sometimes ideas that you aren't serious about when you first jot them down turn out to be enjoyable and interesting to work on. If you don't record ideas as and when they come to you, you will lose them. Most professional writers carry notebooks to jot down their ideas, and many of these ideas remain undeveloped. Nonetheless, many a tale is told about the idea that was nearly dismissed but that in fact became the basis of a successful piece.

■ Planning basics

The mark of good planning is that you should know precisely what you're going to express before you start actually writing. A useful plan will take time, but the payoff is improved writing. If you are sitting down to write without knowing what it is you're saying, then you haven't planned enough. It may help to think of planning as the thinking stage – you should not have any thinking about what to say left to do once you've planned. Thinking in the writing stage should only be about exactly how to convey the ideas you've had.

> Planning = what to say   Writing = how to say it

A good plan is specific and detailed, it shouldn't be a shopping list of basic ingredients. Look at these two plans for a newspaper article pointing out how teenagers are commonly represented.

Both plans follow similar lines, but it is likely that the second one would produce a better piece of writing and take less time to write. Thorough planning helps avoid vague comments or waffle, and often results in better ideas, as you are focusing only on what to say. When you write without a detailed plan, you're thinking about the wording of things as well as the ideas, so your attention is divided.

Intro:	use quote from negative source and discuss how negatively it shows teenagers
Para 1:	argue against points made in opening quote
Para 2:	gives examples of teenagers being nice
Para 3:	write about stereotype of violence/aggressive teenagers
Conc:	end with strong points about being fair

Fig. 1 *Plan A*

Intro:	start with quote 'teens roam the streets in packs, picking on the weak and defenceless'; contextualise as typical, note stereotype of teenagers
Para 1:	metaphor of teen/wolf – unpick connotations – vicious, predatory, wild, numbers; connotations of 'picking on' – for amusement
Para 2:	figures about teens and positive contributions (CHECK) – membership of voluntary organisations, involvement in charity etc.; contrast with figures of convicted/asbo'd teens (CHECK)
Para 3:	mini-bio of Harry Castleton (volunteers in shelter as well as playing clarinet in county orchestra and studying 4 A2 levels)
Conc:	return to quote and connect to reality – true for small minority of teens; equiv minority of 20–40 yr old men are rapists, but standard image of man that age not rapist

Fig. 2 *Plan B*

■ Types of plan

There are many different ways of planning work, and the one you use is entirely your choice. The only ways it can be 'wrong' are if it doesn't give you enough detail or if it doesn't make sense to you. Plans are only written for your own use, not for anyone else, so you only need to think about what is logical for you. Some people like linear plans, like the examples above. Others use a mind-map style of diagram to note and connect everything relevant, then order the clusters of ideas to produce a coherent path through the material. There are some examples of this on the next page.

■ Planning and commenting

For this particular task, you have to produce a commentary as well as the text itself. If you plan the text carefully, you can make sure that it helps you to produce a good commentary. Your commentary needs to briefly contextualise your piece – i.e. explain where it would be published and who your audience would be – and it should also explain in a detailed linguistic way how you have achieved what you set out to. To help you with this, a plan for this task should include a reminder of features you could use as well as details of the content. A plan for your production work, in other words, needs to help you with the *how* of writing as well as the *what*.

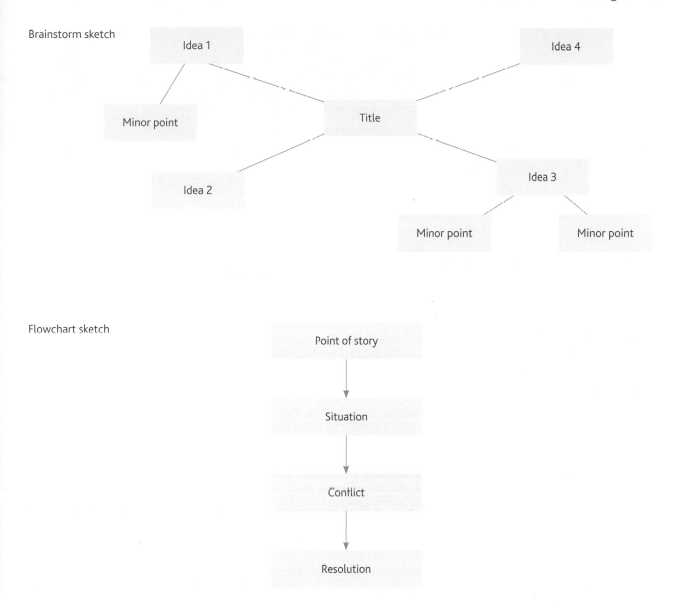

Brainstorm sketch

Flowchart sketch

Fig. 3 *Examples of brainstorm and flowchart sketches*

■ Common errors

It's important that all your written work is accurate, so make sure you know the difference between these commonly confused homophones:

- ■ *There* = anything to do with a place (note that it contains the word 'here') and in sentences about the existence of something. For example: 'There are many metaphors in this text …'
- ■ *Their* = belonging to them.
- ■ *They're* = they are.
- ■ *It's* = it is.
- ■ *Its* = belonging to it. For example: 'The text shows its persuasive intent through …'
- ■ *Whether* = if.

AQA Examiner's tip

Your teacher will probably mark spelling and expression errors in your work. Take note of these and do not repeat the same mistakes. It's not worth losing marks for something that can so easily be fixed.

■ *Weather* = rain, snow, etc.

■ *Which* = relating to a specific one.

■ *Witch* = worker of magic.

There are many other words that are commonly misused or misspelled, so watch out for these too:

■ *A lot* and *in fact* are **always** two separate words.

■ *Maybe* is not the same as *may be*. If 'might be' would make sense in its place, then you need 'may be' (*may be* is a verb phrase, *maybe* is not). For example: 'Maybe you should try it for once. It may be something you'd like.'

■ *Effect* and *affect* are not interchangeable. *Effect* is a noun – things have an effect. *Affect* is a verb – something affects something or someone. There is a verb *to effect* but it has a different meaning: to bring about – it's often used with the noun *change*. For example: 'The effect of this would be … These changes would affect millions.'

🔦 Checking and editing

Many students fail to check their work. This costs marks, since it cuts off the editing part of the process and results in far less polished work. When you check your writing, you are assessing a number of things at once, but primarily you're checking for accuracy of expression (i.e. spelling mistakes, etc.) and for sense. It helps to read aloud. This is not something you can do in an exam situation, but for your coursework it's well worth getting into the habit of reading your work aloud, especially if you have any thoughts of writing as part of your career later. Reading aloud helps to catch overlong sentences or those sentences that you never quite finished, especially if you make sure you pause after each sentence and consider each as a single unit. If spelling is an issue, it can help to check backwards, one word at a time from the end to the start. This works because when reading sentences, we don't always notice the words within them. If you pay attention to each word individually, however, it's easier to see those errors.

Checking and editing go together – there's no point spotting changes that need to be made, if you're not going to make them! Some people like to correct anything they spot straight away, others just note that something's wrong and come back to it another time. That can be a good way of separating the critical, fault-spotting work from the creative rewriting work. It can be helpful to run through several edits of a text, especially if it is long or, like this coursework, needs more than one kind of check. Novelists sometimes run through separate edits to look at aspects such as each character's development, the setting and plot development. For the production piece, you'll probably need to edit it for accuracy and sense, and separately for the effect. You're supposed to be deliberately creating or questioning a particular representation, and it's worthwhile doing a read-through and edit specifically asking yourself whether you've achieved that aim to the best of your ability. The commentary needs an edit for accuracy and sense as well, of course, and also a check to make sure you've included the best possible features and sufficient analytical detail.

Coursework activity 1

Rewrite the piece below, correcting the errors. Check your ideas against the feedback (page 199).

The way women are represented in the tabloids is discusting. There looks are always wrote about. Although mens looks aren't comented on very often. There always linked to there families, how many children theyve got and thats not always relevent.

Producing and challenging representation

There are several ways of challenging existing representations. You can write something critical that explicitly highlights and questions the representation in question. This kind of text is likely to appear in a media context. Alternatively, you can write something that ridicules the representation in a subtle or exaggerated way, using satire or reversal. This kind of text has a far wider range of possible genres, including comedy routines, children's stories and literary writing, as well as also possibly appearing in the media. The texts you've encountered in Unit 1, Section A Language and mode and Unit 2, Section A Investigating representations will have given you some ideas about the range of texts available to you, but there are other possible genres not included in this book.

Topic revision summary

- Keep a record of *all* possible ideas for your production work as you work through this section.
- Plan your content *in detail* before writing.
- The format of your plan needs to make sense *to you*.
- Include possible linguistic features to use in your plan, to start your commentary later.
- It *is* important to write accurately.
- You must leave *time* for checking and editing.
- Expect to check and edit *separately* for accuracy and effectiveness.

Producing representations for a media audience

In this topic you will:

- examine some existing media texts that produce and challenge representations

- explore the range of contexts within the bracket of the media

- begin to collect some ideas for your coursework production.

Representation in the media

The media are a key place that representation is examined and debated. In preparing for your investigation in the last section, you have encountered many examples of representations. Some were produced unthinkingly by the simple use of stereotypes and unquestioned assumptions, such as the sentences in Data response exercise 1 on page 130. Other texts, however, deliberately question the use of particular words and phrases to represent groups of people, individuals and institutions, such as Eve Kay's piece 'Call me Ms' on page 144. In your production coursework, you are required to create a 'positive intervention', so if you choose a media text, you must write one of the second type. Your media writing needs to question, challenge or argue for particular usage.

In this topic, you will look at some texts to get a feel for the genre features needed. You will also engage in activities to get you thinking about what kinds of writing are possible for this part of the coursework, and will practise writing some extracts and begin to develop your commentary skills.

Types of media writing

'The media' is a broad label and seems to include more kinds of text all the time. Newspapers, magazines, the radio and television are what we first think of, but web-based material must also now be included.

Coursework activity 2

List a range of possible media texts that could be used for this coursework activity. Do not only note the ones you'd like to use, but include everything at this point. When you run out of ideas, think about the following:

- Where would you look for a text for a specialist audience?
- Have you included spoken media texts?
- What kinds of text are specific to the internet?

Check your ideas against the feedback (page 199).

Writing feature articles

Since feature articles are such a large part of this field, we will look specifically at how to write those here. The basic ingredients in terms of parts of the text (textual segments) are similar for newspapers, magazines and websites.

Coursework activity 3

1. Gather a range of at least five feature articles from various sources on any topic. Ideally you would include broadsheet and tabloid newspapers, different magazines and website pieces.

2. Note the graphological features that they all have in common (refer to The linguistic frameworks toolkit on page 206 if you need to check terms).

3. Note the features or segments that at least two of them share.

4. Note how many of them address the audience directly.

5. Note what kinds of evidence they offer for their claims/statements/opinions.

Check your ideas against the feedback (page 199).

Extension activity

Compare the linguistic detail of the feature articles to get a more detailed picture of how each relates to its context. Look for tone, audience positioning and mode features in particular, but you may also notice uses of imagery or particular grammatical patterns.

 Examiner's tip

If you choose to write a text not discussed in this book, repeat this exercise for 'your' genre. Remember the texts you examine for this purpose do not need to have anything to do with representation or your topic – it's the form, structure and style you're looking at.

The more specific linguistic detail of these feature articles is likely to vary a lot more. You can get a good sense of the genre or form features by looking at a wide spread of texts; but to see, for example, what kind of lexical register to use, or whether imagery is frequent, you need to go to the specific context you want.

Positioning yourself and your audience

When writing media texts, students frequently struggle with getting the voice right. As you saw in Language and mode (page 27), and in Investigating representations (page 156), texts represent the writer in a particular way, and also make assumptions about the audience. This is true no matter what the genre, but if you choose to write a media text about representation, it's particularly important to give this some thought.

Data response exercise 1

The extract below is the beginning of a feature article on the way people react to a stay-at-home father. How does the writer represent herself and her audience?

'Oh, can't he get a job?' says the irritatingly nosey woman on the bus. I've just told her, after a series of increasingly rude and personal questions, that my husband stays at home with our two daughters while I work full time. 'No, it's not that,' I reply flatly (this isn't the first time). 'It's his job to take care of the girls and the house.' 'Oh' she replies, not getting it at all.

It's not particularly hard to understand, but somehow something about our domestic arrangement is just Too Much for some people to cope with. It isn't even that unusual anymore – government figures show 189,600 men fulfilling home and care responsibilities instead of being 'economically active' in spring 2005. It intrigues me, the reactions we get, because it really says something about the stereotypes people clearly still cling to, despite living in these modern times 'n' all.

■ **Data response exercise 2**

Now have a look at the following extract from a commentary relating to the article above. It's a good example of how to comment on your own writing. What do you think is good about it?

Check your ideas against the feedback (page 199).

In my article, I have created a friendly tenor between myself and the reader in several ways. By opening with the reference to the 'irritatingly nosey woman', the audience is clearly taken into my confidence. I'm letting them know that they are not like her, so they are positioned with me. The detailed description of her fleshes her out quite quickly and in a strongly negative way, using the adverb 'irritatingly' to modify the adjective 'nosey'. This pattern is repeated with 'increasingly rude' on the next line. The generally conversational style of the article also supports the friendly tenor. I capitalise the phrase 'Too Much' to emphasise its importance and to use blended mode features. I also use speech-like syntax in 'It intrigues me, the reactions we get …' by delaying the subject.

■ **Audience issues**

As you saw in Coursework activity 2, there is a huge range of possibilities in the field of the media. Each has its own conventions and it is worth exploring a range before making any final decision. Also in Coursework activity 2, 'specialist audiences' were identified as a category, and the extract below is taken from such a website. PinkNews states on the site: 'We cover stories we believe to be of interest to a primarily gay UK audience … if a story passes the office, "I'd find that interesting" test, we will spend the time to research and write an article on it' (www. pinknews.co.uk).

COMMENT: Not all representation is positive

25-August-06
Tony Grew

Should we be happy that the rather shallow humour of *Little Britain* is being exported to America? Or that more and more companies are commissioning 'gay' adverts to appeal to homo-consumers?

Representation is always a slippery issue. Tony Grew muses on whether more adverts and more gay jokes are a good thing.

The announcement today that *Little Britain* is to be remade for an American audience has generally been interpreted as a triumph for UK comedy talent.

The rationale seems to be that Americans have taken to British humour for the first time since *Monty Python*, and we should all be proud that our comedy is being appreciated once again. While I welcome exposing US audiences to Julia Davis' darker-than-dark *Nighty Night*, I am more troubled by *Little Britain*.

Gay audiences have warmed to the characters of Daffyd, Emily Howard and Sebastian, the Prime Minister's bitchy assistant.

But what do these characters actually say about gay people? Well first, let's examine Daffyd.

The 'joke' in the Daffyd sketches – and let's be clear, with Lucas and Walliams there is only one joke – is that he is so obviously gay but thinks no-one else is.

Fair enough. Much of the comedy comes from Matt Lucas' outrageous costumes, and it is brave of him to display himself in them, but I wonder how much of the comedy in Little Britain is actually laughing AT gay people, not with them.

The fact that Lucas is gay is not a get-out-of-jail-free card against accusations of fostering homophobia. It is all about context.

When *Little Britain* was a cult programme, it was easy to argue that its brand of humour was aimed at a BBC3-type viewer, one with a discerning taste and a deeper understanding of the actual reality of gay life.

When it is some Essex white-van man with a can of Stella resting on his belly, chortling at the funny fat faggot mincing round being flamboyantly gay, it becomes much harder to argue that the programme is having a positive impact.

www.pinknews.co.uk

In this example of writing for a specialist audience, the conventions of feature article writing largely apply. Audience positioning is to some extent easier when writing for a context which explicitly defines its audience. It is probably best to only consider writing for specialist audiences that you happen to belong to naturally, though, unless you explicitly take the stance of writing as an outsider.

■ Extension activity

Follow the URL in Data extract 3 and read the whole PinkNews piece as a model of writing about representation in the media. Use it as a basis to think about texts you could produce – connecting to its form and style (a feature article for the web), its topic (homosexuality and its representation) or its approach (how is more visibility of x good/bad?)

■ Coursework activity 4

Think about the specialist audiences that you belong to and research possible outlets. For example, you might start with your gender and age, then other social categories and finally interest groups. You will almost certainly find web material for most of these audience groups, and there may be radio and print outlets.

Once you have a collection, look at their audiences more closely and determine whether you do really fit. Alternatively, you could start by looking at the media sources you already use and do this exercise backwards – why does xx magazine appeal to you, or how do you fit into its audience? Once that's done, still try to find media outlets that are new to you whose audience you fit into

Check your ideas against the feedback (page 199).

■ Spoken media

Speeches are probably the most popular choice in this category, although it is also possible to write for a radio audience for this topic. Speeches can be used to engage with and challenge an existing representation, or you may choose to contribute to the representation of someone or something. If you want to write a speech, check the planned speech section of Unit 1 again (page 19) and think carefully about the precise context. Who would be giving the speech, where and to whom?

■ Data response exercise 3

The next extract is Tony Blair's statement to the press following the death of Diana, Princess of Wales in 1997.

How does this speech use the conventions of planned speeches to create a representation of Diana?

Check your ideas against the feedback (page 199).

Fig. 4 *Tony Blair's statement to the press following Diana's death*

I am utterly devastated. The whole of our country, all of us, will be in a state of shock and mourning. Diana was a wonderful, warm and compassionate person who people, not just in Britain, but throughout the world, loved and will mourn as a friend. Our thoughts and prayers are with her family, in particular with her two sons, and with all of the families bereaved in this quite appalling tragedy.

I feel like everyone else in this country today – utterly devastated. Our thoughts and prayers are with Princess Diana's family – in particular her two sons, two boys – our hearts go out to them. We are today a nation, in Britain, in a state of shock, in mourning, in grief that is so deeply painful for us.

She was a wonderful and warm human being. Though her own life was often sadly touched by tragedy, she touched the lives of so many others in Britain – throughout the world – with joy and with comfort. How many times shall we remember her, in how many different ways, with the sick, the dying, with children, with the needy, when, with just a look or a gesture that spoke so much more than words, she would reveal to all of us the depth of her compassion and her humanity. How difficult things were for her from time to time, surely we can only guess at – but the people everywhere, not just here in Britain but everywhere, they kept faith with Princess Diana, they liked her, they loved her, they regarded her as one of the people. She was the people's princess and that's how she will stay, how she will remain in our hearts and in our memories forever.

Topic revision summary

- 'The media' covers a huge range of texts, not just newspapers and magazines.
- Research the genre features of the form you choose to write in.
- Use your own experiences in deciding who/what to write for and about – do explore niche publications and outlets that cater to your interests.
- Consider how you position yourself and your reader in writing.
- Be specific and detailed in your commentary.

Producing representations for children

In this topic you will:

■ explore how some existing children's texts work with representations

■ examine some issues in writing for children.

An opportunity to challenge expectations

Children's texts are often examined for representation and stereotypes. Older texts especially are interesting to look at in terms of outdated assumptions, while many recent texts for children play with representation and challenge more traditional and stereotypical ideas. Fairy tales offer particularly fertile ground for revisiting and challenging expectations, and even quite young children can appreciate the humour in twisting a fairy tale to produce unexpected characterisations and outcomes.

In this topic, you will consider fiction and non-fiction for children and gather some ideas about possible texts for a coursework submission. You'll also be able to think about how people write for children (what techniques and features to use), plan a text, and examine an existing non-fiction text for children about disability.

Writing for children

In writing for children, many people assume that you need to write simply in short sentences. This is just not true. Even early graded reading books are not solely in simple sentences, as they would be so boring to read. It's also not true that the lexis in children's books is simple – there are many complex words used even in picture books, especially if they contribute to a phonological effect. In a sense, children are accustomed to not understanding every word spoken, so they are better at letting language wash over them than adults. In completing the following exercises, remember that you can be more adventurous and playful with language, especially with phonology, in texts for children. If you do decide to make your coursework text one for children, don't worry about the graphology. You may of course indicate that your text is for a picture book, for example, but you should not produce the illustrations yourself.

In this topic you will explore some of the possibilities for writing representations for children. There are examples of texts here that can be parodied, and others that deliberately challenge representation, to help you build up your ideas collection. You will produce some short pieces of text for children, and practise your commentary skills.

Coursework activity 5

Make a list of possible texts for children that could be written for this section of the coursework. When you run out of ideas, think about the range of texts you've encountered in this unit so far, and consider whether equivalent texts for children are possible.

Check your ideas against the feedback (page 199).

Working with fiction

Fiction offers the chance to consider other viewpoints, in some cases literally to visit other worlds. It is often through fiction that we begin to understand other people's way of life. It is thus an ideal way to offer positive interventions into the representation of particular groups or cultures, allowing children to experience something outside themselves.

If we start with the youngest age group, we must consider picture books – that is, the storybooks for preschool children that feature colour illustrations on every page, with only a sentence or two of text. Examining how babies' books represent the world would be a less useful task for this coursework, since there is often only a single word or phrase for each picture.

Coursework activity 6

Discuss with a partner some ideas for early storybooks that offer positive interventions into representation. Create a list of possibilities together that includes different groups to be represented.

Check your ideas against the feedback (page 200).

Coursework activity 7

Three concerns are mentioned in the feedback to Coursework activity 6. Check that each idea on your list addresses at least one of them. If you have gaps or imbalances, try to address those now. Does one type of intervention appeal to you more than the others? Note down the things that occur to you, as they may be helpful in your planning and decision making later on.

Check your ideas against the feedback (page 200).

How to get fiction ideas

Fiction of all kinds revolves around conflict – and for children, that conflict must always be resolved within the story. It's also one of the golden rules of writing for children that the child or children must resolve the conflict without adult intervention. If everything is normal and happy and going along nicely, there's no story – you need something to happen to your characters in order to give you a plot.

One way of coming up with possible plot ideas is to use the 'what if?' technique. Fiction is all about 'what ifs?' In your case, since you're producing your text for a specified purpose (to contribute to the representation of someone/something), you need to keep that in mind as your theme.

Stories for older children

If you were going to write for a picture book audience, you could produce a whole story, as the 600-word limit would work for a picture book. For an older audience, however, you'd only be able to produce part of a text – perhaps a chapter of a book for seven to ten-year olds, or a couple of pages of a novel for 'older readers'. The most effective way of approaching this is either to write the beginning of something, or to have a clear plan, so you know where the extract you're producing will slot in. You could also consider producing a short story for this age group, perhaps with the genre of a children's magazine or comic in mind.

Obviously, writing for older children has different challenges to writing for the preschool age group. The representation aspect of your text has more scope with the older ones, too – you could more easily write about 'issues' for a slightly older audience. Think about Jacqueline Wilson's work, for example – she has done a great deal for the representation of children under state care, but her sometimes gritty realism would not be considered appropriate in picture books.

Getting the voice right

Many stories for the 'middle market' (ages seven to ten) are written in the third person, with the main character's thoughts being represented in the writing. This is known as third-person limited narration, as opposed to third-person omniscient narration, where the narrator is godlike and knows everything. Some are written in the first person, with a child character addressing the audience directly and explaining their situation and thoughts. How to narrate your story is another decision to be made.

Working with non-fiction

This area is broader than you might at first think. There are media outlets for children, so you could try a newspaper, magazine or radio piece addressing a representation issue directly. If you're interested in tackling an issue or institution, a 'Horrible Histories' style treatment might be appropriate. For the representation of issues and groups of people, there are children's books explicitly about these subjects. The extract below comes from a book called *What do you know about people with disabilities?* intended to encourage children to discuss and think about the issues involved.

Coursework activity 8

Imagine you've decided to write the opening of a novel for seven to ten-year-olds. Think about and note the advantages and disadvantages of each kind of narration. Remember that representation is the focus of your writing and consider specifically how first- or third-person narration would impact that.

Check your ideas against the feedback (page 200).

A DISABILITY IS OFTEN DESCRIBED AS AN IMPAIRMENT OR MEDICAL CONDITION WHICH PREVENTS SOMEONE FROM PERFORMING A SPECIFIC TASK OR FUNCTION

However, many people consider that it is not the impairment itself which is disabling, but the fact that society often limits the opportunities which are available to disabled people.

An impairment may be caused by the loss of part or all of a limb, or by an organ or mechanism of the body not working properly. A physical impairment affects the working of the body. A learning impairment or difficulty restricts a person's mental development. People become disabled when, as a result of their impairment, they are faced with physical and social barriers which make it difficult for them to participate fully within the community.

Wheelchair users may be 'disabled' by an environment which denies them access to places simply because they are not accessible to wheelchair users.

■ **Data response exercise 4**

Which features does the extract on the previous page use to appeal to its child audience? Pay attention to graphological features as well as the language used.

Check your ideas against the feedback (page 200).

Non-fiction for children tends to introduce terminology and jargon gently – you should expect to define any technical lexis you use. You should also be thinking about the graphology (although, remember, you don't need to produce any diagrams or illustrations), as children's non-fiction is usually very well laid out, with various sections, and careful use of colour and images. For this issues-based kind of writing, you need to be careful about your tone – giving any kind of information or instruction on how to treat people is tricky, and a patronising tone will not offer any kind of positive intervention.

Q **Topic revision summary**

- There are many possible texts for a child audience, including media, non-fiction and literary texts.
- Do not patronise or oversimplify in writing for children.
- Use creative brainstorming techniques to get ideas for fiction – ask 'what if?'
- Make sure your topic is age-appropriate for your chosen audience.
- In children's non-fiction, you should explain key terms.

Producing representations to entertain

In this topic you will:

- explore the use of humour in working with representation
- develop an awareness of the range of possibilities in writing to entertain
- encounter some literary representations.

■ The freedom of literary texts

This area, producing literary texts that are intended to entertain as well as provoke and challenge, probably offers the most freedom of all the areas explored here. Literary texts may break rules and taboos that others must observe, and literary audiences often expect such writing to challenge and provoke. Comedy as a form frequently questions society and its assumptions, and it is possible to address serious issues through comedic writing. Media texts aren't able to be quite as free in style, and children's texts naturally have a greater need for clarity.

In this topic, we'll look at some ways in which texts for entertainment can represent and be about representation. Some writers – especially those from groups who have historically been unfairly represented – deliberately play with ideas of representation. As well as literary writing, you will examine writing for performance and consider how humour can be created in texts. At the end of this topic, you will have explored ideas and texts from several key areas.

■ Challenging representation through humour

Humour as a rule frequently operates through gaps. The gap may be between what is expected and what is delivered, or between what there should be and what there is. Often it works by setting the audience up to expect one thing, but giving them another. This is true from the simplest of children's jokes, which often work on puns based on a word with multiple meanings (a word is used in an unexpected way), through to observational comedy that highlights the absurdity of everyday life (behaviour is shown to be irrational or bizarre).

Humour can therefore be a good way of exploring issues of representation, because of its natural association with these gaps and its ability to mock the 'norm'. For example, in the following extract the humour derives from the clearly inappropriate nature of the questioning of the mugged man.

Fig. 5 *Even children's jokes can rely on sophisticated linguistic understanding*

> *Defence lawyer*: So you say you were attacked walking down King's St, sir?
>
> *Victim*: Yes, that's right.
>
> *Defence lawyer*: And it was dark at the time, wasn't it?
>
> *Victim*: Yes, it was around eleven and it was dark.
>
> *Defence lawyer*: And had you heard about the mugging in that area last week?
>
> *Victim*: Yes, I had, but I'm often in that area and it's always been ok before.
>
> *Defence lawyer*: So there you are, walking around on your own in the dark in an area known for muggings. Surprised you were attacked, were you?
>
> *Victim*: Well, yes,…
>
> *Defence lawyer*: And what were you wearing at the time, sir?
>
> *Victim*: Sorry, what? What was I wearing? A suit, a bit like this one.
>
> *Defence lawyer*: I see, so you're strolling around in a dodgy area wearing a suit that screams 'I've got money', right?
>
> *Victim*: Well, er, I hardly think that's …
>
> *Defence lawyer*: Quite right, sir. Bit foolish, weren't we? Could you also confirm your charitable donations for the last year for me, please?
>
> *Victim*: Sorry, what? No, I don't think I can remember them all. I er give regularly to the NSPCC and the RSPCA and…
>
> *Defence lawyer*: Precisely, sir. You are known as a charitable giver. Is there any way we can be certain that the accused did actually have the intention of robbing you? Is it not possible that perhaps he thought you might be willing to give him some of your wealth, knowing that you give regularly to several charities and were displaying your wealth in a very deliberate way?

Student sketch

There is humour here because the situation is clearly ridiculous. The challenging effect, however, is achieved through reference to stereotypical rape victim questioning in which similar arguments have been used to suggest that rape did not take place.

■ Data response exercise 5

Describe and comment on three features that make the extract above effective.

Check your ideas against the feedback (page 200).

■ Writing to fill the gaps

Some writing that is done with the intention of dealing with representation is about filling a gap. Looking at the literary canon – the collection of works generally regarded as 'great' – there are proportionally more books by white upper-and middle-class educated males than other groups. This is now not as true as it once was, and there have been campaigns to discover and study works by non-canonical writers to try to balance things out. The situation has led, however, to some areas of human experience being under-represented in literature, which in turn has prompted some writers to try to fill these gaps. Writing by women is now better represented, but there remain areas of women's experience that are less 'written' than others. This is what prompted *The Vagina Monologues* by Eve Ensler. This work, first performed in 1996, is a performance piece put together from interviews with 200 women about their vaginas. It attempts to correct the fact that for many women and girls, words for their genitalia are taboo.

AQA ✓ Examiner's tip

If you choose to close a representational gap, especially if you use comedy, remember that not all representation is automatically positive. Look again at the PinkNews piece on *Little Britain* and homosexuality at www.pinknews.co.uk

Coursework activity 9

Think about any gaps in representation that you might be able to tackle in your coursework. Note down anything that occurs to you, even if you think you might not be able to use it. Don't be afraid to use your own experience – there is also an issue with people representing 'others', however well-meaning the attempt.

Check your ideas against the feedback (page 201).

Data response exercise 6

The following extract is from one of Ensler's monologues, entitled 'I was there in the room', which describes a birth.

This monologue is structured like a poem and is primarily a piece to be performed rather than read. Select three features from at least two linguistic frameworks and comment on their effect.

Check your ideas against the feedback (page 201).

> I was there when her vagina changed
> from a shy sexual hole
> to an archaeological tunnel, a sacred vessel,
> a Venetian canal, a deep well with a tiny stuck child inside,
> waiting to be rescued.
> …
>
> We forget the vagina, all of us
> what else could explain
> our lack of awe, our lack of wonder.

■ Literary forms

Literary writing is not just novels and short stories. A poem or series of poems could be a successful submission, and don't forget about performance texts. A radio story or play is possible, and the monologue is also a suitable form for this coursework activity, because its length is quite flexible and a 600-word text is usable as a short performance piece. Monologue is also well suited to challenging representation through its direct address to the audience.

Style and literary writing

As noted above, you can be a lot freer with literary writing than with other forms. There are no rules as such but there are standard pieces of advice in writing creatively, the most repeated of which perhaps is to avoid excessive description. Strings of adjectives often slow down the pace of writing and make it less clear what you are trying to say. An oft-repeated guideline is to cut rather than add – less is more. If you have two words of the same class together, maybe you don't really need both; or maybe you need to replace both with one that does the job in a punchier way.

For example: 'The tall, old, twisted tree stood in the graveyard' is less effective than 'The gnarled tree loomed over the graveyard.'

A related piece of advice is to avoid *-ly* adverbs like 'he ran rapidly'; replace the verb with something more specific – 'he sprinted' is better.

Challenging through surprise

Many literary texts tackle representational issues by using an element of surprise or by describing things and people in an unexpected way. The *Noughts and Crosses* trilogy (Marjorie Blackman) achieves this very effectively with its race-reversal theme. Similarly, Jeanette Winterson in *Written on the Body* never reveals the first-person narrator's gender, and it is an interesting exercise to try reading it both ways. In *The Passion of New Eve*, Angela Carter plays with gender representations in numerous ways, but the novel closes with this bizarre individual:

> Here, only seabirds swooped over great cliffs and there was no sign of life until the road brought us to a broadish bay with a wide beach of pebbles, and then petered out into the track it had threatened to become for the last few miles we had been upon it. On this beach, a lone, mad old lady sat in a wicker garden chair that had once been painted bright pink … She did not turn her head to look at us, perhaps she didn't hear us.
>
> It was an impressive head. The hair was dyed a brave canary yellow and piled in an elaboration of many tiers of curls, giving the general impression of a very expensive ice-cream sundae. All was decorated with peek-a-boo bows of pale pink silk ribbon and would have looked well under a glass dome on grandmother's mantlepiece. She was wearing a two-piece bathing costume in a red and white spotted fabric and, round her shoulders, a stole of glossy and extravagant blonde fur but her flesh was wrinkled and ravaged and sagged from the bones. Her face was very dirty but magnificently painted; a fresh coating of white powder and scarlet lipstick and maroon rouge must have been added that very morning. She sang of the lights of Broadway, of foggy days in London Town and how she'd learned her lesson but she wished she were in love again. Her swimming eyes had retreated deeply into her head down cavernous sockets frosted

> with glittering turquoise eye-grease. Her fingernails were fully six inches long and lacquered a glinting red, though badly chipped and scratched. She wore high-heeled silver sandals on her gnarled old feet and sat facing the ocean like the guardian of the shore; her fissured high soprano mingled with the slumbrous chords of the sea.

A. Carter, The Passion of New Eve, *1982*

Data response exercise 7

Read the extract on page 193.

1   Note the typical feminine symbols in the passage.

2   Note the ways her feminine aspects are undermined.

3   Explain briefly how the overall effect is created.

Check your ideas against the feedback (page 201).

Coursework activity 11

Plan and draft a piece of literary writing that deals with representation. Remember to plan for linguistic features as well as for content. Write about 300 words, and follow it up with a commentary of about 200 words.

Check your ideas against the feedback (page 201).

Topic revision summary

■ Literary writing offers more freedom than many other forms.

■ Comedy can work well to challenge representation (but be careful you're not inviting an audience to laugh at the person/group/event you're representing).

■ The representation of under-represented groups is worth considering.

■ Literary texts are not only written to be read – consider radio plays and monologues as well.

■ Do not overdescribe in literary writing.

Coursework preparation

Making a choice

Through the last three topics, you have explored a range of texts that work with representation. You should now feel in a position to narrow down the possibilities that you have collected, to make your final choice about coursework pieces. Before starting on your own work, this topic will enable you to check the requirements for the production work and examine these against some sample work, before producing your plan.

AQA's requirements

Your writing for the production piece must:

- be about 600 words

- challenge or produce a representation of a person, group of people, event or institution

- have a clear genre – literary or non-literary

- not be an essay.

Your commentary must:

- be about 400 words

- explain the representation you have created

- show how you have used your knowledge of language to create an effective text.

How the work is assessed

The relevant assessment objective here is:

AO4 Demonstrate expertise and creativity in the use of English in a range of different contexts, informed by linguistic study.

The production and commentary together are worth 20 per cent of the AS marks (i.e. half of the coursework submission). The production piece is marked out of 20 (10 marks each for 'form and content' and 'style and structure'), and the commentary is marked out of 10. The full mark scheme is available in the specification on AQA's website. Accurate writing and a logical structure are just as important as what you're saying. You'll notice also that graphological features are not very important at all – if you spend ages planning layout and colour, and skimp on the actual writing, you won't do very well.

What to do next

You will have amassed a range of ideas in working through the last three topics. If you already know what you want to do, that's great, but if you don't, don't worry, there are a few things you can do to help you decide. Try asking yourself the following questions, and note down your first, gut-reaction answers:

- Is there a genre or form I particularly do or do not want to write in?

- Are there areas of representation that I am especially interested in?

■ Are there areas of representation that I don't care about at all, or don't really understand?

■ What kind of text do I normally like to read or write?

Now go through the ideas you collected in the previous topics and reject those that you don't want to do at all, or rank them according to how much they interest you. Maybe you can instantly reject anything literary, or satirical, or for children? Try to narrow it down, but don't forget that the ideas covered here are not the only possibilities. Try thinking *around* the activities here – what other things might be feasible? Discuss the options with a friend or with your teacher. It will make a difference in your marks if you are interested and engaged in your writing.

💡 A sample answer

Have a look at this student response to the task. As you read it, think about how he achieves what he's trying to do. Identify some language features he uses that he could discuss in his commentary.

A Letter from a Ghost

Representation Creative Writing

I'm only a ghost. A shadow of a human; ostracised from the public wherever possible and spat on by those who dare. Thirty long years have passed, each day melting into the last and yet, I find myself happy.

I didn't mean for it to happen. It just sort of … did. I didn't ask for any of it, didn't want any of it. Life plays out that way, you know? I thought, a few days, that's all it'll need to be. I'm still waiting for that deadline to finish. But whilst I live out here, you live in there, mocking me.

You think you're so good, don't you? You walk around with an air of dignity, and you think you're better than me. If you can bring yourself to acknowledge my existence, your eyes bore into mine, filled with hate, disgust or sympathy. But either way, you still think you're higher then me.

Why?

Why do you think of me as a piece of dirt? I've seen some TV, and know that you worry about those in Africa who are filthy, starving and dying. Yet you conveniently forget to wonder about our hygiene; our stomachs; our lives. You care more for them than your fellow Englishman. You give £3 a month to the WWF but order me to 'move on' when I'm in your sight. You enjoy a nice cold beer at the local pub but turn in disgust when you see me with a can. You are shocked and horrified when a person commits suicide but couldn't care less if I've 'disappeared'.

I didn't come here by choice, you know. My life is nothing but trial after trial. Occasionally I'll talk, asking for the pennies people are willing to part with. Other times I'll just sit there, looking up to the Lord, arms clasped in 'prayer', whilst I hear the occasional sound of money being dropped in front of me.

So what if I waste it? If you lived in the streets, had no friends or family, wouldn't you try any way you can to improve it? We're not all druggies you know. I buy alcohol. I buy cigarettes. But only *after* I've eaten. So when you walk past me and look away as if that means I don't exist, know this. My parents abused me. I was a punch bag that took nine months to personally make. If you would continue to live there, be my guest. As for me; I wanted out. As a child, my naivety led to the belief that going away for a while would make everything better.

My brother died the night I left, killed when my parents' anger reached an incredible height after my departure.

Now, thirty years on, I've found peace. There's discomfort here in abundance, but there's no more physical pain. Sure, the teenagers will come and throw things at me because I'm an entity lower than the mud they run away on, but it's heaven compared to my former existence.

I have no idea what my name is, and would you care? People see my meagre possessions and conclude that I've found them or stolen them, because I couldn't possibly have brought them from my home or brought the items to keep me company during the long, winter nights. You people see a homeless person and conclude that I'm stoned on drugs and therefore dangerous, that I'm there deliberately to be a nuisance or an ignorant shit that needs to be ignored and hastily retreated from, or that I'm so drunk that trying to make sense out of me would be just downright stupid.

You don't like me. You never will. I have an image set down in imaginative stone. Indisputable. Unchangeable. Regardless of the circumstances that brought me here, I'm nothing to you. Yet you know what? I don't care. I'm only a ghost.

Examiner's comment

This is a very effective piece in many ways. The strongest feature is probably the voice – he uses the first-person narrative very effectively and addresses us with the second person in a powerful way. The syntax is also strong – the snappy simple sentences offer sharp and sometimes shocking comments. As for marks, this would score highly – 9 out of 10 each for form/content and style/structure.

A sample commentary

Have a look at this student's commentary now and see whether he selects the same things for comment as you would.

A Letter from a Ghost

Commentary

The audience of this piece was aimed at around 16 onwards, but particularly adults, because they probably have a stronger negative viewpoint of the homeless. I have deliberately danced around the phrase 'I am a homeless person' because I've tried to get the audience to figure it out themselves. However, in the seventh paragraph, I mention 'living in the streets', because by this point I hope they have realised the idea.

Repetition is used a lot in this piece, like the use of 'our ...' in the fifth paragraph, as well as the use of triadic lists, like the second sentence in paragraph nine. This is mainly for emphasis, but also to add emotion. The narrator is trying to teach the reader that their view of the homeless is unjustified and, as the fifth paragraph also details, sometimes hypocritical.

The reason I decided to label him 'a ghost' was because we do tend to ignore and depersonalise them. I wanted the reader to know from the beginning that he understands what we see in him, and repeated 'I am a ghost' at the end to leave you on a note. It was designed to have you reconsidering your views on the homeless; that, actually, they are humans, and that it probably was exceptional circumstances that led to their lives on the streets.

There are a number of rhetorical questions throughout too. This is to reinforce the idea that we should rethink our prejudices. For example, in the ninth paragraph, I dehumanise the narrator by stripping him of a name, which we should care about, but we don't, because of his lifestyle.

Paragraph four is one word, 'Why?' This is because in the third paragraph I've outlined how he feels the population views him, and after this he shows us what we feel isn't right.

Also, I use both the first and the second person in this piece. The first person makes it personal, for example 'my brother died … after my departure' is highly emotional. The second person is used because it directs it to the reader. 'You don't like me. You never will.' This involves you in the piece and makes you know that he is talking about the way society treats him. Moreover, there are two examples of 'you know' in the piece, because this makes it more like a conversation, and again including the reader.

Overall, I do feel this piece flowed well. It is supposed to be persuasive, and I've deliberately used shock words like 'shit' for real impact. It was designed to have you question your thoughts on the homeless, which I feel it does.

Examiner's comment

Again, this is good work, although it's less strong than the production piece. The positive things are:

■ he explicitly discusses representational aspects – dehumanisation, labelling, how this piece fits with 'typical' representation of the subject

■ he identifies specific linguistic features – repetition, triads, first/second person.

The things it's missing in the higher bands are:

■ grammatical detail – word classes are not identified

■ syntax – no sentence functions or types are noted.

Overall for the commentary, it balances out at around 6 out of 10. It has top band characteristics in terms of explaining the representation, but the linguistic detail is more like 4 out of 10. However, this does give him a total of 24 out of 30, likely to be a high grade.

■ Beginning your own work

Having worked through the material here, you should now be ready to get started on your own piece. Remember to refer to other sections in this book to help you – Unit 2, Section A Investigating representations shows you plenty of other texts; Unit 1, Section A Language and mode may help you with genre features; and The linguistic frameworks toolkit on page 206 will help you with your identification of features for the commentary. Remember also to produce a plan before you write anything – a cohesive structure is part of the assessment criteria, and planning really helps to get this in place.

■ Topic revision summary
■ Choose to produce work you can be enthusiastic about.
■ Do not unthinkingly select an idea you've seen in this book.
■ Remember to plan the commentary as well as the production piece.
■ Include grammatical detail in the commentary for high marks.

Feedback

This part of the book provides all the feedback for the Coursework activities and Data response exercises in Unit 2, Section B.

Writing skills

Coursework activity 1

The correct version is:

The way women are represented in the tabloids is **disgusting**. **Their** looks are always **written** about, although **men's** looks aren't **commented** on very often. **They're** always linked to their families, **for example** how many children **they've** got and **that's** not always **relevant**.

Producing representations for a media audience

Coursework activity 2

Possible genres or categories:

- Broadsheet-style features – newspapers and online.
- Tabloid-style pieces – newspapers and online.
- Articles for a specialist audience – magazines, radio and online.
- Web-only venues – blogs, social networking sites.
- Spoken texts – radio plays, speeches.

Coursework activity 3

You should have a clear idea now of how feature articles are put together, and perhaps also of how they differ in various contexts. You probably found the following features in your sample:

- Catchy headlines/titles.
- Introductory paragraphs that explain the topic and introduce the writer.
- Pull quotes.
- Satellite or inset articles or text boxes.
- Synthetic personalisation.
- Anecdotal as well as 'hard' evidence.

Data response exercise 1

Feedback for this activity forms part of Data response exercise 2.

Data response exercise 2

This commentary is successful because it connects a general point (the friendly tenor) with further specific linguistic points, each with examples and labels. These labels do vary in their detail (the grammatical detail is far more precise than the 'speech-like syntax'), but on the whole the commentary contains sufficient precise detail to score highly.

Coursework activity 4

This is such a personal exercise, it's difficult to give useful feedback. You should have found possible written, online and radio contexts – there is a wealth of niche radio operators available online, as broadcasting on the web makes it easier to run a small station. This exercise may give you your context for the production piece. For example, if you are a skater, you might consider writing a piece about how skaters are perceived in the mainstream media. Or, if you are interested in the environment, you might come up with a radio piece about green politics and how those behind them are represented

Data response exercise 3

The speech represents Diana as:

1. warm and compassionate – this is supported by the listing of 'the sick, the dying, with children, with the needy'

2. important – the speech creates a sense of her death affecting many with several examples of parenthesis offering elaboration: 'The whole of our country, all of us, …'; 'who people, not just in Britain, but throughout the world, loved'; 'the people everywhere, not just here in Britain but everywhere …'

3. 'the people's princess' – this alliterative phrase has survived this speech, because it is a compact image used in the closing sentence that summarises the paragraph that precedes it, bringing the speech to a climax. It is also effective because of its use of the possessive, suggesting that the princess belongs to 'the people'.

Producing representations for children

Coursework activity 5

Fictional writing for children is perhaps the most obvious area. Within that, you may have listed:

- picture books that allow children to see the world through others' experience
- books for older children featuring marginalised groups
- stories exploring issues through metaphor (e.g. using fantasy races or aliens to explore racism)
- revised fairy and folk tales that challenge popular stereotypes
- reclaimed folk traditions, e.g. African and Asian tales.

In the area of non-fiction you may have considered:

- children's media-style writing on particular words or representations
- non-fiction books for children about particular groups, institutions, etc.

■ Coursework activity 6

There are three main concerns for writers to do with representation in picture books. First, children should have access to books that have familiarity to them. That means that books should represent the experience of all groups in society, showing different family settings, different cultures and heritages, and different values. Second, children should be exposed to the experience of other groups as well. If children are able to see their own experience as part of a wide range of experiences, they will accept that wide range as normal and be less likely to buy into -isms later. Finally, picture books should avoid perpetuating stereotypes and contributing to inequality.

Your list of possibilities may contain all three types of intervention, for example:

■ a family story where the father is the main carer for the child

■ a story focused around a particular religious or cultural festival

■ a revised fairy tale where Little Red Riding Hood and Grandmother work together to kill the wolf.

■ Coursework activity 7

You should have a few ideas for children noted now, and maybe you already have quite clear ideas about what you'd like your coursework to be. Remember to keep an open mind and to use all the practice exercises to improve your writing skills generally, whatever kind of text you're going to focus on for coursework. You will be expected to produce texts at A2 Level as well, and it is important that you don't narrow your experience of writing too much at this stage. You may find it helpful to discuss your ideas with others.

■ Coursework activity 8

First-person narration	
Advantages:	*Disadvantages:*
It's good for directly representing a particular situation or culture. It's easier to get your audience 'on-side' and sympathising with your character's point of view.	It doesn't allow you to explain much background realistically (you have to stay 'in character'). You can only write about what your character can see, experience or know about.
Third-person narration	
Advantages:	*Disadvantages:*
You can describe characters' thoughts and feelings clearly (rather than showing everything through one point of view). You can explain background, e.g. why a particular festival is celebrated or a family situation.	There can be less reader-identification with the character. It can be more descriptive and less immediate.

■ Data response exercise 4

You may have noted some of the following:

Graphological features:

1 heading in graffiti-style writing

2 photos featuring children

3 comic-strip story

4 small amounts of text

Language:

1 The heading is a simple question – no existing knowledge is assumed.

2 The first answer to the question offers what seems like an 'official' answer, because of its formal style with relatively complex lexis, such as 'impairment' and 'function'.

3 On the left-hand page, the nouns are balanced between abstract, e.g. 'impairment', 'condition', and concrete, e.g. 'limb', 'body'. On the right-hand page, there are fewer abstract nouns as this comic-strip section is more direct and less theoretical.

4 The explanation of the social view of disability is also in formal language, and this use of formal language helps children to see the issue as serious. Technical terms are used in children's books in order to help familiarise them with the necessary jargon.

5 The comic-strip section is a contrast linguistically to the facing page, and it contextualises the issues for its child audience. The language here is far simpler and more colloquial – many of the sentences on this page are simple, e.g. 'It was Friday evening', whereas on the left-hand page, most sentences are complex, e.g. 'A disability is often described as an impairment or medical condition that prevents someone from performing a specific task or function.'

■ Producing representations to entertain

■ Data response exercise 5

You may have noted some of the following:

1 The key to the way the text operates is intertextual reference. If the reader doesn't understand the reference to rape victim questioning, the effect is lost and it becomes merely absurd. Some of the humour, and the entire challenge to representation rests on the realisation that the text is parodying the way rape victims have been treated.

2 The lawyer's control of the situation is shown through his use of closed and leading questions, e.g. 'And it was dark at the time, wasn't it?' Several of the questions asked only allow the victim to agree with or reject the lawyer's statement, allowing the victim no control over the conversation at all.

3 The lawyer's certainty and confidence is shown linguistically by his use of discourse markers, e.g. 'so', and his control of the topics via his questions.

4 The way nouns are changed and modified is also under the lawyer's control. For example, 'King's St' becomes 'an area known for muggings', then a 'dodgy area'. This move from straightforward name to complex post-modification to simple pre-modification shows how the lawyer is manipulating and colouring the facts. Taking the complicated post-modifying phrase and reducing it to a simple adjective shows that the lawyer is presenting this idea as fact – it becomes part of the identity of the area. A similar thing happens with the man's suit.

5 The victim's growing uncertainty is shown as his first few responses take the form of 'yes' with an explanation, while he later becomes less sure. This is represented by hesitancy features such as the non-verbal filler 'er' and his indefinite response to some questions with 'Sorry, what?' as though he hasn't understood, or the question is unexpected. His surprise at the questions asked encourages the audience to see them as unusual.

Coursework activity 9

If asked to do this task, the author of this book would perhaps consider writing the experience of working mothers, or of non-drivers. In a sense, what this task really asks is 'In what way(s) do you belong to a minority?' Asking students, the author received a range of ideas including: British-born Asian people; Muslims living in the UK; Christian teenagers; unemployed people; the family of a person with a disability.

Data response exercise 6

Some possible comments include the following:

1 When read aloud, the many fricative sounds, e.g. '<u>sh</u>y <u>s</u>exual', '<u>s</u>acre<u>d</u> ve<u>ss</u>el', 'Vene<u>ti</u>an', in the first stanza create an overall softness.

2 The first stanza uses a lot of imagery in the form of metaphors. These metaphors are mostly related to space, and show changes from the small 'hole' to the larger 'canal', 'well', replicating the opening up of the birth canal.

3 The repetition of 'lack' at the end, which is firmly identified as 'our' by the use of the possessive, shows that it is our – the audience's – fault that the vagina is not perceived as incredible. The abstract nouns 'awe' and 'wonder' are presented as the natural response to it, using the technique of presenting these responses as normal and commonsense.

4 The image of the tiny child stuck in the well reminds us that this is a poem about birth, and that there is in fact a tiny child due to emerge from this 'well'. The image of a well also reminds us of the vagina's connection to life, as the birth canal.

Coursework activity 10

There are many possibilities for this exercise. Allowing a character to speak directly to the audience does enable you to explicitly comment on and perhaps correct the existing representation of them. You can also do this quite effectively by seeming to conform to a stereotype in your characterisation, then suddenly undermining such a stereotype.

Data response exercise 7

1 Typical trappings of femininity in the passage include her hair (dyed blonde and very elaborately 'done'); pale pink ribbon; glamorous symbols of bikini and stole; make-up, and her song of lost love.

2 These aspects are undermined primarily by her age and the dirtiness of her face. Many of the individual descriptions are immediately undermined in place, e.g. the hair is dyed 'a brave canary yellow' – the adjective 'brave' implies that it shouldn't be that colour (that shade is perhaps more associated with youth).

3 The passage produces a grotesque image because the feminine aspects are exaggerated, distorted or out of place. The way that aspects of age are used to undermine the feminine aspects may lead us to question why older women 'should not' display femininity in the same way. Linguistically, the text is dominated by concrete nouns with detailed description (sometimes we have to know the rules to know when we can break them!), and the 'mad old lady' is the subject of many of the sentences, but we see her only through the narrator's eyes – we never hear her voice directly.

Coursework activity 11

Your piece will be highly individual and specific. Hopefully you have developed your understanding of the requirements of this task sufficiently to have produced something that could be developed further into your coursework submission, should you wish to do so. By now you probably have a fairly clear idea of what you'd like to produce, or at least a reasonable set of ideas to choose from. Check the detail in your commentary – for a good mark, you must have grammatical detail, ideally including word class and comments on sentence use.

Answers to Topic revision exercises

Unit 1, Section A Language and mode

Note: these answers are offered as possibilities only. Others may be equally valid – if you can justify them.

What is mode?

1 Mode as a term refers to whether a text is primarily spoken or written or neither.

2 Texts are more complex than the black/white approach of 'either spoken or written'. Many written texts, even quite formal ones, share features with the spoken mode, and some texts seem to fit more naturally at the unexpected end of the continuum.

3 List the following:

a Two 'spoken-style' written texts:
- Shopping lists – they are not intended to be permanent and are written for a known, small audience
- Diary/journal entries – they can be very personal and informal, and are produced for a known, small audience.

b Two 'written-style' spoken texts:
- Lectures, political speeches – both are prepared in advance and delivered to a large, wide, not personally known audience.

c Three 'spoken-style' electronic texts:
- Chatty e-mails – they are informal and personal in tone, and produced for a known audience. Also, interaction is possible – an e-mail may well contain the text of the e-mail it is replying to.
- Text messages – they are not permanent, they may not follow spelling or grammar rules, and they are personal in tone, written to a known audience.
- msn conversation – it is a conversation, and thus two-way interaction, using turn-taking. It also follows the same pattern as text messages above.

d Three 'blended-style' electronic texts:
- Blogs – these can have permanent archives, their audience is broad and unknown, but the content is often personal and very informal in style. Since the audience can respond and leave comments, there is some interaction.
- Forum postings/bulletin board – these can be personal and directly answering an individual, but they are also public and often archived, so permanent.
- Text messages from the network – these are not personal, and are likely to use more standard spelling than casual text messages, but in most ways they are like other texts.

e Three 'written-style' electronic texts:
- Official websites, e.g. government information – they have a wide audience, formal tone and clear structure.
- Commercial e-mails – they have a wide audience, make use of visual elements and offer no interaction.
- Help screens in software – they have a wide audience and a formal and practical tone. They also offer highly organised information and may include diagrams/screenshots.

f Features of the written mode:
- Formal tone.
- Audience not known to writer – you can't predict who will read your book or article.
- Visual elements used, e.g. diagrams, images, colour.
- Planned – there is more than one stage to producing a written text.
- Permanent – you can return to a book and it will be the same.

g Features of the spoken mode:
- Informal tone.
- Speaker and receiver can see each other, so audience is known, even if they're strangers.
- Interactive – all participants contribute.
- Ephemeral – conversation not recorded.
- Spontaneous – participants do not plan their contributions.

The written mode

1 Graphology relates to the visual, non-linguistic aspects of a text, i.e. the things that create an impact but are not actually linguistic decisions.

2 Use of colour, layout features like lists or text boxes, and any images.

3 The centred image of a glass of juice with the box visible behind clearly identifies the product. The blue background connotes clarity and freshness, and is a key product colour, helping brand recognition. The Eyecare Trust symbol used high on the right-hand side implies official endorsement of the product. The eye chart feature, as discussed, links with the concept of eye health being supported – this is visually reinforced by the fact that the type is clearer where seen through the glass. The clear font also uses the brand colours, helping customers to recognise the product in shops.

The spoken mode

1 Transcripts do not include conventional punctuation, and they represent exactly what was said. Non-fluency features like repetitions and fillers, which we normally screen out when listening to speech, are therefore included.

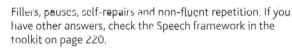

2 Fillers, pauses, self-repairs and non-fluent repetition. If you have other answers, check the Speech framework in the toolkit on page 220.

3 Interruptions occur when someone tries to take control of the conversation. Monitoring devices like 'you know' are used to check someone is listening. An adjacency pair is two utterances that naturally belong together, like a question and answer or apology and acceptance (or rejection). For other possibilities, check the Interaction framework in the toolkit on page 213.

Blending modes

1 *Syntactic parallelism* is a kind of patterning where the same syntactical structure is used repeatedly, often with some words repeated. *Triads* are patterns of three, either the same word/phrase repeated three times, or a set of three related ideas. *Contrasts* are often combined with *mocking the opposition*, to show where 'they' went wrong and what 'we' will do to put it right. For further possibilities, check the Rhetorical framework in the toolkit on page 219.

2 Typical spoken mode features borrowed by written texts are direct address (known as synthetic personalisation in mass audience texts) and informal, more colloquial language.

3 Simulation of the spoken mode allows written adverts to seem more personally directed to their audience and thus to be more persuasive.

4 Electronic texts are truly in the middle of the mode continuum, and even the most like spoken language (e.g. chats) use graphology for effect. Equally, the most like written language (e.g. formal websites, commercial e-mails) are too interactive and temporary to be considered 'written mode'.

Context and mode

1 Audience, purpose, genre and mode.

2 **a** Convergence is moving linguistically closer to another speaker, by adopting some of their speech habits. Divergence is moving further away from the other speaker, by emphasising individual speech habits.

   b You converge upwardly by adopting speech habits of a speaker who uses more standard speech than you do.

   c You diverge upwardly by making your speech more standard in order to distance yourself from someone who speaks using non-standard features.

3 **a** 'Face' is the persona projected or acted out in a conversation.

   b Positive face needs are to be liked and accepted as part of a group.

   c Negative face needs are to be allowed freedom of choice and individuality.

   d Using terms of endearment or nicknames is a positive politeness strategy.

   e 'Would you mind terribly...?'

Lexis, semantics and mode

1 Colloquialism, jargon, metaphor, idiom, euphemism.

2 Rabbit, cat, elephant, giraffe, deer.

3 **a** Using extra words to soften what's said: I don't really like him very much.

   b A word or phrase used to gain attention and show you're changing the subject: *So,...*

   c A word made up of the initials of other words, which can be pronounced as a word: *ASBO*.

   d Describing an object as though it were human: the trees shake their branches in anger.

   e Being imprecise, often by adding extra words or parts of words: that *thingummy* over there.

Phonology and mode

1 The IPA is needed because there are more sounds than letters, and letters do not match up exactly with sounds, e.g. 'c' may be hard or soft (*circle* has both).

2 Fricatives: *sh, sss, zzz*; nasals: *mmm, nnn*.

3 Alliteration, rhyme, onomatopoeia, elision, emphatic stress.

4 In written mode texts, alliteration and assonance are more likely to be deliberately used for effect. In the spoken mode, stress and non-verbal features are worth examining. In the blended mode, phonetic spellings may be interesting.

Grammar, syntax and mode

1 With the imperative first sentence, Raworth asserts an authoritative tone, matched by the simplicity and brevity of the second declarative sentence. The interrogative third sentence introduces the topic of the article and positions the reader as someone concerned about the ethics of consumerism and globalisation.

2 The second-person pronoun 'you' allows Raworth to address the reader directly, further supporting her positioning of the audience as interested in trade issues and ethics.

3 The second paragraph uses the present tense for immediacy, e.g. 'You want to know', together with a sense of the future through the auxiliary verb 'will' to question the likelihood of the scenario she describes.

4 Keeping the first clause short and simple – 'The technology is simple' – and having a long coordinating clause following it has the effect of increasing how silly the retailers' behaviour seems. The 'washing instructions' is a real anticlimax to that sentence, so concern with such things is trivialised.

5 Abstract nouns – 'globalisation', 'employment', 'jobs', 'conditions', 'right', 'trade unions' – are frequent in this passage because the argument focuses on ideals and issues of power. Thus there are few concrete nouns – 'people', 'women', 'countries'.

6 Adjectives in the extract as a whole are frequently negative – 'poor', 'appalling', 'excessive' – and serve to highlight the issues. There are a few comparative adjectives used in the fourth paragraph: 'faster', 'cheaper', 'more flexible' – all in the context of the retailers' demands. This contrast between what's best for business and the workers' experience is a constant theme in the text.

■ Unit 1, Section B Language development

Lexical and semantic development

1 Proto-words are sounds created by children that bear a resemblance to lexis used by adults, but which don't necessarily have a meaning. Children often make sounds that resemble adult words, but until those sounds are applied consistently to the things they are describing, they are not really meaningful or 'proper' words.

2 Nouns are some of the most easily assigned word classes as they often relate to concrete objects in the real world or to people around the child. It is easier to label physical objects than to describe a feeling or a grammatical relationship between other words.

3 Overextension is a process by which a child uses a lexical term (a word) in a wider way than an adult. For example, a child may overextend the use of the word *truck* to include *buses*, *lorries*, *fire engines* and *vans*. There are three main forms of overextension: categorical, analogical and mismatch.

4 Children, according to Aitchison, label, package and network build. They actively develop a sense of which labels apply to which objects, what a label means and then how it relates to other labels and categories.

Grammatical development – syntax

1 Syntax is a part of grammar. It means word order and the ways words are placed in order to create different meanings.

2 After the pre-verbal stages, most children go through the proto-word, one-word/holophrastic, two-word, telegraphic and post-telegraphic stages.

3 These structures require a more sophisticated manipulation of syntax and can often confuse children. For example, while many questions swap subject and verb word order to become interrogatives (*I am tall. – Am I tall?*), others do not (*You walked to the shops – Did you walk to the shops?*)

4 Tense and aspect require the manipulation of different elements of syntax and can be tricky for children to grasp. Past tenses can be overgeneralised and there is often confusion between the past tense form of a verb and its past participle (*I done it – I did it – I have done it*).

Grammatical development – morphology

1 A morpheme is the smallest meaningful grammatical unit. It can be a whole word (*dog, person, guitar*) or a unit that is attached to a word to change its meaning (*dogs, walked, singing*).

2 Inflectional morphology is about adding morphemes to create new grammatical meanings, i.e. turning words into other grammatical forms: present tense to past tense; singular to plural. Derivational morphology is about creating new words from existing morphemes: *walk – walker*; *cycle – cyclist*; *ghetto – ghettoisation*.

3 Overgeneralisation is the process through which children apply grammatical rules to words for which the rule does not apply, e.g. *mouse – mouses*; *run – runned*.

4 'Wugs' are imaginary creatures invented for an experiment into children's application of the plural rule.

Phonological development

1 Phonemic contraction is the process through which the child's range of sounds decreases as he or she becomes more 'tuned in' to the sounds of the main language/s spoken in the immediate environment. While children are capable of producing the sounds of any human language when they are born, they tend to lose this ability as they get older and as they are exposed to the sounds of one main language.

2 Children's early pronunciation 'errors' are often to do with substituting easier sounds in one area of the mouth for more difficult sounds in the same area. Children often reduce combinations of consonants (consonant clusters) to make them easier to say. Children also leave out unstressed syllables and final consonant sounds.

3 The 'fis phenomenon' was noted by Berko and Brown, and it involves a child being able to hear what's wrong with an adult's mispronunciation of a word, while not being able to articulate the correct sound him or herself. So a child will know that an adult is wrong when he or she says 'fis', but cannot say 'fish' to correct them.

Pragmatic development

1 Pragmatics might be defined as what we are 'getting at' as opposed to what we actually say. It could also be defined as the unwritten rules of conversation. It's important to communication because we rely on mutual understanding to make ourselves clear. Much of the subtlety of human communication is in the shared understanding of situations and the ways in which language can convey more than just simple, literal meanings.

2 Halliday noted: instrumental, regulatory, interactional, personal, heuristic, imaginative and representational functions.

3 Each of these is an example of how language can be used in a particular way to signal more than its literal content. Idioms are sayings – often metaphors – that rely on shared understanding to work: expressions such as 'it's raining cats and dogs' (it's raining heavily) or 'it's brass monkeys out there' (it's very cold) depend not on literal semantic interpretation but on a grasp of English idiom. Sarcasm operates by meaning the opposite of what it suggests, so, again, a literal semantic interpretation would lead to confusion. Indirectness is often a social strategy to avoid putting upon other people, to get what you want via implication, but is something that children often fail to grasp until they're older.

Children's early reading and writing

1 Different theorists propose slightly different stages, but the most recognisable stages children go through are probably scribbling, emergent writing, copy writing and then independent writing. Kroll proposes four stages of development: preparation; consolidation; differentiation; and integration.

2 Spoken and written language are very closely linked. Much of a child's early writing will exhibit the same virtuous errors as his or her spoken language, and the written orthography will reflect some of the patterns in the child's spoken phonology. As children get older, they learn the differences between the two modes and can write in a different style.

3 A range of other factors is important. Once children can accurately organise their ideas on the page, they then need to get used to the different forms and genres that exist in writing – stories, comprehension exercises, lists of ingredients for recipes, poems, etc. – and the various audiences and functions of written language.

4 Teaching and interaction are very important in children's development of reading and writing. While spoken language is acquired without explicit instruction, reading and writing are much more reliant on teaching. To progress confidently, children need to be aware that reading and writing are valued, and shown the various ways in which language can be used for different purposes. Because of English's inconsistent spelling patterns, certain spelling rules need to be taught explicitly and other patterns learned by memory.

Language development theories

1 'Nature' theories foreground the role of inherited abilities, while 'nurture' theories place more emphasis on the influence of the child's environment.

2 There is some evidence that children imitate adult writing at the 'scribbling' stage, and also that they repeat words and phrases they hear without fully understanding their meanings. There is evidence that children pick up local accents too, suggesting that a form of unconscious imitation is at work.

3 There is a great deal of evidence. Children's use of categorical overextensions, overgeneralisations, derivational morphology and syntax formation all point to language development as being governed by rules.

The linguistic frameworks toolkit

Like any other complex subject, English Language has its own system of labels – a language of its own. This section is about those labels and helping you to understand the relevant terminology. Some of the terms, like *simile*, *alliteration* and *noun*, may be familiar from your past studies, but many will be new, or used in a more specific way. Take the time to learn them as you work through the course.

These sets of words are described as frameworks because they help us to see how texts are put together. It's like using scaffolding to examine how a building is constructed. Each framework gives a different view of a text or set of data, but we need to use several or all of them together to get a full analysis.

In the main text of this book, each key term is defined in the margin the first time it is used. The key terms reappear in the frameworks, but often with more detailed definitions and examples. Not all the terms explained here are used in the main text, but you do need to understand them.

💡 The frameworks

- **Contextual** terms allow you to consider things like who the text is for (audience) and what it's trying to achieve (purpose).
- The **Grammatical and morphological** framework covers terminology about the grammatical classification of words, e.g. nouns, adjectives and verbs.
- The **Graphological** framework contains terms for the visual aspects of texts.
- The **Interaction** framework covers how we use language to relate to others, like taking turns in speech or IM.
- The **Lexical-semantic** framework is about words and their meanings, and offers a range of words for describing types of vocabulary and effects to do with meaning, such as imagery and puns.
- The **Phonological** framework is all about sound, and is used to examine effects created by sound devices, e.g. alliteration and onomatopoeia.
- The **Rhetorical** framework is mainly concerned with persuasive texts, written or spoken, and covers features intended to make texts more memorable.
- The **Speech** framework is concerned with language used only, or primarily, in speech, e.g. terms for words like 'um' and 'y'know'.
- The **Syntactical** framework describes how sentences are put together.

Each framework gives a different lens to examine language through – whether it's the mechanical grammatical level or the practical, real-world, contextual one. To work with language efficiently, you need to be able to combine these lenses to gain a clear understanding of what a text is doing at all relevant levels.

Note: *relevant* is a keyword here. Although examiners might well be impressed if you can correctly identify the word class of every word in a text, once you've done that you'll have no time to discuss why they're there, what it all means, and how those words connect to contextual factors. Without that second step, you can only ever get half marks.

■ Contextual terminology

Asynchronous communication	A communication in which participants do not need to be present simultaneously, e.g. e-mail.
Audience positioning	The concept of how the writer/author or speaker seems to be imagining the audience. To analyse this, look at assumptions made about the audience and also at the tenor of the text.
Blended mode (or mixed mode)	A term that primarily expresses the mode of new electronic forms of communication, e.g. e-mail, txt, web pages and chat. Texts that are clearly either written or spoken but use features from the other are not truly of mixed or blended mode – it's more useful to comment on how and why such texts use such features.
Channel differences	The mode differences related to how a text is received (e.g. via eyes or ears).
Context	The context of a text is the set of conditions around that text's production – who is it for? (audience); what is it for? (purpose); what kind of text is it? (genre); how is it received? (mode).
First-person narrative	A story or account written from the 'I' position.
Genre	The category or type of a text. These categories all have sets of conventions that texts can adhere to or use in creating meaning and effect.
Implicature	Expressing meaning indirectly.
Inference	Drawing out meanings from others' speech.
Mode	This is usually used to mean whether a text is spoken or written. It has become an area of study focusing on the features that characterise written and spoken texts.
Pragmatics	Pragmatics is a broad term often used to relate to a gap between what the words used actually mean and what the intended meaning is. We understand 'pragmatic meaning' by reference to the context of the words. For example, 'What time do you make it?' could be a straightforward question, but if it's a parent asking a teenager who's arrived home an hour after the agreed time, the actual meaning is likely to be different.
Subject position	The perspective from which events or issues are perceived and recounted.
Synchronous communication	A communication in which both/all participants are present at the same time, e.g. a chat.
Tenor	A text's tenor is related to the relationship between the participants in a conversation or between the writer and audience in a less interactive text. The tenor may be described as 'professional', 'informal', 'intimate', etc.

■ Grammatical and morphological framework

Abstract noun	A subcategory of nouns – the name of an abstract idea, concept, emotion or belief, e.g. *difficulty*, *paganism*, *love*, *virtue*.
Active voice	A name given to grammatical constructions that relate to the rules of subject and object in a clause. In an active sentence, the subject acts as the agent of the verb (basically 'doing' the verb), e.g. 'the dog chewed the bone'. *See also* Voice.
Adjective	A modifier used to add detail, usually to a noun. They normally occur as pre-modifiers directly before the noun, or follow a stative verb, e.g. 'the big tree'; 'he seems happy'.
Adverb	The easiest adverbs to spot are the *-ly* ones, but there are many more. Adverbs modify a verb, or an adjective, or a whole clause, e.g. 'He ran *swiftly*'; 'She's *very* quick'; '*Fortunately*, he arrived on time'.

Adverb type	Adverbs can be divided into groups relating to: – manner: *how* something is done (e.g. *rapidly*) – time: *when* something is done (e.g. *tomorrow*) – frequency: *how often* something is done (e.g. *frequently*) – place: *where* or *in what direction* something is done (e.g. *backwards*) – degree: *to what intensity/how much* something is done (e.g. *very*; *quite*) – comment: adding an *opinion* to a clause or phrase (e.g. *fortunately*) – linking: used as *connectives* (e.g. *however*). Adverbs can move around in clauses far more than other elements, so it's worth noticing precisely what the effect of the adverb's position is. Compare 'Happily, he bounced into the room' with 'He bounced happily into the room'. In the first, we're happy he's arrived, and in the second, he came into the room in a happy way.
Adverbial	A word or phrase acting like an adverb. Adverbials can modify the same parts of the sentence as adverbs and are as mobile as adverbs. Examples: 'We'll see her in a while'; 'He's running as fast as he can.'
Agent	The person (or thing) carrying out the action of the verb. The agent usually comes before the verb, but not always. Examples: 'I hit him'; 'The thieves were caught by a gang of youths.'
Aspect	Aspect relates to the duration of events or how an event should be viewed in relation to time. Verbs are usually in either the perfective or the progressive aspect. Both are formed with an auxiliary verb (e.g. *am* walking, *was* shopping, *have* eaten). The perfective aspect relates to actions that are completed, while the progressive aspect relates to actions that are, or have been, ongoing.
Attributive adjective	An adjective used to pre-modify a noun. The adjective is being used to define an attribute of the noun. Examples: 'The empty bottle'; 'An excessively large clipboard.'
Auxiliary verb	A verb that supports or 'helps' another. If there is more than one verb in a clause, usually only one is a main verb and the other(s) must be auxiliaries.
Bound morpheme	A morpheme that can only have meaning when attached to a free morpheme. Examples: *-ed* to show past tense; *-s* to show plural.
Collective noun	The name for a number of things as one unit. Be careful not to label all plural nouns collective. A collective noun acts like a singular. Examples: 'The herd is on the move'; 'The team is ready.'
Common noun	The name of an object, type of animal, person or idea. Common nouns can usually be used with determiners, e.g. *the goat*, *a star*; and they may change in the plural by adding *-s/-es*, etc. Examples: *dog*; *boy*; *country*; *shoe*.
Comparative	Adjectives inflected with *-er* or combined with 'more' are in the comparative form. Examples: 'She's bigger'; 'He's more helpful.'
Complement	An element that adds information to a subject or an object. A subject complement usually follows the verb and can be used with a stative verb. Examples: 'She seems really annoyed'; 'That boy is a pain in the neck.' An object complement usually follows the object and is clearly related to it. Examples: 'I made her really annoyed'; 'I find that boy a pain in the neck.'
Concrete noun	A subcategory of common nouns – the name of a tangible, physical object. Examples: *book*; *elephant*; *cheese*.
Conjunction	A function word that connects elements and clauses together.
Coordinating conjunction	A conjunction that connects main clauses together to form compound sentences. Can also be used to connect other elements together, so don't assume that an 'and' makes a sentence compound. The most common coordinating conjunctions are: *and*, *but*, *or*.

Copula verb	A verb used to join or 'couple' a subject to a complement. The most common is *to be*.
	Examples: 'I am happy'; 'That kid seems strange'; 'That song sounds great.'
Demonstrative pronoun	Pronouns used to differentiate between possibilities. Usually there is a spatial relationship between the possibilities. They are: *this, these, that, those*.
Determiner	Function words and phrases that are used before nouns to determine their number and specificity.
	The important ones are:
	– the indefinite article – *a/an*
	– the definite article – *the*
	– possessives – *my, your, his, her, its, our, their*.
	There are also many words that can replace articles, and words expressing quantity that can be considered determiners.
Evaluative adjective	An adjective that implies a judgement about what it's describing. Evaluative adjectives are a means of leading the audience and are worth commenting on.
	Example: compare *dark* to *gloomy*.
Factive verb	A verb used to express a truth, or conviction that what follows the verb is true.
	Examples: 'He *discovered* that his wife was having an affair' presupposes that his wife was, in fact, having an affair; 'The administration *learned* that there were weapons hidden in the forest' presupposes that there were weapons there.
Free morpheme	A morpheme that can stand independently and act as a meaningful unit on its own.
	Examples: *dog*; *run*.
Functional word/ grammatical word	A word that has a grammatical function, but doesn't carry as much meaning as the lexical words. The functional classes, also known as closed classes, include: *pronouns*; *determiners*; *prepositions*; *conjunctions*; and *auxiliary verbs*. They are called 'closed' because new functional words are hardly ever created.
Future	English has no future tense as such. We most commonly express the idea of the future by using:
	– *will* or *shall* as an auxiliary, e.g. 'I'll eat it later.'
	– *be going to* with the infinitive, e.g. 'He's going to buy a car.'
	– the present progressive (this refers to the near future), e.g. 'We're leaving at eight.'
	– the simple present (this often suggests something definite), e.g. 'He goes at ten.'
Grammar	The word 'grammar' is used in this subject primarily to refer to word class and morphology. It does not mean punctuation, or rules, but patterns of usage.
Grammatical cohesion	Grammatical cohesion is often achieved by ellipsis, or through the use of pronouns to avoid repetition.
	Example: 'Simon woke slowly. Rubbing his eyes, *he* remembered what had happened.' (It wouldn't sound right to repeat the name.)
Infinitive	The 'base form' of the verb.
	Examples: *to eat*; *to sing*; *to be*.
Inflection	A word is said to be inflected when it has a suffix attached to change the meaning. Nouns inflect to show number (*cat/cats*), while verbs inflect to show person, tense, and number (*go/goes*; *eat/eaten*).
	Nouns and verbs can also be inflected to derive new words (*see* Derivational morphology in Glossary).
	Example: *to text* (verb) – I am a fast *texter* (noun).
Interrogative pronoun	A pronoun used to ask questions and stand in for an unknown noun. They are: *who, whom, whose, what, which*.
	Examples: 'Whose did you borrow?'; 'What did you take?'
Lexical word	A word that carries meaning. If you omit the functional words in a sentence and have just the lexical ones, it can still be understood. The lexical classes, also known as open classes, are: *nouns*; *verbs*; *adjectives*; and *adverbs*. They are called 'open' because new ones come in all the time.

Main verb	The verb that is the focus of the clause. Verbs that are only ever main verbs can also be called lexical verbs. Examples: 'I am *eating*'; 'He'll be *arriving* soon'; 'She *sleeps* far too much'; 'He couldn't have *done* any more'; 'I *have* three children.'
Mean length of utterance (MLU)	A calculation based on the average number of morphemes used across a number of utterances.
Modal auxiliary verb	This group of verbs can only function as auxiliaries; they never appear on their own. They are used to express possibility, probability, certainty, necessity and obligation. Examples: *will*; *would*; *can*; *could*; *shall*; *should*; *may*; *might*; *must*.
Modality	The degree of certainty or doubt conveyed by a text.
Modifier	A word, usually an adjective or a noun used attributively, that qualifies the sense of a noun, e.g. *old* and *factory* in 'the old factory building'. Adverbs of comment also act as modifiers, e.g. *obviously*.
Morpheme	The smallest unit of grammatical meaning. A morpheme can be a single letter, such as the '*s*' often used to indicate a plural in English.
Morphology	The study of word structure, especially in terms of morphemes.
Nominalisation	The process of turning an event or action normally expressed as a verb into a noun that can then be used at the head of a noun phrase. It is often used in headlines and journalism as a compressed form of syntax. Examples: '*Mayor's tube outburst* provokes outrage' – the Mayor has made an outburst about the Tube …; '*Baby snatch mother* tells of heartbreak' – a mother has had her baby snatched … .
Object	The person or thing that receives the action of the verb, or has the verb done to it. The object usually follows the verb, but not always. Examples: 'I hit him'; 'The dog caught the ball.'
Participle	The past participle is the *-ed* or *-en* form of regular verbs. Examples: *eaten*; *walked*; *gone*. The present participle is the *-ing* form of regular verbs. Examples: *screaming*; *leaving*; *being*. They can be used as modifiers as well as part of a verb element. Examples: 'The *dancing* girls'; 'The *hidden* room.'
Passive voice	A name given to grammatical constructions that relate to the roles of subject and object in a clause. In a passive sentence, the subject of the clause has the action of the verb carried out on it. Example: 'The bone was chewed by the dog.' In a passive construction, the agent of the verb (the person or thing 'doing' the verb) need not actually appear. Example: 'The bone was chewed.' *See also* Voice.
Person	Verbs inflect to show the person or the subject – i.e. who is carrying out the action of the verb. Examples: *I go*; *you go*; *he goes*; *we go*; *you go*; *they go*. *I am*; *you are*; *he is*; *we are*; *you are*; *they are*.
Personal pronoun	A pronoun used for a person. They vary according to person, number and whether they refer to the subject or object of the clause. You should know the difference between the various personal pronouns. Singular subject pronouns: *I* (first); *you* (second); *he/she/it* (third) Plural subject pronouns: *we* (first); *you* (second); *they* (third) Singular object pronouns: *me* (first); *you* (second); *him/her/it* (third) Plural object pronouns: *us* (first); *you* (second); *them* (third)
Plural	The marking of a noun to indicate how many are being talked about.
Possession	The marking of a word to indicate that it possesses or owns something.

Possessive pronoun	The possessive words: *mine, yours, hers, his, its, ours, theirs,* They are used to stand in for the noun phrase. Examples: 'That's *mine, yours* is over there.' Note: possessive words used with a noun, e.g. 'That's *her* bag', are determiners rather than pronouns.
Predicative adjective	An adjective used as a complement following a stative verb. In this case, the adjective relates to the subject of that verb. Examples: 'He is devastated'; 'The table is bare.'
Prefix	A beginning that adapts the original word in some way. Examples: *pre*fix; *un*happy; *re*turn.
Preposition	A function word that expresses a relationship between words, phrases or clauses. Prepositions usually relate to space or time. Examples: 'He's *in* the house'; 'It's *between* the green one and the red one'; 'I'll be there *at* eight.'
Primary verb	This small group of verbs can be main or auxiliary verbs. They are: *be, have, do.* Compare: 'Do you eat cheese?' with 'I do karate.' 'I am leaving' with 'I am a teacher.' 'I have bought a new car' with 'I have a cat.'
Pronoun	A function word that stands in place of a noun. Instead of repeating our own names endlessly, we use *I* as the subject and *me* as the object.
Proper noun	The name of a specific person, animal, place, work of art, day, etc. Proper nouns always have a capital letter at the start, and can rarely be put into the plural. The proper noun category is not divided any further. Examples: England; *Pride and Prejudice*; Friday.
Reflexive pronoun	A pronoun used to refer the action back to the subject, often emphatically. Examples: 'I can bath *myself*, you know'; 'He bought it for *himself*.'
Regular/irregular	Verbs' behaviour can be described as regular (i.e. following the usual pattern) or irregular (i.e. unusual) in their formation of the past tense or past participle. In all languages, the most irregular verbs are the ones used most often; so the primary verbs are usually irregular, together with other common verbs.
Subject	The main focus of a sentence. In the active voice, the subject will be the agent as well; in the passive voice, the subject may be receiving the action of the verb but remain as the main focal point for the sentence. Examples: 'Smith has the ball … Smith's beaten two defenders … Smith's been tackled by Marques.' In each of the clauses above, Smith is the subject, but only in the first two is he also the agent.
Subordinating conjunction	A conjunction that connects a subordinate clause to a main clause. There are many subordinating conjunctions, including: *because, although, until, while, when.*
Suffix	An ending that adapts the original word in some way. Examples: walk*ing*; happ*iness*; work*aholic.*
Superlative	Adjectives inflected with *-est* or combined with 'most' are in the superlative form. Examples: 'She's the biggest'; 'He's the most helpful.' (**Note:** the definite article 'the' is usually added as well.)
Tense	Tense relates to where we locate a verb's action in time. There are two tenses in English: present and past. The simple present tense implies an action that takes place regularly or habitually. Examples: 'I take the train to college every day'; 'I speak English.' The simple past tense relates an action in the past. Examples: 'I took the train to college yesterday'; 'I spoke to my mother.'
Tense and aspect	Tense and aspect combine in different ways to create a range of different time frames. Taking the verb 'to do' as an example, here are the various combinations that might be created: |	Simple	Progressive	Perfective | | --- | --- | --- | --- | | Present | *I do* | *I am doing* | *I have done* | | Past | *I did* | *I was doing* | *I had done* |

Verb	A 'doing word', but we need to be much more precise. Verbs may be *dynamic* and describe action or process, or they may be *stative* and describe states. As a rule of thumb, stative verbs are not used in the present progressive form (I am _____ing).
Voice	This refers to the verb as active or passive. In an active construction, an active voice verb is used together with a subject. In the active voice, the subject also acts as the agent – the thing or person performing the verb. Examples: 'I ate the apple'; 'The minister changed the immigration policy again.' A passive construction is formed by the auxiliary verb *be* together with the *-ed* or past participle. The subject of the sentence now becomes the object as well. The agent is optional. Examples: 'The apple was eaten (by me)'; 'The immigration policy was changed again (by the minister).' It's worth commenting on passive constructions, especially when they hide the agent.
Word class	Words that have the same formal properties. Examples: nouns; adjectives; verbs.

■ Graphological framework

Colour	The connotations of different colours are often used in texts to contribute to the overall meaning.
Deviant spelling	The deliberate use of a non-standard spelling (i.e. not the dictionary norm) for effect, e.g. *Kwik-Fit*; *Phones 4 U*.
Font	The typeface chosen, which may contribute to the writer's self-representation.
Grapheme	The smallest functional unit in a writing system, e.g. *a, m, !, ;*
Graphological cohesion	A graphologically cohesive text uses an appropriate layout and set of graphological features, e.g. a letter in columns would be unlikely to 'feel right' – it wouldn't be cohesive.
Graphology	This relates to the visual and layout features of a text – the things you can see but that aren't actually linguistic features.
Headline	Mainly used in newspapers, a headline may summarise the story to follow or offer a pun that often makes complete sense only after the story has been read.
Image	Pictures may be used in texts for many different reasons. Note: 'imagery' has nothing to do with pictures.
Inset article	Similar to a satellite article but appears within the main text, usually within a box.
Layout	The shape of a text – it may be in columns, a list or continuous prose. A particular cluster of layout features may help identify the genre of a text, e.g. a headline, subheadings and columns probably indicate a newspaper or magazine article.
Lists	These may be bulleted, numbered or left plain. Those in the body of a text – e.g. 'He was surrounded by market vendors selling fruit, cheese, clothes, toys …' are not graphological features.
Orthography	The way in which letter shapes are formed on a page and the characters used.
Phonetic rendition	When words are spelled as they sound, e.g. *queen* is spelled *kween*.
Pull quote	A phrase or sentence selected from an article to be enlarged at the side or between columns of the main text.
Satellite article	A kind of sub-article, connecting to the subject of the main article. It may be at the side or bottom of the main piece, usually separated by a line and may have its own heading.
Subheading	These lead the reader through a text, indicating what the main topic of each section is.
Text box	A box drawn within a text, with text inside that contributes to the whole but does not follow on directly from the main text surrounding it.

■ Interaction framework

Accommodation	The process of adapting one's speech to make it more or less similar to that of other participants in a conversation.
Adjacency pair	Two utterances by different speakers that have a natural and logical link, and complete an idea together. There are several types, including *question/answer, greeting/greeting, apology/acceptance, suggestion/agreement*. The second utterance is limited by the first.
Backchannel behaviour	Also known as support or feedback to the speaker and describes a range of ways in which a listener encourages the speaker to continue, through: *gesture* (e.g. nodding, hand gestures); *minimal response*; or *engaging* with what they're saying (e.g. echoing words/phrases, commenting, asking questions, such as 'really?').
Closed question	A question that limits the range of possible responses. Example: 'Do you do French at college?'
Cohesion in speech	A spoken text can be cohesive through the other frameworks, but also through: – smooth turn and topic management – recycling and mirroring.
Convergence	When a person's speech patterns become more like those of the other person in a conversation. Convergence reduces social distance and can be either upwards or downwards.
Declarative used as an interrogative	This is fairly common in speech – the question is marked only by rising intonation, but the utterance is grammatically a statement rather than a question. Example: 'And you take French at college?'
Discourse marker	A word or phrase that indicates a change in topic, or a return to a previous topic. Examples: *so; getting back to …; anyway; right*.
Divergence	When a person's speech patterns become more individualised and less like those of the other person in a conversation. Divergence increases social distance and can be either upwards or downwards.
Downwards	When applied to convergence/divergence, movement away from Standard English.
Face	The persona or role a person projects or acts out in a conversation.
Face-threatening act	A communicative act that threatens someone's positive or negative face needs.
Facework	The way people work together to protect and support each other's 'faces' in conversation.
Interaction	The linguistic aspects of how people relate to one another.
Interruption	Beginning a turn while someone else is talking, in a competitive way. It's often done to change the topic or to take control.
Intervention	An attempt to take part or engage in a debate.
Latch	Turns that join and follow immediately after one another without pausing or with overlap are described as latching.
Mirroring	When a speaker uses words, phrases or other features previously used by another speaker. It may be done unconsciously, but still shows support for the first speaker.
Monitoring device	A feature used to check someone is listening, e.g. *y'know*; rising intonation; tag questions.
Negative face need	The need to be allowed independence and to do your own thing.
Negative politeness	Strategies that recognise the independence or the status of the person you are speaking to.
Off-record	Dropping a hint, saying something without really saying it.

Open question	A question that allows a range of possible responses. Example: 'What do you do at college?'
Overlap	Beginning a turn while someone else is talking, in a cooperative way. It's often done in agreement or to encourage the speaker.
Positive face need	Our need to be liked and to feel part of a group.
Positive politeness	Strategies that emphasise social closeness.
Questions	Questions can be used to direct the topic of a conversation. Forms of question worth commenting on specifically are open, closed, declaratives used as interrogatives, and tag questions.
Reformulation	Rephrasing what someone else has said, perhaps summarising their idea to clarify it to yourself, or echoing that you agree with them. Teachers frequently do it to support good answers.
Simultaneous speech	Two or more participants speaking at the same time.
Tag question	A brief ending tagged on to a statement that turns it into a question. To truly be a tag question, the tag must contain either the same verb as the original statement or an auxiliary verb, and the statement must change from positive to negative or vice versa. Examples: 'You don't want to go, do you?'; 'He wants to go, doesn't he?' There are other words and phrases that are colloquially used as tag questions. They are worth commenting on but must be clearly defined as behaving like tag questions. Examples: 'You'll do that for me, right?'; 'He'll be round soon, yeah?'
Three-part exchange	A sequence of three linked utterances between two speakers following an initiation–response–feedback structure. These structures are common in classroom speech. Note that adjacency pairs and three-part exchanges can be concluded and a new one begun in a single turn. Example: A: alright B: yeah thanks (.) you A: good (.) cheers (0.5) goin' out tonight? B: think so (.) got loads of homework though In this example, B concludes an adjacency pair and opens a new one in the second line, as does A in the third line. These pairs are said to be *chained*.
Topic management	The control of a conversation in terms of speaking and topic.
Turn	A turn in conversation is one person's utterance. Most conversations naturally observe turn-taking.
Upwards	When applied to convergence/divergence, movement towards Standard English.

■ Lexical-semantic framework

Antonym	A word with the opposite meaning to another word. Example: *up* and *down* are antonyms.
Cliché	An overused expression. Traditional examples: 'In for a penny, in for a pound'; 'Every cloud has a silver lining.' Contemporary example: 'At the end of the day'; 'It ticks all the boxes.'
Coherence	A measure of how a text makes sense.
Cohesion	A measure of how a text fits together as a whole. A text can be made lexically cohesive by repeating keywords and/or by maintaining an appropriate register, i.e. by not mixing formal and taboo language, unless done for effect.

Collocation	A set of words – often a pair, or a phrase – that have become strongly associated. **Note**: many collocations are also clichés.
	Examples: 'A vast majority', 'A sweeping generalisation', 'Son and heir.'
Collocational clash	A play on words where one item in a collocation is replaced by another word, usually which sounds like the original in some way. These are often found in tabloid headlines and some kinds of shop names.
	Examples: *The Codfather* (a fish and chip shop); *Hair Today Gone Tomorrow* (barber's).
Colloquial language	Everyday, spoken-style language. Typically, it's what you wouldn't expect in a formal written passage.
Connotation	The associations something has: the value that a word has, but would not be found in the dictionary. Connotations can be personal and specific, but usually we're interested in connotations that can be assumed in an audience, i.e. shared connotations.
	Example: 'house', 'residence' and 'home' have similar denotational meaning and would seem to be synonyms, but the word 'residence' has connotations of grandeur for most people, and 'home' is somehow more than just a house.
Deictic reference	A reference to something not in the text; a word that changes meaning according to context.
	Example: the demonstrative pronouns *this* and *that* refer to different things depending on the context.
Denotation	The meaning of a word as you would expect to find it in the dictionary.
Discourse marker	A word or phrase that indicates a change in topic, or a return to the previous topic.
	Example: 'Well, ok then, as I was saying.'
Dysphemism	A sort of negative euphemism, often emphasising the negative for a comic, abusive or ironic effect.
	Examples: *worm-fodder; got the bullet; butt-ugly.*
Euphemism	A word or phrase that tries to avoid saying something unpleasant. There are many in use for concepts like sex and death, but there are a growing number used in the business world and in politics.
	Examples: *passed away; downsized; surgical strike; friendly fire.*
Figurative language	Language used in a non-literal way. Several specific techniques or features can be described as figurative language.
Filler	A word, phrase or sound used to fill a gap, e.g. *er; like; y'know.*
Formal/informal lexis	*See* Lexical register.
Hedge	A word or phrase used to pad out and soften what's being said.
	Examples: *sort of; could you possibly; perhaps.*
Homonymic pun	A play on words based on words that look the same but are not.
	Example: 'Being a mortician is a grave business.'
Homophonic pun	A play on words based on words that sound the same but are different. A particularly clever example is using phrases that sound the same, as in the Two Ronnies' *Fork 'andles* sketch (fork 'andles/four candles).
	Note: sometimes a homonymic pun is a homophonic pun, if the words are spelled and sound the same – don't get bogged down in which it is.
Hyperbole	A figure of speech involving exaggeration. Hyperbolic language, like similes and metaphors, is found in everyday speech, in newspaper headlines and advertising, although we would often link it with a poetic or literary register.
	Example: 'I've told you a thousand times not to do that!'
Hypernym	A category into which other words fit: in effect, the title of a semantic field.
	Example: *fish* is a hypernym relating to cod, herring, goldfish, pike.

Hyponym	A word within a hypernym's category: a word within a semantic field (i.e. a lesser/lower or more specific word).
	Examples: *vodka*, *wine*, *Shiraz*, *Red Stripe* are all hyponyms of alcohol; *car*, *truck*, *Ford Focus*, *JCB digger* are all hyponyms of vehicle.
Idiom	Metaphorical or non-literal sayings common in their cultural context – they don't translate well, but anyone sharing a linguistic background understands. They are often clichés in that they tend to be overused, but not all clichés are idioms – it has to be not literally true or not possible to decipher from the actual words used in order to be idiomatic. The use of idiom can also be seen as part of pragmatics – what you are 'getting at' rather than what you are literally saying.
	Examples: 'Pull your socks up!'; 'He was really taken to the cleaners.'
	In both these examples, if you hadn't heard the expression before, you wouldn't be able to work out what was meant, even if you understood all the actual words.
Imagery	An interchangeable term with figurative language. **Note**: it does not have anything to do with actual pictures presented in a text, usually described as images.
Jargon	Technical language in any field. We often think of it as relating to technology, but all fields have their jargon.
	Example: hypernym is linguistic jargon; bouquet is a jargon term from the field of wine tasting.
Lexical register	A cover-all term relating to the general level of formality of a passage, together with the complexity of vocabulary (or lexis) used. A high-register text is formal and complex, a low-register one is informal in style and would use colloquial, chatty language, perhaps with some degree of taboo language too. Many texts are mid-register or mix it up, perhaps combining a high lexical register (complex lexis) with a chatty style and direct address. It is possible and valid to talk about a legal/medical/educational, etc. register to mean a text that is typical of those contexts.
	Examples: formal register – *police officers*; colloquial register – *cops*, *coppers*; very informal – *pigs*.
Lexis	The total stock of words in a language; synonymous with vocabulary. 'Lexical' means relating to the words, so 'lexical complexity' is how complex the words are and 'lexically varied' says the text is using a range of types of vocabulary. **Note**: *lexeme* = word; *lexicon* = dictionary.
Marked term	A term in which the gender of a person is (often unnecessarily) foregrounded through a gendered pre-modifier or suffix.
Meiosis	A figure of speech involving understatement. It is the opposite of hyperbole.
	Example: 'The burning down of the school was the result of a prank.'
Metaphor	A figure of speech or figurative usage where an object or person is described as being something else. We often think of these as poetic or literary, but they do also feature in everyday speech, in newspaper headlines and advertising. A dead metaphor is one that's been so overused, we've forgotten it's not literally true – like 'I'm freezing/starving/going to kill you.'
	Examples: 'Your bedroom's a tip!'; 'He's a dead man walking.'
Metonymy and synecdoche	Synecdoche is when a part of a larger object or institution stands symbolically for the whole.
	Examples: 'Give us this day our daily bread', where bread stands for food; 'A nice piece of ass' stands for an attractive woman/man.
	Metonymy is when we substitute one usually related idea for the thing it is representing.
	Example: *The Whitehouse* stands for the US government; *the Crown* stands for the monarchy.
Perforation	A process whereby words 'slide down' the scale of acceptability and pick up negative connotations over time.
Personification	A figure of speech where an animal or inanimate object is described as having human characteristics.
	Example: 'Our woodland cowers under the threat of global warming.'
Pun	Simply put, a play on words (this feature straddles phonology and semantics, since it involves sound and meaning). *See also* Homonymic pun *and* Homophonic pun.

Secondary semantic field	A semantic field that is not directly related to the subject matter of the text. Example: battle terms used in a football match report.
Semantic cohesion	Texts can cohere semantically by: – using semantic fields related to the topic – using a semantic field as an extended metaphor. Example: 'The House of Commons was like a battleground today, with the Prime Minister ambushed by the leader of the opposition, his backbenchers offering covering fire with a series of irrelevant questions.'
Semantic field	A group of words related by their meaning. Examples: the words novel, play, poem all belong to the semantic field of literature.
Semantics	This relates to the meanings of words or a text – how words relate to one another by meaning, or how we use words to mean different things.
Simile	This is a figure of speech comparing two things in a more explicit way than a metaphor, usually using *like* or *as*. Again, these are often associated with a literary style, but can in found in most contexts, e.g. in newspaper headlines and advertising. Example: 'For skin as smooth as silk …'
Slang	Informal vocabulary more usual in spoken than written language, often associated with a particular group or context.
Synecdoche	See Metonymy and synecdoche.
Synonym	A word meaning the same as another word. Thanks to the English language's mixed heritage, there is often more than one word for a broad concept, although usually there are subtle differences in meaning, so it's difficult to come up with exact synonyms. A word may have synonyms that are different in terms of register or formality, or there may be different connotational meanings between them. Examples: *sofa*, *settee* and *couch* are synonyms.
Taboo language	Technically, this applies to words that cannot or should not be said in their context. Naturally this varies according to context, so beware of labelling mild swearing as taboo in a colloquial conversation taking place in a pub between close friends. Taboo words have tended to relate to particular fields: body parts; urination and excretion; religion; sex; and death. Currently some of the most taboo words (i.e. taboo in most contexts) are racist terms.
Tail	A word or phrase added on to the end of a sentence.

■ Phonological framework

Accent	The specific way words are pronounced according to geographical region.
Alliteration	The repetition of a sound at the beginning of words. Note that it's about the sound, not the letter, so 'crunchy chocolate' is not alliteration, but 'kicking cats' is.
Assonance	The repetition of vowel sounds, or of similar vowel sounds. Again, it's about the sounds not the letters, so 'loud brown cow' does have assonance, but 'all ages' does not.
Collocational clash	A play on words where one item in a collocation is replaced by another word, usually which sounds like the original in some way. These are often found in tabloid headlines and some kinds of shop name. Example: *The Codfather* (a fish and chip shop).
Consonance	The repetition of consonant sounds. Again – the emphasis is on the sound produced, not the letter. Example: *lazily buzzing*.
Consonant clusters	Groups of consonants pronounced together. Examples: *strong*; *tractor*.

Consonants	Sounds created by some kind of closure of a part of the vocal tract. All sounds apart from vowels. Examples: *b*; *d*; *r*; *k*; *p*.
Emphatic stress	Emphasising a word or phrase in speed (usually indicated by bold type).
Falling intonation	Pitch going down at the end of an utterance, often associated with making a statement (but dependent on accent and other factors).
Fricative	A sound that is created by the slow and controlled release of air through the mouth, creating friction. Examples: *thick*; *then*; *fat*; *vet*; *sat*; *shot*; *treasure*; *dizzy*.
Half-rhyme	Words that almost or nearly rhyme, or look like they should rhyme but don't (sometimes called 'eye rhyme'). Examples: *come* and *run* (half rhyme); *love* and *prove* (eye rhyme).
Homonym	A word that looks like another word, but is in fact different. It may sound the same, or be pronounced differently. Example: the dog's *lead*; a *lead* pipe.
Homonymic pun	A play on words based on words that look the same but are not. Example: 'Being a mortician is a grave business.'
Homophone	A word that sounds the same as another word or words. Example: *there*, *their* and *there* are all homophones.
Homophonic pun	A play on words based on words that sound the same but are different. A particularly clever example is using phrases that sound the same, as in the Two Ronnies' *Fork 'andles* sketch (fork 'andles/four candles). **Note**: sometimes a homonymic pun is a homophonic pun, if the words are spelled and sound the same – don't get bogged down in which it is.
Intonation	The way the pitch of our voices goes up and down as we speak.
Nasals	Sounds produced by resonance in the nasal cavity. Examples: *more*; *none*; *going*.
Non-verbal aspects of speech (NVAS)	A commonly used term for prosodic (*See* Prosodic elements).
Non-verbal communication (NVC)	A key part of face-to-face speech that conveys meaning without the use of words. It includes body language, facial expression and prosodics.
Onomatopoeia	A word that creates the sound it's describing. Sometimes these words are newly made up in a text, to produce exactly the right effect. Examples: *Sqwaark! Phwoooar!*
Paralinguistics	The things that add to the meaning of a text that aren't actually language. Examples: graphology; non-verbal communication; prosodics.
Phoneme	The smallest unit of sound in a language.
Phonetic rendition	When words are spelled as they sound, e.g. *queen* is spelled *kween*.
Phonological cohesion	Texts may be phonologically cohesive by using phonological devices to create patterns, e.g. a rhyme scheme or consistent alliteration.
Phonology	This relates to sounds and patterns of sounds. We use 'phonetics' when we're talking about the specific study of sound, perhaps in children's language or accent; 'phonology' is more about patterning or the deliberate use of sound for an effect.
Pitch	High or low sounds (i.e. a high pitch might be a whistle, a low pitch might be a rumble).

Plosives	Sounds that are created by a sudden release of air (like an explosion) from the mouth.
	Examples: *cat*; *tin*; *pan*; *goat*; *bat*; *dog*.
Prosodic elements (also known as prosodics)	Paralinguistic vocal elements of spoken language used to provide emphasis or other effect. In other words, aspects controlled by the voice but not actually words. Also known as non-verbal aspects of speech (NVAS).
	Examples: stress; pitch; volume; tone; pace.
Pun	Simply put, a play on words (this feature straddles phonology and semantics, since it involves sound and meaning). *See also* Homonymic pun, Homophonic pun and Collocational clash.
Rhyme	Rhyming words end in the same sound.
	Examples: *bed* and *dead*.
Rising intonation	A pitch that goes up at the end of an utterance, sometimes associated with asking a question (depending on accent and other factors).
Stops	Sounds where the air flow is completely stopped. They are created in the throat (e.g. glottal stop), at the back of the mouth (e.g. *ck*), at the alveolar ridge (e.g. *t*) or by the lips (e.g. *p*).
Vowels	Sounds created with an open mouth.
	Examples: *a*; *e*; *i*; *o*; *u*.

■ Rhetorical framework

Balanced structure	This is (usually) a sentence where the two halves balance each other. It may also be a contrast or antithesis.
Contrast/antithesis	Many speeches present reality contrasted with what the speaker offers or is fighting for. Such constructions may also come into the category of balance or mocking the opposition.
Figurative language	Language that is not used in a literal way; features like metaphor, simile and personification. (*See* Lexical-semantic framework for more detail.)
Hyperbole	A figure of speech involving exaggeration, used in everyday registers as well as in poetic and rhetorical ones.
	Example: 'I've told you a million times.'
Repetition	Rhetorical speech frequently uses repetition to help the audience retain the key points.
Rhetoric	Related to the art of public speaking, or oratory. Rhetorical features tend to be included for persuasion or to make the speech memorable.
Rhetorical cohesion	Cohesion in rhetoric may be achieved through syntactic parallelism, repetitions and phonological patterns.
Rhetorical question	A question that is not intended to be answered, or which the speaker/writer answers him/herself.
Syntactic parallelism	The repetition of sentence structure.
	Example: 'If she trusted him, she had to believe him. If she loved him, she had to trust him.'
Synthetic personalisation	The technique where a writer/speaker uses the second-person pronoun to synthesise or fake a personal relation to the audience.
Triad	A pattern of three words or phrases.
	Examples: 'Education, education, education'; 'The good, the bad and the ugly.'

■ Speech framework

Accent	The specific way words are pronounced according to geographical region.
Dialect	The language variety of a geographical region or social subgroup. It may include specific words, e.g. 'aye/yes', and grammatical features, e.g. 'he weren't there'.
Discourse	A continuous stretch of language (especially spoken) that is longer than a sentence.
Discourse marker	A word or phrase that indicates a change in topic, or a return to a previous topic. Examples: *so*; *getting back to* …; *anyway*; *right*.
Elision	The missing out of sounds or parts of words.
Ellipsis	The missing out of a word or words in a sentence. Also common in written language.
False start	When a speaker stops what they're saying and begins again, changing tack somehow. It may be because the way they started just isn't working, or to avoid saying something inappropriate. A false start is therefore a kind of self-repair involving going back to the start of the utterance. Example: 'I'm uh we're doing this next week.'
Filler	A word, phase or sound used to fill a gap. Examples: *like*; *you see*; *uh*.
Idiolect	An individual style of speaking, made up of choices in all frameworks.
Micropause	A period of silence of less than half a second, usually indicated by (.).
Minimal response	A single word, very short phrase or non-verbal filler used in response. Examples: *yeah*; *uhuh*; *I see*.
Non-fluency features	Features of spoken language that are due to spontaneity and the speed of normal speech. The label 'non-fluency' is not very helpful as it implies a lack of clarity or care on the speaker's part.
Non-fluent repetition	When a speaker repeats him/herself, but not deliberately or for effect.
Non-standard English	Words, phrases and constructions not usually seen in formal texts. They may be colloquial words or phrases, or related to a dialect. Examples: 'He ain't coming'; 'They takes them all.'
Non-verbal filler	A filler that isn't a word, e.g. *um*, *er*. Also known as a 'voice-filled pause'.
Pause	A gap in the flow of speech, or a period of silence. It is indicated in a transcript by a number in brackets, showing the number of seconds of silence, e.g. (2).
Received pronunciation (RP)	The 'poshest' UK accent, used now by few people.
Recycling	Reusing the same words. It can be simple repetition, or reusing the same word or phrase in otherwise different sentences.
Self-repair	When a speaker corrects him/herself. Example: 'We've got to go to the shops after breakfast (.) after lunch.'
Speech features	Features common in spoken but not written language.
Standard English (SE)	A universally accepted dialect of English that carries a degree of prestige.
Transcript	An accurate written record of a conversation or monologue, including hesitations and pauses. Transcripts have their own conventions and do not employ usual punctuation.
Voice-filled pause	*See* Non-verbal filler

■ Syntactical framework

Clause	A clause is a unit of meaning. A sentence can be a single clause, or it can be made up of several. Clauses are composed of five different types of element (subject, verb, object, complement, adverbial), and there are seven basic types of clause: SV – I ate. SVO – Simon climbed the tree. SVC – He is dead chuffed. SVA – They live over there. SVOO – I gave the balloon to him. SVOC – The boy made me angry. SVOA – You need an apple every day.
Complex sentence	A sentence consisting of a main clause with one or more dependent clauses, often connected with a subordinating conjunction. Example: 'If you donate £2 a month, we can help hundreds of people.'
Compound sentence	A sentence consisting of two or more main clauses, connected by coordinating conjunctions, or sometimes just separated by punctuation (semicolon). Example: 'I went to the park and (I) played on the swings.'
Compound-complex sentence	A sentence consisting of two or more main clauses and at least one subordinate clause. Example: 'When the party was over, the kids cleared off and the parents cleared up.'
Coordinate clause	A coordinate clause is also a main clause, in a sentence containing more than one main clause. Coordinate clauses are introduced by coordinating conjunctions such as *and*, *or* and *but*.
Main clause	A clause that can stand alone as a simple sentence. Every major sentence contains at least one main clause.
Minor sentence	A grammatically incomplete sentence. It might be missing a subject or a verb. Minor sentences are usually used to create a spoken mode feel, e.g. working for you all year round
Modifier	A word, usually an adjective or a noun used attributively, that qualifies the sense of a noun, e.g. *old* and *factory* in 'the old factory building'. Adverbs of comment also act as modifiers, e.g. *obviously*.
Mood	*See* Sentence function
Noun phrase	A phrase with a noun as its main word. Examples: 'The long sandy beach'; 'An exceptionally intelligent young woman.'
Phrase	A group of words functioning as a single unit.
Post-modification	The placing of modifiers such as adjectives and adverbs after a noun. Examples: 'The policy, *utterly repugnant to many*, went through Parliament yesterday'; 'The tree – *tall, magnificent, ancient* – had stood there since he could remember.'
Pre-modification	The placing of modifiers such as adjectives and adverbs in front of a noun. Examples: 'The *smallest* thing', 'It's an *utterly repugnant* policy.'
Relative clause	A subordinate clause that is used to add more information about another clause element. It acts like an adjective. Examples: 'The man *who lives at the end of my street* is a postman'; 'I finished reading the book *that you gave me*.'

Sentence function	There are four sentence functions (also known as moods):
	Declarative sentences are the most common and they make statements. They usually have a SVO order (subject, verb, object).
	Example: 'He washed the car every Sunday, no matter what.'
	Interrogative sentences are questions. The subject and verb may be inverted in an interrogative, or a 'dummy do' (de-lexical auxiliary) may be used.
	Example: 'Why on earth *did he wash* the car every Sunday?'
	Imperative sentences are directives, more commonly known as commands, although they may also offer advice or invitations. They usually omit the subject, although it is occasionally used for emphasis.
	Examples: 'Wash the car'; 'Come out with us this time.'
	Exclamatory sentences are often incomplete or simply don't fit elsewhere. **Note**: an exclamation mark does not necessarily make an exclamatory.
	Examples: 'What a terrible day!'; 'If only I hadn't eaten that!'
Sentence type	This refers to the structure of the sentence, i.e. minor, simple, compound, complex or compound-complex. Don't confuse it with sentence function – (declarative, interrogative, imperative, exclamatory). Don't describe sentences as long or short – this is meaningless and a waste of your time.
Simple sentence	A sentence consisting of a single main clause, e.g. 'The soldiers advanced.'
Subordinate clause	A subordinate clause is not able to act as a main clause, and forms part of a complex sentence, together with a main clause. Subordinate clauses are introduced with subordinating conjunctions such as *if*, *when* and *because*.
Syntax	The linguistic framework dealing with word order and sentence structure. Grammar is a word-level framework, while syntax deals with larger units.
Verb phrase	A phrase with a main verb as its main word.
	Examples: 'We *had been waiting* for hours'; 'The babies *might have been born* in the car on the way to hospital.'